Roge
adults
won
Liver

'The
is th

'Zestf
been

'Thi
C
pae

'A me

'An extraordinary lrely

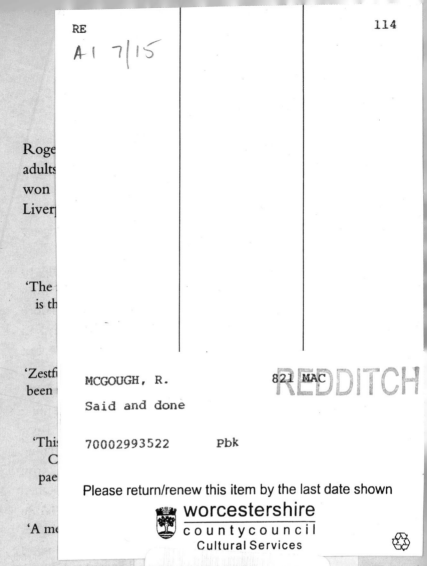
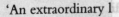

Said and Done

Roger McGough

arrow books

Published in the United Kingdom by Arrow Books in 2006

1 3 5 7 9 10 8 6 4 2

Copyright © Roger McGough 2005

Roger McGough has asserted his right under the Copyright, Designs
and Patents Act, 1988 to be identified as the author of this work.

First published in the United Kingdom in 2005 by Century

Arrow Books
The Random House Group Limited
20 Vauxhall Bridge Road, London, SW1V 2SA

Random House Australia (Pty) Limited
20 Alfred Street, Milsons Point, Sydney,
New South Wales 2061, Australia

Random House New Zealand Limited
18 Poland Road, Glenfield,
Auckland 10, New Zealand

Random House (Pty) Limited
Isle of Houghton, Corner of Boundary Road & Carse O'Gowrie,
Houghton 2198, South Africa

Random House Publishers India Private Limited
301 World Trade Tower, Hotel Intercontinental Grand Complex,
Barakhamba Lane, New Delhi 110 001, India

The Random House Group Limited Reg. No. 954009
www.randomhouse.co.uk

A CIP catalogue record for this book is available from the British Library

Papers used by Random House are
natural, recyclable products made from wood grown in
sustainable forests. The manufacturing processes conform to
the environmental regulations of the country of origin.

ISBN 9780099478751 (from Jan 2007)
ISBN 0 09 9 47875 7

Typeset by SX Composing DTP, Rayleigh, Essex
Printed and bound in the United Kingdom by
Bookmarque Ltd, Croydon, Surrey

Said and Done

When all's said and done
There'll be nothing left to say or do.

For my children

ACKNOWLEDGEMENTS

Collected Poems published by Penguin Books in 2003 contains the complete poems from which the following extracts have been taken:

'The Railings' (page 81), 'In at the Kill' (page 134), 'Cinders' (page 137), 'The Way Things Are' (page 139), 'Let me Die a Youngman's Death' (page 155), 'At Lunchtime' (page 209), 'Discretion' (pages 245, 246), 'Huddersfield' (page 280–1), 'Cardiff' (page 280–1), 'The Identification' (pages 283), 'Out of Sequence' (page 286), 'The Rot' (page 290), 'Here I Am' (pages 355, 359, 387).

Extract from 'The Moon's Last Quarter' (page 375), by Robert Graves, kindly reproduced by permission of Carcanet Press.

My thanks to Kate Watkins, my editor at Century, to Peters, Fraser and Dunlop, to Adrian Mealing at UK Touring and to Phil Bowen whose story of the Mersey Poets, 'A Gallery to Play to' (Stride Publications), reminded me of details I might have forgotten.

CONTENTS

LETTER FROM THE POET

'Dunrhymin'
London
England

Ladies and gentlemen,

I apologise sincerely for being unable to attend this evening's performance. Owing to pressure of work, an increasing sense of unreality, and the fear of drowning in a sea of upturned faces, I have employed an out-of-work actor to impersonate me.

On my behalf he will read poems, answer questions, sign books, get drunk and generally keep up the poetic image.

Of course, there will be weaknesses in performance, the overeagerness to please, the nervous mannerisms too consciously affected, and it goes without saying that he lacks the charisma, charm, wit and raw animal sexuality of the real poet.

I trust, however, that you will enjoy the evening, and forgive my underpaid stand-in should the mask slip and his true self show through.

Yours faithfully,
Roger McGough

This is a letter I often read out before a performance, usually in a foreign country where I am unknown, and where the only photographs of the author available are those on the back covers of books published long ago. Occasionally it will result in puzzled mutterings in Czech or Portuguese which I interpret as *'Is he really an actor?'* . . . *'Is he really the poet?'* . . . *'Does it matter either way? I'm only here for the wine and canapés.'*

It has long been a daydream of mine to have impersonators going around the world at other people's expense, reading my poems in packed auditoria, selling my books, forging my signature, and popping a huge cheque and a thank-you letter to me in the post. In that way I could stay at home and quietly get on with writing works of flawed genius. My dilemma is that I have always regarded the creative impulse as something pure and seen a paradox in the need to show off the result, to have it published, sung, or hung on the wall. The shy extrovert, or the wheedling introvert 'Look at me, look at me', I have never fully resolved the conflict between the privacy of the poet and the public face of the performer, and the trick has always been to try to achieve a balance between the two.

I have been quoted as saying (a risk you take when someone asks for a quote and you oblige) that my favourite journey is not the one over Hammersmith Bridge on a summer's evening, or the one on the ferry crossing the Mersey, but the one I make at the end of a show from the microphone centre stage to the dressing room. It's terribly coy isn't it? The image it conjures up of the performer in a hurry to escape the warm embrace of the audience to the solitude backstage, the empty dressing room, the unforgiving mirror. It is true, however, that I'm not very good at bowing and saying thank you, and coming back for encores because I feel embarrassed, afraid of overstaying my welcome, but it's equally true that one of my favourite journeys is the one from the wings to the centre of the stage – but please don't quote me on that.

Inevitably, the older the writer–performer becomes, the more difficult it is to achieve that balance between having the time and space in which to write, and the need to go out and earn some money. Friends who are actors and musicians are at a loss when the engagement diary is empty, and it's not only the wage they miss it's the prospect of being isolated, passed over, of not being up there in front of an audience, doing what they do best. But for me the dilemma is that although I enjoy being on stage I don't like people looking at me and, with age, the business of packing a bag and taking the bus, tube and train, of checking into a hotel, turning up at the theatre for a sound check and performing has become wearisome, and most times I'd rather be at home brooding.

And long-haul travel has certainly lost its allure. My eldest son Finn, who writes and directs films for television, is for-ever dashing around the world, from Arkansas to Azerbaijan he's off at the drop of a contract. If he has time off between projects, he travels to Laos, Vietnam, wherever the fancy takes. Funnily enough, Tom, who is three years younger and generally studio-bound as a TV film editor, rang me just now to tell me he's leaving for Rio de Janeiro on Friday. Every opportunity they get, it's up, up and away – as far away from north London as they can get. Ah, youth! Ah, genes! Ah, DNA! I can see where they get it from, this wanderlust, this need to travel and explore. (Their mother,

3

obviously. Living 12,000 miles away at the time of writing.)

Yesterday I turned down an invitation from the Christchurch Book Festival to spend a week in New Zealand in August, followed by a trip to Melbourne. My first reaction was yippee! Travel and adventure. Book signings and bungee jumping, unlimited kiwi fruit and lionisation. Then Captain Cautious kicked in with '*Ooh, it's a long flight, and it will be their winter, and you've been before and . . . Pardon? Bungee jumping? Are you mad?*' I declined on the grounds that I was already committed to appearing at the Edinburgh Festival, which is true, except that as I'm only doing two nights in the Book Tent and as it's not yet contracted, I could easily have pulled out. But I didn't. Why? Whale watching off the Kaikoura coast or bagpipe watching on the Royal Mile, which would you choose? Over the last twelve months I have turned down invitations from literary festivals in Bratislava, Olomouc, Medellín in Colombia (at the third time of asking), Buenos Aires and Chicago. Nearer home, an exciting opportunity was the offer of a part in *The Twelve Just Men*, which played at the Assembly Rooms during the Festival. The show starred a giggle of comics playing it straight, including Bill Bailey, Stephen Frost and Owen O'Neill, so I gave it some serious thought. A new challenge, the chance to hang out with the cream of British comedy for a month. The offers that would come winging in from film and television producers. It's Edinburgh, after all, and who's to say that's not Steven Spielberg out there whispering to his aide, '*Who's the bespectacled baldy guy? We could use him in our next film.*'

'*You mean* The Night of the Bespectacled Baldy Guys?'

'*That's the one.*'

But the prospect of untold excitement, not to mention all that rehearsing, resulted in a polite refusal. What is happening to me? Am I so happy here in south-west London that I can't tear myself away? I don't think so. My mates in the pub don't understand and, to be honest, neither do I. Buenos Aires? Chicago? And you're getting paid to go there? You're mad to turn them down. I think back to those days in the early sixties when I was a schoolmaster wearing down-at-heel spectacles and a brown corduroy jacket with patches at the elbows. Not a penny to my name but fit as a fiddle, fancy free and not a care in the world. Where were the gilt-edged invitations then to cavort in sunny climes? The warm overtures to mingle with the glitterati, read my poems and sign my books? Not having published anything at the time may have had something to do with it, but even so, it does seem to be poetic sod's law that by the time you're famous enough to be invited anywhere you are too old to take advantage. And now I can't raise the enthusiasm for long-haul travel because I remember the reality of those far-off festivals and book bangs. Leaving a family behind, I could never extend my visit and so it was never a holiday, but rather a vortex of public readings, interviews, hangovers, more interviews, school visits, more hangovers. I've made a good living out of impersonating myself, but that 'pretending to be a poet' syndrome that Larkin worried about can be very debilitating. In fact, maybe I'm developing a Larkinesque agoraphobia? Experiencing the first ominous signs of an all-enveloping psychosis? What bad luck finally to settle down and write the story of my life while succumbing to clinical depression. I can see the chapter headings: 'Poetry. What's the point?' . . . 'The Darkness at the End of the Tunnel' . . .

5

'Scaffold. The Wasted Years' . . . 'The Sound of One Hand Booing'. . . 'Overdose or Over Beachy Head?'

I wish I had kept a journal in the sixties. What was Reg Dwight, before he became Elton John, wearing at the Scaffold recording session when he was a backing singer? What did Bob Dylan actually say that night in the Adelphi Hotel? *'Roge, I'm gonna tell you something now I ain't ever told anyone . . .'* Did I really have a threesome with Marianne Faithfull and Julie Christie, or was I just dreaming? (Just dreaming.) Did Keith Moon and I jump fully clothed into the pool at his twenty-first birthday saturnalia? Did John Lennon ever give me back the half-crown he took off the table in Thelma's flat in Princes Avenue? Questions, questions – and I don't have the answers. As Adrian Henri once remarked, plucking a scintilla of nostalgia from his paint-stained beard, 'If I'd have known that I was living in one of the most exciting periods of recent history, I'd have taken more notice.'

ACHTUNG, MINEN!

I live in a tree-lined suburban road near the River Thames as it runs from Chiswick to Barnes. Looking out of my study window, which is at the back of the house, I see limes, sycamores and silver birches in various states of undress. At the bottom of the garden a plastic swing, no longer used, hangs forlornly from the branch of a pear tree. Trees, however, played no part in my Liverpool childhood; in fact, I can hardly recall any. The roads around where I lived suggest a verdant, arboreous neighbourhood: Ash Road, Elm Drive, Beech Grove, Poplar Grove, Lime Grove, Alder Street, all within easy toddling distance. But no trees. There must have been trees of course, in the local parks – Hatton Hill in Litherland and Bowersdale in Seaforth – but if there were any, they remain shadowy and forbidding. Railed off and out of bounds: 'Keep off', 'Keep out'. Grass was what you kept off, trees were what you steered clear of. Railings we had in abundance. Fences and barbed wire. Walls with broken glass cemented into the top. Rusting iron lamp-posts cold to the touch. But no trees.

We had sand though, if not coming out of our ears, then out of our shoes, socks and sandwiches. Before the Container Port was built in the sixties, Gladstone Dock was the last dock running north from the Pier Head. From there

7

Seaforth Sands would stretch up and away through Waterloo, Crosby, Formby, Ainsdale, Birkdale and as far as Southport. The further you went, the bigger the sand dunes, the softer the sand, although the sea was never more than a wet promise, a mile or so in the distance. But as a child, what I associated with sand was not buckets, spades or donkeys, but bristling barbed wire strung out like fishing nets in which to catch shoals of Nazis, and a phalanx of concrete pyramids stretching into the distance to keep the enemy tanks from rolling up the beach and blowing us all to smithereens.

I was about three years old, maybe younger, and playing on Seaforth shore with Aunty Kathleen who would have been in her early teens. Probably there were others with us: Brenda, perhaps, in her pushchair and a couple more aunties. Suddenly, I was chasing a red ball across a wide patch of very flat, wet sand. There were screams and Kathleen came racing across the sand: 'Stop, stop, stand still. Roger, stand still.'

Sensing this was not a game, I did as I was told as Kathleen, dark hair streaming, raced towards me. It was only after I had been snatched up and was being carried gingerly away that I noticed the dark metal buttons in the sand: parallel lines of what looked like rusty cricket studs stretching away into the distance. Although too young to be able to differentiate between happiness and hysteria, I remember Kathleen pointing to what must have been an MOD notice. I couldn't read the words, but the black skull and crossbones triggered off a fit of screaming. To this day I still can't believe that I found a gap in the barbed wire and ran across a minefield, but I did. Maybe some of the mines were past their explode-by date, but I doubt it. Light on my feet, perhaps I subconsciously avoided stepping on the cracks in the pavement; kept out of range of the bony fingertips of witches waiting to catch me by the toes and drag me down into the fires of hell below.

This is such a dramatic memory that I wondered if it were really true, and when I met Kathleen in Liverpool recently and recalled the incident she said yes, it was all just as I remembered it, with one glaring omission. A golden retriever racing ahead of us had been blown up, obliterated in one ear-splitting instant. She thinks that I must have chased the dog through the wire and into the danger area, and that there was no red ball. But how strange, for I can smell the sea, and I can feel the wind as I run into it, and I can see this red shiny beach ball bouncing ahead of me. A case, perhaps, of the Magician in the Brain taking care of me, with sleight-of-hand conjuring up a warm friendly image to hide a terrible truth.

GEOGRAPHY

Whenever I heard the Liverpool comedian Robb Wilton on the wireless begin his act with 'The day war broke out . . .' I always thought he meant that the war lasted for a day. As I was too young at the time to understand the jokes that followed, I would ponder on this day-war, and because the studio audience would greet his opening catchphrase with hoots of laughter, I assumed that the joke lay in the fact that the war was still going on, and on, and on.

I was two years old when the Second World War began and had been at primary school for two years when it ended, so I think I can speak with some authority about life in war-torn Ruthven Road during Hitler's offensive. I wasn't that small child in the sepia photograph, or the one running and skipping in a grainy black-and-white film. My world was as vivid, noisy and multicoloured then as it is for any child growing up today. Grandma McGarry and my aunties were huge fans of Charlie Chaplin and often took me to watch his films at the Palladium Cinema in Seaforth, and I fondly imagined that before the Talkies came in, everybody was silent and walked with a stutter. My own children still refer to my early childhood as the 'black-and-white days'.

Despite the absence of bananas and the constant threat of

being slaughtered, I had a privileged upbringing, not in terms of wealth certainly, but of loving parents and a large pool of close relatives. It was made clear to me from the beginning that I was a very lucky boy. Lucky to have been born into the one true faith, lucky to have been born in Liverpool, to have a roof over my head, food on the table, a beautiful mother, a brave, strong father and a kind sister. And although I wasn't told how lucky I was to have been born and brought up during the terrible years of the Blitz, it may well have been implied. Ruthven Road, where I lived until my early twenties, is off Bridge Road, the main thoroughfare that runs south from the lift-bridge over the canal to the docks at Seaforth. Three years ago when I was in Liverpool making a radio programme about local railways, I took a cab out to Litherland to revisit the old homestead, pausing perhaps to admire the blue plaque on the front of number 11 Ruthven Road, but the house is no longer there, having been pulled down to make way for Princes Way, a flyover in the ointment.

Talking of ointment, I was standing on Bridge Road remembering Spofforth's, the barber shop where I had to go every other Saturday morning to sit on the wooden plank laid across the arms of a leather chair and passively smoke. One time the barber, chattering away to the reflection in the mirror of one of the men waiting and making a point with the scissors, snipped the top of my left ear. Out squealed the blood. No harm done, he said, staunching the flow with the cotton wool he kept handy for such occasions. A slick of Germolene ointment and Bob's your uncle. As I was recoiling at the memory, my hand to my ear, a voice called out from behind, 'All right, Roger, writing one of yer little poems, are yer?' A friendly passer-by. 'It's all changed since you were a lad, eh?'

Some, but not all. To my right I could still see the lift-bridge that spans the Leeds-to-Liverpool canal and below it, running parallel to Ruthven Road, is Jubilee Road where my paternal grandmother lived. Born Margaret Boland, she married James McGough and bore him seven sons and a daughter. Of Irish stock, they were living in a country that didn't welcome immigrants and they would have seen those welcome notices in lodging-house windows: 'No Blacks. No Irish. No dogs'. So perhaps it was no surprise that all the children were given safe old English names. In chronological order: William, Roger, James, John, Francis, Andrew, Edward and Ella. No Seans, Siobhans or Patricks in our street, thank you very much. Living only 200 yards away, we would always be popping over to see Grandma McGough and whatever uncle was on leave: John in the RAF, Frank in the Navy, Andy and Ted in the Army. There was a time early on in my life when I thought that the difference between men and women was that men wore uniforms. As I got older my visits grew less frequent, for she was a tough old bird who'd stand for no nonsense and I think she'd kept her sons in check with a rod of iron, if not a belt of leather.

I never knew my paternal grandfather and he was seldom mentioned. Airbrushed out of the family tree, was James. So completely, in fact, that I can't recall seeing a photograph of him. Who did he look like? Any resemblance to my father? Perhaps he looked like me. *'That's Jimmy on the right with his mates outside the Pig and Whistle. The one with the ponytail and the green glasses.'*

At family gatherings the dreaded word 'drink' would be mentioned in hushed tones. I gathered, too, that he was one of those men who would spend his wages on beer as soon as he got his hands on them. So every Friday night, Grandma would be one of that band of suffering women waiting outside the dock gates to grab the wage packets off their husbands before they disappeared into one of the bottomless pubs. With crystal-clear blue eyes that seemed to challenge the world, it was evident that Grandma McGough had been hardened by life, and there seemed to be a shell round her, a sort of coldness that kept even her sons at bay.

Looking left down Bridge Road I could still see the railway bridge, beyond which were the River Mersey and the docks at Seaforth. Carry on down the hill, under the bridge, and you'd come to Alder Street on the left. That's where my other grandmother lived, Grandma McGarry. Born Mary Hughes, she had married a young widower called William McGarry and bore him thirteen children. The ones that survived infancy were William, Hettie, Mary, Joseph, Winifred, Frances, John, George, Magdalen, Kathleen, Eileen and James. My mother, christened Mary Agnes, was called Aggie at home, which she always thought common – '*Aggie, yer tea's ready*' – and became Mary on leaving Alder Street.

If there was a certain anaglyptic chill in the back-to-back up by the canal it was fireworks down by the docks, and the living room downstairs is where it all happened. Grandma McGarry was deaf, had cataracts and was crippled by arthritis, but she was the benevolent planet round which all the related stars revolved. Her secret was seeing the absurdity in everything and using her deafness to comic effect:

AUNTY EILEEN   Ooh, that Hilda Johnson, yer tell her something and it runs like water off a duck's back.
GRANDMA   Runs like duck's water off her back?
ALL (*Voices raised*)   No, like water off a duck's back.
GRANDMA   That's what I said.

The living room was large and dominated by a kitchen table that always sported a white tablecloth, numerous cups and saucers, at least one teapot, sugar bowls, a bottle of sterilised milk and a deck of playing cards. Off the living room were a small kitchen, a pantry and a room in which the coal was stored. Sounds strange now, but at the time it seemed like a great idea. Need more coal? Out into the yard on a cold winter's night, or cross the lino and grab a shovel full? I know which I'd have chosen.

It also housed Uncle Jim's war souvenirs, which included a 303 rifle. Uncle Jim, who had joined the Royal Marines at seventeen and seen action at Dunkirk, was the youngest of the family, with gas–flame blue eyes and dark curly hair, his gypsy looks and charm had the women of the family fluttering around him: 'Lash me, but I'm tired,' he'd yawn, cueing his sisters to put the kettle on, plump up his cushions and push his armchair nearer to the fire.

As my first school was a hundred yards up the road and the church wasn't much further, plus the fact that the McGarrys were at the heart of our social life, Alder Street is where I spent a great deal of time. Uncles Bill, John and George were married and living away, so it was the aunties who ruled the roost. Gossip, gossip. Cluck, cluck. Kathleen and Eileen, the pretty ones who taught me how to jive and jitterbug at thirteen. Gossip, gossip. Cluck, cluck.

Magdalen, known as Marge, who had been disfigured by a dental operation in childhood, which left her with a twisted jaw, was everybody's favourite aunt and a babysitter extra-ordinaire. On a Friday evening, once Mum and Dad had left for the cinema, the playing cards would come out and by ten o'clock Brenda and I, falling asleep over pontoon, would be red-eyed and begging to be taken to bed.

'Ah, just one more game of snap,' she'd plead, magicking two toffees from behind our ears.

I would love to regale you with tales of musical evenings. Those nights spent around the piano in the parlour singing the songs of auld Ireland with Uncle Billy on the accordion, Aunty Winny on the fiddle, me mam on the penny whistle and Grandma herself beating it out on the bodhrán. But alas, I cannot tell a lie. When people played the piano or sang, it would be a friend of the family, Arthur Kennedy, Joe McDonnell or Father Hughes himself:

GRANDMA   Will you have a smidgen of whisky, Father?

FATHER HUGHES   No thanks, I'm forswearing it for Lent.

GRANDMA   You're swearing for Lent?

ALL (*voices raised*)   No, Father's forswearing the drink for Lent.

GRANDMA   That's what I said.

My father enjoyed sitting down at the piano at home and going through his short repertoire of airs but he played for himself, never socially, for he was a shy man and it's from him I inherited that fear of the jolly compère pointing and saying: 'Your turn now, give us all a song. Quiet everybody.'

And where was Grandfather McGarry when all the shenanigans were taking place in the parlour, when the carpet was rolled up and everyone joined in for a spot of lino dancing? Sadly, he'd gone before I could talk to him. Not dead, but his mind had gone. Delayed shell-shock they all said, the result of the horrors he'd gone through in the Great War, and I didn't know any better. Senile dementia? Possibly, but his symptoms seemed nearer to some sort of extreme psychosis. He'd worked all his life at the Bryant and May factory and had a framed scroll to prove it, but by the time I knew him he was a spent match, choking on fish bones and walking round the yard with a broom handle at his shoulder. He didn't seem to know who I was. He would talk to me but he made no sense, it was as if he was talking to someone else. Someone who lived in a different age. He shambled around the neighbourhood mumbling to himself and, as far as I'm aware, nobody laughed or pointed at him because they remembered him as a good bloke. At this time, too, just after the war, a new younger generation of shell-shocked ex-servicemen were taking to the streets.

The first seventeen years of my life were spent within a half mile radius of 11 Ruthven Road, in an unlovely, unfashionable part of north Liverpool. Word was to reach us later of the drumbeat of Toxteth and the scally, Scouseheart of Dingle, the coolness of Woolton and the smugness of the Wirral, and I would be drawn inevitably to the heart of the city, but, for those early years, this was my geography:

North:

*Jubilee road. Near the canal by the lift-bridge
in Litherland, a frying-pan's throw away
from the Richmond Sausage factory,
grandma McGough, having raised seven sons
and a daughter lived alone. No jubilation.
All done and dusted. Frost on the aspidistra.*
Helsinki.

South:

*Alder Street. In a roomy back-to-back
in a cul-de-sac near Seaforth docks,
grandma McGarry, having borne thirteen
was deaf to the noise of grandchildren,
giddy aunts and messmates. 'Put the kettle on.'
'It suits you.' 'Who's for a game of cards?'*
Naples.

*For those early years this was my geography.
My north, my south, I sailed between the two.
Since then I've travelled the world and found
that everything I learned, I already knew.*

MY LITTLE EYE

I wish I could remember my coronation, the day I was crowned overall winner of the Litherland Baby Show at the age of eighteen months. I wish I could remember that morning in the backyard, when I stood up in my pram to dip my dummy into a cloud and fell out, landing on my head, or that time I was kidnapped and held to ransom by Hungarian gypsies . . . All right, I was kidding about the kidnap, but I clearly remember being woken up in the middle of the night, and my sister and me being put into dressing gowns, the ones with silken rabbits stitched on, carried downstairs and hurried off to the air-raid shelter at the bottom of the road.

> *The cord of my new dressing-gown*
> *he helps me tie*
>
> *Then on to my father's shoulder*
> *held high*
>
> *The world at night with my little eye*
> *I spy*
>
> *The moon close enough to touch*
> *I try*

Silver-painted elephants have learned
to fly

Giants fence with searchlights
in the sky

Too soon into the magic shelter
he and I

Air raids are so much fun
I wonder why

In the bunk below, a big boy
starts to cry.

Although the fear of those adults around me may have been contagious, the only feelings I can remember were of excitement. The bunk beds in the shelter would have been crammed with children, the young ones laughing or crying, the older ones reading stories to them or singing, and the grown-ups coming and going, trying to make light of the situation. My father would have been a volunteer fireman, perhaps on duty outside, where the sky would have been fizzing with light and noise.

Whenever the sirens went off and there wasn't time to run down to the shelter, we would hide in a small cupboard under the stairs. Brenda and I would be put into a cot that took up all the space, and Mother would lie on top of us with my dad covering us all. As my sister and I drifted off to sleep they would listen to the aircraft thundering overhead, to the ack-ack fire and to the explosions that seemed to be drawing closer and shudderingly closer. It must have been terrifying for them and no doubt the Hail Marys came thick and fast. The idea of our hunkering down there was that should the house be bombed and collapse, my sister and I would stand the best chance of survival. Luckily my father's brave, and perhaps foolhardy, attempt to withstand the full force of Hitler's *Luftwaffe* was never put to the test.

The alleyways that ran between the backs of the houses, or 'jiggers', as they were known, were good places to find the tail fins of enemy incendiary bombs that many boys collected, but you had to be careful when picking them up for some mornings they would still be white hot. It was scary but reassuring to know that once handed in, the tail fins would be melted down to make incendiary bombs that could be dropped on German houses. Barrage balloons, the pride and joy of the ARP (Air Raid Precautions), were moored in a field close by and when lowered by metal cables they seemed to perch on the roofs of the house opposite, like alien spacecraft, or elephants grazing. In the first published version of that poem about my dad giving me a piggyback to the air-raid shelter, I had described them as: 'Unheard of silver elephants have learned to fly', which made perfect sense to me, because as a child, I remember someone saying 'a herd of elephants' and my mishearing it as 'unheard of elephants', and years later assumed that the reader of the poem would also make the connection. Several of my poems have sprung from a creative dyslexia, but in this case I changed the line to 'A herd of silver elephants' and again to 'Silver-painted elephants' in search of a less confusing image.

There is a little town in north Wales called Chirk, and when the bombing was at its fiercest my mother took my sister and me to stay there with a local family. It was an evacuation of sorts, but I don't know how it was organised, and we certainly didn't have our names written on luggage labels and attached to our coats. The Hulse family took us in, Alma and Orlando, who had two older children, and they were so welcoming and warm that I've never been very good at Welsh jokes. Uncle Lando, as we called him, worked down the coal mine and was built four-square, with arms and legs like sawn-off pit props. He would come home from the shift covered in coal dust with his blue eyes sparkling and teeth shining, and chase Brenda and me round the living room pretending to want a big hug until Aunty Alma chased him upstairs for a bath. He would take us into the fields at first light to gather mushrooms and for long walks along the banks of the River Vernwy, where the smell of wild garlic was almost tangible.

My memories of that period seem to belong to a child of another time and place. Of distant mountains and open skies, and greenness in every direction. Of the tuneful clamour of birds as I walked with Brenda and Aunty Alma through hedge-lined country lanes to Old Jack in his grocery shop, a caravan on wheels, seemingly in the middle of nowhere. Of the flickering black-and-white films and the noisy projector, as we all sat on wooden benches in the village hall. Another twelve months or so down there and I might have become a Welsh Laurie Lee and, instead of *Summer with Monika*, my first book would have been 'Cider with Blodwyn'. But Hitler had other ideas, the bombs stopped falling and we moved back to the city.

LEARNING TO READ

Seriously, Roger, do you think for a moment that anybody is going to be at all interested in the fact that you won a baby show?

I don't know, but the fact that I did may go some way to explaining my later interest and moderate success in show business. You know, baby show, show business? More important, how many autobiographies have you read in which the writer was not only the winner of his class, but Best Baby of the show?

Under hypnosis I can still smell Johnson's baby powder, gripe water, cheap scent and eighty-four filled nappies, mine remaining clean and dry, as I preferred to wait until I got home and use the potty as I'd been trained. A very fetching velvet romper suit was one of the prizes and an electric iron (which would have come in very useful once we'd switched over from gas). But that must have taken a while, for Mum continued to use an old flat iron for ages; unless she couldn't be doing with all that newfangled electrical nonsense. I would have been a toddler standing on a chair in the back kitchen, watching her doing the ironing. I loved the fresh smell and the warmth, and the way creases disappeared in the wake of the black iron ship as it sailed across the open sheets. I loved especially the gas rings on the stove, out of which the blue tongues of dragons came hissing to lick the base of the iron until it was red hot. That morning, when Mother eventually turned off the gas, I watched the dragons slink back into their lair and, in an attempt to catch their tails, put my hand on top of the ring, still glowing. I think I heard the hissing sound before I felt the pain, and I do remember my palm sticking to the gas ring as she pulled it off and shoved my fist into a pot of cold tea.

To have entered me for a competition before I was out of nappies clearly illustrates my mother's loving pushiness, and it was to show itself again eight years later when I was happily doing well at junior school and she learned from a friend that her son was leaving to go to St Mary's College, the Catholic grammar school that all the local RCs aspired to. Once admitted to the preparatory school, her friend said, a boy stood a better chance of passing the scholarship. Because her friend was a close friend, she had kept the information close to her chest until her own boy had got in, so we had missed the deadline. Never mind, said my dad, he'll probably pass the scholarship exam anyway and so it won't cost us a penny. Mum, though, was taking no chances, and it took a lot of courage for someone who had little education to breeze through the posh school gates, buttonhole the intimidating secretary and wheedle an interview with Brother Thompson, the other-worldly Headmaster. I don't know what she said, but that same afternoon I was sat down at a desk by Mr Keating and given the school entrance papers. I passed and proudly entered St Mary's College, as Brother Thompson would always put it, 'through the back door'.

Up until then I had attended Star of the Sea School, Seaforth, a name rich in assonance. It was a large Gothic building divided into two sections, Infants and Juniors, each with its own entrance and playground. The Infants' playground was small, but to the little infants it seemed very spacious, whereas the Juniors' playground was large but seemed small to the big juniors. There must be a lesson there somewhere. Miss Crooke and Miss O'Brien were the teachers I remember with fondness and, although I have very few memories of my formative years there, I was very happy. Always assuming, of course, that the Magician in the Brain hasn't blotted out the frequent beatings, the bearded nuns, the sexual abuse, the bullying and the afternoons spent locked in rat-infested cellars.

I was bright enough to enjoy learning and my mother, true to form, had made sure I could read and write before starting school. How well I remember during the early nights of the Blitz the two of us cuddled up together in the blackout, curtains pulled back and her reading bedtime stories by the light of a blazing factory or a crashed Messerschmitt. In school, wall charts were very popular and that was how we learned our times tables, chanting out the numbers as teacher pointed to the chart. Learning by rote. My very favourite chart was a large laminated one that had probably been in the school since the twenties. It was the alphabet in which each letter was incorporated into the colourful illustration and accompanied by a caption. For instance, 'Tired Mother says "h"' which showed a flapper sitting wearily on an h-shaped chair. 'Ronnie's red rattle says "r"' with a wholesome young tyke rattling his r-shaped red rattle. Others I seem to recall, although my memory could be playing me false, were 'Poppy's pink potty says "p"' and 'Norman's naughty nudger says "n"'.

I loved the art lessons, and was good at drawing and painting, but not the best in the class. A quiet, good-looking boy called John Askew was the Michelangelo of our year and he never seemed to do anything else. Whenever the rest of us would be slaving over a hot sum or stringing sentences together to see what happened, he would be encouraged to sit at the back of the classroom and paint. Even though John and I obviously had something in common, we couldn't be described as having shared interests. At that age, seven or eight, we weren't interested in art, we were just good at it. So we weren't mates and when I left Star of the Sea a year later to go to St Mary's our paths never crossed again. I was to hear and read about him, though, not as an artist, but as a pop star. On leaving school he joined the Merchant Navy, as so many of our contemporaries did, and learned to play guitar (as so many of our contemporaries did). He was eventually signed up by Larry Parnes, rechristened Johnny Gentle and enjoyed a short career as a pop idol. His biggest claim to fame was a two-week tour of Scotland in 1960 when the Beatles, then billed as the Silver Beatles, were the support group. If only he'd practised his guitar at school instead of doing all that cutting and pasting, he might have had a longer career. Alternatively, if he hadn't gone into the Merchant Navy he might never have become a pop star of the sea.

CLOCKWORK CHEESE

What was your favourite toy when you were a child? A doll's house? An electric racing car? A wooden Noah's Ark with animals? That teddy bear in the cupboard who can't understand why you don't take him out and play with him any more? Mine was a toy cheese. Toy cheese? Yes, it's difficult for me now to comprehend, let alone explain. I see a mechanical toy, a metal cheese portion that when wound up did things like . . . er . . . well, . . . er . . . make cheese noises? Perform nifty cheese-like movements? I don't remember. But it certainly kept me amused for hours when I was tiny. It was more fun to play with on the lino than the carpet because it made the whirring clockwork noise seem louder, and I loved the red colouring of the label and even the oily, metallic smell. Who needs computer games? Bring back mechanical cheese, I say.

Being a boy and well aware of my chromosome make-up, I enjoyed war games. I had a set of lead soldiers (the ones we used to suck the paint off), but mine remained stupidly at attention all the time, even when I ordered them to charge or kneel down and fire at will. So I much preferred playing with my father's collar studs and cuff-links. I would kneel in front of the easy chair by the fireplace and the back cushion would become the mountain where the cuff-links would lie in wait to ambush the studs as they crossed the plain below. Rummaging around in Mum's sewing box would reward me with bra clasps and suspender fastenings that could be thrown into the fray, often changing the course of battle.

I sense that I have always preferred books and radio to film and television because the latter are too prescribed and specific. If you are imagining, as I was, real soldiers, then lead soldiers are no more realistic than bra clasps.

As I grew older and began to play outside with other kids, I wanted a gun so that I could shoot them. During the war metal toys would have been hard to find . . . (Come to think of it, where did that cheese portion come from? Could it, horror of horrors, have been second-hand? Had Santa pulled a fast one?) . . . so my dad carved me a wooden revolver and painted it black. Light and easy to use, it did the job perfectly, as countless German soldiers and Red Indians will testify.

Flicking through my junior school exercise books, I see that on almost every page I have drawn Spitfires blasting Messerschmitts out of the sky, while below, one of our lads machine-guns a platoon of Japanese soldiers. I assume that the Japanese outnumbered the Germans in these early Bayeux tapestries because as baddies they were easier to draw. Like most boys of my age I always carried around with me a little plane-spotting book and from the silhouettes could recognise Dorniers, Fokker Wulfs, Mustangs, Hurricanes, Lancasters, as well as obscure Italian and Ibizan aircraft. At seven I longed to be able to do my bit for Britain, perhaps as a plane spotter on top of the Liver Buildings, but my war effort was restricted to collecting milk-bottle tops. In those days, milk-bottles had a wide two-inch neck and the tops were cardboard discs that fitted inside and could be recycled. I forget, now, how it worked but you were given a badge with a military rank for the number you had collected. I think I got to be a lieutenant-colonel, but that could be a case of over-promotion on my part.

After the Second World War (we won, by the way), metal and plastic toys started to reappear in the shops, and I was given a box of Meccano. A lot of my friends loved their Meccano and every year upgraded their sets to include winches, crowbars, stopcocks, electron guns, internal combustion engines and I don't know what else. My set was the basic '0' reg., which included strips of red metal with holes punched in them, some nuts, bolts, a spanner and a pair of wheels. It kept me amused for minutes. Dad would sit with me and get all enthusiastic about constructing a pair of ladders and a luggage trolley, but little Isambard Brunel would soon drift off to rummage in Mummy's sewing box. For a short while I collected and swapped Dinky toys, but playing with miniature Lagondas, Aston Martins and Ford Prefects made me carsick, so I gave them all away.

A Ford Prefect of the non-Dinky variety was the only car we ever owned and there was great excitement when my dad bought an over-used one. In his bachelor days and the early years of marriage, he'd been mad keen on motorbikes, and there are lots of photographs of him astride BSAs, Triumphs and a favourite of his called a Scott, sometimes with Mum on the pillion and Aunty Win in the sidecar. But for years he could only afford a bicycle and so this splashing out on a car when Brenda and I reached our teens must have been cause for celebration.

We didn't have it for long, though. The one notable

journey we made in the old jalopy was a trip down to London to visit Mum's brother George and his wife, Helen, who lived in Eltham. I don't know what time we set off from Liverpool, but we only got as far as Whitchurch in Shropshire when Dad decided we wouldn't make it before dark so we slept overnight in the car. Whether the car's lights failed or we had run out of petrol I don't remember, the only good news was that as there were no motorways in those days there were no Little Chefs either, so we didn't have to eat in one.

THROUGH THE KEYHOLE

'Number eleven in the centre of the terrace is a small house with a bow-window in the front overlooking a tiny garden surrounded by a low privet hedge. Open the front door and in we go, to find ourselves in a small vestibule with what is obviously the "parlour" on the right-hand side. Let's have a look. Neat and tidy as one would expect. Not a trace of dust, and the smell of Brasso and beeswax furniture polish tells us that there is a house-proud mother somewhere. Notice the framed pictures of Rio de Janeiro in which a collage of butterfly wings has been used as a background, the Moroccan pouffe and the procession of miniature ebony elephants, suggesting that whoever lives here has travelled abroad. I think much of the furniture polish will have gone on the radiogram over there, and on the upright piano, obviously much in use on account of the sheet music propped up and the lid left open. Let's have a quick peep at the LP on the turntable and see what their taste in music is. My money is on Glenn Miller. Joseph Locke perhaps? No, I'm wrong, Beniamino Gigli. Ooh. Aren't we posh!

'*We can lose that I think. Let's move on to the living room, and mind the crucifix on the wall as you back down the hall.*

'Living room, recently redecorated and very much up to the standard of cleanliness we've already come to expect. In the centre of the room a square dining table with four chairs, and two tapestry easy chairs by the fireplace. Low oak sideboard, on top of which are a pair of brass candlesticks and a pewter tea service consisting of a teapot, sugar bowl and milk jug. Probably a black iron grate over there once upon a time, with a hob and an oven. Gorgeous, weren't they? But a devil to clean, so it's been replaced by this geometric fifties version of brown and beige tiles. A pair of hunting prints on the wall? No, I rather doubt if a Master of the Hunt lives here, but they do provide a glimpse of the countryside. Rather a dark room being overlooked by the backs of those houses opposite; and while we're by the window, notice the pane of glass at the bottom here has recently been replaced, the putty is still soft. Would I be right in suspecting a small boy playing with a ball in the backyard? We shall see. A small bookcase above a writing bureau. Let's have a look . . . *Family Medical Encyclopaedia* . . . World Atlas . . . *Adventures on the Roof of the World,* some *National Geographic* magazines, P. G. Wodehouse . . . Mazo de la Roche . . . Some authors I don't seem to recognise . . . Novels about the sea, which surely gives us a further clue . . .

'Leading into an extremely small kitchen, which is very dark indeed, overlooked by the house next door. Gas stove on the left, standing next to a green-and-cream-painted kitchen cabinet complete with glass-fronted cupboards and a fold-down table. On the right, below the window and with a sumptuous view of the backyard wall, a chest of drawers with a spotlessly scrubbed surface, on which the lady of the house no doubt does her baking. And hanging from the ceiling what looks like two iron coat hangers with wooden slats fitted in, and a rope-and-pulley system, one of those fabulous contraptions they used for hanging out the washing to dry. Absolutely of its time!

'In the far right-hand corner the kitchen sink with the inevitable Ascot heater providing the hot water. And not only for washing-up, because along the length of the far wall is an iron bath, with a low curtain of yellow gingham to hide its modesty, and a removable lid of plywood covered with Formica. No central heating, of course, and even now there's one helluva draught blowing under the back door.

'Is it time for a coffee-break do you think, or would you rather carry on? Yes, so would I, so let's continue upstairs.

'Its dreadfully narrow, so do be careful, Giles.

'And the stairs lead directly into a small bedroom, a girl's by the look of it. I should imagine this was formerly the bathroom, which has been converted. Linoleum flooring and an empty fire grate. Coming out, we take two steps up to the left into what is obviously the boy's room. One large wardrobe with a full-length mirror that seems to glower over the room. Again, it's very dark in here, the only view being a sky the colour of old saucepans reflected in the dull grey roof tiles of the house opposite. It's about thirty metres away and it's got its back to us. Another unused iron fire grate and the inevitable linoleum. In the recess next to the fireplace what used to be known as a tallboy, a high chest of drawers made in two sections and placed one on top of the other. Alongside the bed what would appear to be a home-made bookcase. Let's have a shuftie. Comics mainly: *The Wizard, The Hotspur, Adventure, Rover,* and some abbreviated classics, *A Christmas Carol, A Tale of Two Cities, Treasure Island,* the usual boy's stuff. No sign of any particular hobbies or interests, unless you count Owzat, a sort of rolling-dice game that is set out on the top shelf, next to the cricket scorebook and pencil stubs. And we can't leave without saying goodbye to the Virgin Mary, whose statue it is on top of the tallboy.

'*And cut! And Giles, please make sure that Toby doesn't lose the bit about the saucepan-coloured sky, I really liked that. Did you? Thank you.*

'The master bedroom at the front of the house is bigger and much lighter thanks to the two windows overlooking the cobbled street outside. Double bed, and bedroom suite consisting of dressing table and matching wardrobe. A painted plaster statue of St Theresa, I think it is, on the mantelpiece and an even larger statue of some saint or other on top of the cupboard.

'*Cut! Who is it, Giles? Anybody know? Saint Anthony perhaps, although it could be Saint Francis of Assisi. That's a gorgeous little town, anybody been there? You have! All right, then, let's make it Saint Francis.*

'A painted plaster statue of Saint Theresa on the mantelpiece, and an even larger statue of Saint Francis of Assisi on top of the cupboard. So there you have it, a quick glimpse through the keyhole of an ordinary working-class house in post-war Liverpool. And it's back to David in the studio.

'*And cut! God, Giles, do you think there'll be a Caffè Nero around here? No, neither do I.*'

A CLEAN SLATE

Open the back-kitchen door and step into the yard. Facing you, six feet away, is the high wall that divides the McGoughs from the Thomases. At the foot of the wall is a 'garden feature' comprising a thin rectangle of soil about the length and width of two coffins laid end to end. No grass as far as I can remember, but for reasons known only to themselves, irises flourished.

Except for our short-stay pet cats, we all kept well away from it and even then I wondered why it was never concreted over. The yard sloped down for about eight yards to the back door. Halfway down on the left was the coal shed, below that the bike shed (formerly the washing shed where Mum kept the mangle, dolly peg and washing tub) and next to the back door the toilet. Having been brought up for seventeen years in a house with only an outside toilet, I always thought there was something unhygienic about one inside the house. I must admit, though, that in winter it was like a frozen tundra down there, for we never had a light fitted until I was ten and, when snow had turned to ice, the slope down from the kitchen door became a treacherous mini-piste. In summer the scourge of Ozzy outback dunnies, the redback and the funnel spider, were never a problem, but daddy-long-legs as big as my fist (small fist, big imagination) used to scare the pants back on to me. 'They're more scared of you, than you are of them,' my dad would say, but I knew that was impossible.

And it wasn't only mini-beasts that scuttled across my nightmares but life-sized ones too.

One of the worst jobs was bringing in the coal. Why was it always on winter nights when it was cold and dark that you had to fetch the bucket and shovel and a torch, and go down the yard? Why not on warm summer evenings? Philosophical thoughts such as these used to take my mind off bogeymen as I did my nightly filial duty. It was 1945 and the war was over, but it was business as usual for the McGough household even with the VJ Day celebrations approaching. I would have been eight years old when I grumbled out of the house and into the yard to fetch the coal. It was pitch-black so I needed the torch as I lifted the latch and swung open the shed door. I shone the beam inside and let out a scream, dropped the bucket and shovel, and shot back into the house. I had seen a ghost, a corpse propped up on top of the coal. A monster in black with a grinning moonface, its arms reaching out to pull me in and drag me deep down under the suffocating coals.

Turns out I had overreacted. The clue lies in VJ Day and the planned street party to celebrate the Allies' defeat of the Japanese. Dad had volunteered to make the guy that would sit on top of the bonfire and in the cold light of the next day I saw the monster for what it really was: a straw-filled suit with a stuffed pillowcase for a head, its face painted yellow with black slanty eyes and a grin. Sayonara. Saynomore.

Open the back door and step into the jigger that runs

between the backs of the houses. Don't dally there because it is dark and claustrophobic, but turn left and hurry towards the light at the end of the tunnel, where you will find the remains of an air-raid shelter and the *Luftwaffe*'s gift to town planning, the 'debris' or 'bommy'. Bommies were the bomb-flattened spaces to be found at the corners of many streets, in pre-skip days the dumping ground for old sofas, garbage and dead cats. If you remembered the houses and shops that had stood there before, these rectangles of brick and broken glass, of blackened toys, wire and shredded linen, were filled with ghosts whose screaming the roar of the bulldozers failed to drown. But if you couldn't remember and they had been cleared, they became not only playgrounds, but battlegrounds for rival gangs. If you were crossing a bommy a few streets away from home, you were liable to be slated. And I don't mean told off. I mean that lads would suddenly appear, pick up handy-sized pieces of shattered roof slate and hurl them at you. It was all done with a sense of fun, you understand, rather than malice, the street urchins' equivalent of toffs throwing bread rolls at each other after supper, but nevertheless the sound of those lethal arrowheads whizzing through the air was one that, like King Harold, I came to dread. Injuries were common, but I was never hit myself, for I realised quite early on that to retaliate by bending down, finding a piece of shrapnel and returning fire made for an easy target, so scarper was the better part of valour.

There were neighbourhood gangs involving older boys, of course, but no fancy names, weird initiation rituals or graffiti tags, and certainly no peer pressure to join up. Nor was there sectarian rivalry, for the 'Proddydogs' and the

'Cattylicks' lived side by side. At thirteen I used to be rather jealous of boys in my class who lived nearer the city centre and couldn't wait for four o'clock so they could gang up and play Sally-O, a game with rules so complicated they couldn't be explained to outsiders. Each night, apparently, worn out after the game, they would all buy chips and a bottle of sarsaparilla and roam the streets until well after ten o'clock. Some lads had all the luck. In our street (apart from Puggy Lewis who spent most of his time in Borstal) there were only two boys of my age: Bunny, who lived in the house opposite, and Vernon, who lived next door but one. My cousins, the McGarrys, lived in the next street, all five of them, but they were younger than me and therefore unplayable-with.

You would imagine that if three boys of the same age grew up and lived within ten yards of each other they would become pals, share sweets and hobbies, roam the streets together, form a tight unit to ward off girls and other undesirables. But no. Bunny Burleigh took after his dad and spent every waking hour taking motorbikes to pieces, oiling, polishing and reassembling the black metal jigsaw. Vernon Carter, on the other hand, took after his mother and wore women's clothes. No, that's unfair, I never saw him in a frock but I always had the feeling that he had just changed out of one. Homosexuality didn't feature at all while I was growing up. There were jokes about queers and there were certain men said to be 'funny', whom Mum told me to keep away from, including a special constable conscripted as the local lollipop man who used to ply me with sweets and cakes on my way home from school. That is, until my dad warned him where he'd stick his docker's hook . . .

'He'll not bother you again,' Dad said.

'But he wasn't bothering me, he was nice.'

'Shut up and eat your corned-beef hash.'

When Vernon left school and joined the Air Force he used to bring a different friend home on every leave and Mrs Carter, all innocence, would serve breakfast to the two of them in bed together and boast to the neighbours how popular her son was: 'I had to say to him, Vernon, no you can't have two friends staying over, that single bed just isn't big enough. But then he looked at me with those big brown eyes and I thought, oh, what the heck, it's Christmas.'

PLAYING CRICKET FOR LANCASHIRE

I perfected my bowling skills in the backyard. Every evening after junior school, weather permitting, I would be out there pitching up a tennis ball, or red sponge ball for hours on end. At first the wicket was the coal shovel stood up against the wall under the living-room window, but that soon became too easy a target and was replaced by a small wooden stump. My run-up began at the back door, two paces and into that smooth overarm action that was to become the envy of bowlers the length and breadth of our street. I modelled my action on Ray Lindwall, the leading Australian of the time, but unfortunately my career as a fast bowler came to an end when a full toss went straight through the window and ricocheted around the living room.

So I turned to spin and in no time at all could land the ball on a pigeon dropping for a ninety-degree leg-break. Needless to say, it wasn't a small boy in short trousers tossing a tennis ball up a backyard ten yards long, but 'Monsoon' McGough leading the attack for Lancashire at Old Trafford. The red leather ball fizzing in my hand as I turn to begin my first spell from the Stretford Road end. Two paces, a silky shuffle, the signature wrist action and 'Owzat?' I've done it again: Yorkshire all out for nought. Brian Statham, not a bone of jealousy in his body, sprints over from long leg and is the first to congratulate me on my ten wickets for no runs. Time for tea. Both teams stand back to applaud me as, head down, I hurry up the steps and into the pavilion. 'I've been calling you for ages,' says mum. 'Your cheese and onion pie will be stone cold.'

By the time I reached my teens I had outgrown the backyard and a choice had to be made, either the family moved to a bigger house with a large garden at the back (preferably leading down to a gently flowing stream), or I made friends with boys who enjoyed playing cricket as much as I did. John Clarke and Bernard Procter, two St Mary's boys and friends from church, were as imaginative as I was and in next to no time we were whipping the Aussies at Litherland Park, which was very much like the Oval except there was no seating for spectators and no pavilion. Oh, and no grass. In between innings we'd discuss the first inklings of philosophy while swigging from bottles of Tizer or Dandelion and Burdock. Not much talk about girls or sex, as far as I remember, more the existence of God and whether eating a chip dipped in beef gravy on a Friday was a mortal sin, or just venial? Venial we decided.

John went on to university to study English Literature, married a local girl and had a successful career in Higher Education, whereas Bernard left school at fifteen to join a seminary and study for the priesthood. We kept in touch intermittently over the years, and I learned about his becoming a Franciscan monk and then about his disenchantment with the monastic life. He was one of three boys in my year at school who went into the priesthood, two of whom, like Bernard, came from poor, one-parent families, and only one still wears the cloth. When they joined the priesthood it was a step up the social ladder and, except for a few orange hot spots, they were respected by the community at large. But then, of course, so were teachers and policemen.

The unimaginable force that governs us, the benevolent energy behind all that we see and do, has been over-simplified in the excitement of evangelism, and in their attempts to personalise God, artists have anthropomorphised a concept that is beyond human comprehension, so many of us have come to reject religion. Except perhaps on those evenings as the light drains away into the horizon, and the old questions rise up again and we lift our eyes from the ground and search for answers beyond the stars. The dead, where are they? All our joys and sorrows must have meaning, surely? And, occasionally, there is a tremor in the soul, a glimmer of revelation, the promise of peace. During my student days I used to love discussing religion, the arguments for and against the existence of God, but now as I listen to people misquoting Stephen Dawkins, who misunderstand the string theory and bang on about war, poverty, AIDS and all the world's problems, which they put down to the failure of religion, I find it so much more of an effort to step in and say 'Excuse me, it's not religions that are the problem, but people . . .' It's like being in the back of a cab with the driver airing his views about politics and immigrants assuming they're yours, and isn't it easier sometimes just to sit back and nod rather than get into an argument? Then he drops you off and you overtip, not because you were afraid to speak up, but to punish yourself for lacking the courage not to tip at all.

Here's a tip: every religion offers a set of rules by which to live your life, and if you break the rules, don't worry, your leg won't drop off nor will you burn in hell for eternity. But if you try to keep to the guidelines, love your neighbour as yourself, you'll stand a good chance of achieving some sort of equilibrium during this life; and in the next, if there is one, you might well be made a prefect and get to wear a badge.

A couple of months ago I was drinking in my local with four guys, all practising Catholics more or less, and when the topic of vocations came up, every one of us agreed (although, like myself, they might have had their fingers crossed behind their backs, but I don't think so) that had it not been for the rule of celibacy we would all have entered the priesthood. We had all been brought up to regard a priest as someone special, a man who could be a power for good in the community both in a social and a political sense. Free housing and away from the rat race. And besides, we were all partial to dressing up and standing in the warm glow of a candlelit altar, the congregation hanging on our every word. But, sadly for us, celibacy was a step too far. Yes, I like to think that my old pal Pete McCarthy was spot on when he said that had the girls not got to me first, I might well have been the first Liverpudlian Pope.

A SNAPPY DRESSER

The backyard was not only my Lord's, my Oval and my Old Trafford, but my cathedral. Long before it became the Kirkstall Lane end, the back wall of the house was the chancel of the church and the windowsill my high altar. I would get my little sister Brenda, and as many tame kids as I could dragoon, to dress as deacons and servers, while I would wrap a white sheet round my waist to make do as an alb and, for the chasuble, put a large towel over my shoulders. The household was a bit short on golden chalices but ran to a pair of brass candlesticks and an old pewter tea service that came in handy during the offertory. My acolytes would lead me out into the yard, where I would celebrate mass with all the solemnity a five-year-old could muster.

Although it was all make-believe, there was no irony or poking fun in our rituals. There was no television in those days and no theatre for the likes of us, so a church was where all the drama took place. The bright colours of the vestments, the incense, the stained glass, the candlelit stage and the singing provided the sensory experiences that at times overwhelmed me. In fact, I fainted in church during mass more than once, a practice not uncommon in those days, having more to do with the compulsory twenty-four-hour fast before receiving communion than to any spiritual paroxysm.

The Latin, too, was sonorous and mysterious, and I could recite all the prayers before I could understand their meanings. I must admit that when English eventually replaced the Latin, much of the mystery and the poetry disappeared. '*Mea culpa, mea culpa, mea minima culpa.*'

I became an altar boy at the age of nine at Star of the Sea church and carried on serving until I was fifteen. It was a social activity as much as anything else, for all my closest school friends joined up as well, and for High Mass and feast days the cast would have numbered about eighteen. There were three priests in charge. The parish priest was Father Timoney – devout and cantankerous, he struck the fear of God into us, but on the plus side he could say mass in fifteen minutes flat. The other, younger priests like Father Flynn, Father Hughes and Father Healey helped run the youth club and organised the annual trips to Galway, the reward for us hard-working, unpaid servers. It was hard work, too, especially if you were on the early shift, which meant leaving the house at 6.30 in the morning to be ready for the seven o'clock mass.

'*Without breakfast, the little chap runs through the mean, cobbled streets, the gas lamps spluttering and dying, as the first shafts of sunlight, edging their way over the smoke-blackened factory walls, find reflection in his eager National Health spectacles.*'

I felt happy about doing it all, though. Making sacrifices and doing good works for no worldly gain, other than for the grace I would be storing up: my own little reservoir of creamy, sparkling stuff that I could dip into in later life. A spoonful to be taken now and again when I was feeling down. 'Grace, the proven existential cure for all known ills.'

I'm not particularly proud of this, but I have always been

what they used to call a snappy dresser. I don't know where I got it from and I wish I were above such trivial pea-cocking, but even as an altar boy I remember always choosing the whitest surplice trimmed with the most lace. Most lads went to the cupboard in the sacristy, grabbed the nearest and slung it on, often back to front, but not me. And you should have seen me as a Boy Scout. We wore those khaki hats that Baden-Powell introduced from the Boer War and I wore mine with the rim of one side turned up, like I was a bush ranger or a soldier on leave from Burma. I fooled nobody. As for badges, I loved them. Artist's badge, Pathfinder's, Swimmer's, Potato peeler's, Pooh-sticker's, Spitter's, I wore them all with pride. If I could wear my CBE medal every day on my hoody I would. And the polished oak chest and decorated scroll that the Lord Mayor of Liverpool presented to me on being given the freedom of the City is something I will always treasure, but where, oh where, is the big gold badge? What is the point of the D.Litt. and Honorary Fellowships if you can't swan around Tesco's in the velvet cap and silken robes?

Our school uniform consisted of an unsnazzy maroon blazer and a cap that had to be worn with the peak pulled down over the forehead. Some hope. What is the point of training a Brylcreemed quiff or a Tony Curtis if nobody interesting gets to see it? So once past the prefects on inspection duty at the school gates, the cap would either be whipped off and stuffed into the satchel, or shoved to the back of the head and worn like a misshapen yarmulke. Come to think of it, it was probably the insouciant quiff and devil-may-care wearing of the cap that first took Joan Taylor's breath away.

These post-war years were not notable for high fashion. Demob suits, trilby hats, belted gabardine raincoats . . . and that was only the girls. Then, overnight, or so it seemed, there were teenagers. How I longed to be a Teddy boy. Unless you were young at the time you can't imagine the impact they had on us all. Standing at a bus stop next to a gang, I wouldn't be able to take my eyes off them. Into a world of beige, brown and grey, aliens wearing outrageous suits of scarlet and midnight blue with velvet collars and bootlace ties seemed to have landed from the planet Rainbow. And the haircuts, usually a DA (or duck's arse, so called because the hair was cut thick at the back and combed into a line from the crown to the nape of the neck to resemble a duck whose arse had been brushed and Brylcreemed). As a sixteen-year-old I didn't hanker after the loose-lipped sullenness, the drooping fag, even the rock'n'roll, it was the tight trousers.

There was a catch-22 situation, however, involving the Teddy boy mystique, for unlike teddy bears there was nothing cuddly about them. Although they dressed in a way that might cause an innocent passer-by to pause and stare, staring would often cause offence. For many of them were nutters in fancy clothing and, like mods, rockers, skins, punks and professional footballers, prone to acts of violence.

It was a Sunday evening jive night at Star of the Sea parish hall where we locals bopped happily and innocently to 78s played on a Dansette record player. Tonight's DJ? None other than the Reverend Father Flynn. The girls, wearing either floral dresses with cardies on top, or black taffeta skirts worn with elastic waspie belts and white blouses, collar up, were dancing demurely in a group, waiting for a couple of us lads to pluck up the courage to move in. Then the Teds arrived. We had our own local Teddy boys, peacocks who preened outside the Ball Hall (snooker rooms) on Bridge Road and would have been horrified to get a speck of dirt on their powder-blue drapes. But these guys seemed like aliens. Gangs from the Bullring and the Dingle would occasionally pop out of town for a spot of bloodletting, and where better to limber up, get the juices flowing, than at a youth club out in the sticks?

They reeked of violence (a mixture of sweat and fear) and their suits with elongated jackets and skin-tight jeans seemed almost a parody of the fashion. They were dirty and I'd never seen hairstyles quite like theirs: black and sculpted. They looked as if their faces were being swallowed by large cockroaches. My instinct was to go right over to them and explain that this was a dance for parish members only, and would they be kind enough to leave. Fortunately, Captain Cautious talked me out of it, and just as well he did. Like something nasty spilled on the floor and spreading, they moved among the couples, mainly girls, who were dancing. Some refused huffily and raced off to the Ladies, but most of them put on a brave face, trying to convince themselves that you can't judge a book by its cover, however dodgy-looking. The ploy of these godless apes was to whip up the yokels into paroxysms of jealous rage at the sight of them pawing our Catholic virgins. But we thought, oh, well, never mind . . . can't be helped . . . soon be over . . . no harm done . . . and other phrases useful for self-preservation that we'd picked up over the years. One lad, though, new to the area, made the mistake of looking at one of the invaders dancing. And boy, could he dance (and here I'm ashamed to admit that Rita seemed to be really enjoying herself, the brazen hussy). He stopped jiving and, leaving Rita in mid-twirl, said: 'Who are you looking at?'

This is a deceptively loaded question beloved of psychopaths because it brooks no answer.

If the reply of your choice is: '*You, yer twat, worra yer gonna do about it?*' He will show you, with gusto. However, you might choose to say: '*You, actually, I was seriously admiring your dancing skills.*' Or, you might opt for '*Your good self, I mean that's a mighty fine haircut, could you recommend a good barber, or in your case, a good entomologist?*' I'm sorry, but whatever answer you give will be the wrong one. The one to release the coil that has wound him up.

I don't know which answer the boy opted for, but he was head-butted before being dragged outside by the gang. Girls were screaming. Father Flynn rushed out to calm things down while one of the mothers phoned for the police. We all went out into Elm Road, hoping that a show of force might deter the inevitable. The gang had formed a tight ring round the lad and were kicking, according to local parlance, seven shades of shit out of him. Then the bicycle chains appeared, and they thrashed and flailed him with such hatred and force, it's a wonder he wasn't killed. A police siren sounded and they scattered in all directions.

'Bastards!' we shouted, 'Come back here and fight!'

One of life's minor tragedies is desperately wanting things when young that you can't afford, and by the time you've grown and are able to afford them, you don't want them. By the time I could afford to buy an expensive Teddy boy suit they were long out of fashion and I had no wish to dress like a colourful flashback. Adrian Henri, painter, poet and bon viveur, claims that the first time he met me was when I stopped him in the street and asked him where I could buy a pair of winkle-pickers. I must say, I don't remember this and really wonder if he was the sort of person I would have stopped in the street to enquire about winkle-pickers. Perhaps the shoes were just a ploy, an opening gambit on my part so that I could find out more about Cannonball Adderley, Kurt Schwitters et al. Also, despite his bulk, Adrian too was something of a snappy, if eccentric, dresser, for this was the man who could alternate between two jackets, one leather, one satin with his poems stitched on the back by nimble-fingered fans.

THE FACTS OF LIFE

Whereas my junior school had been within easy walking distance of home, my new school, St Mary's, was out in the suburbs of Crosby, which meant leaving the house an hour earlier and taking a bus. It also meant going to school on Saturday mornings, sacrifices, I thought, well worth it. My parents obviously did too, because they would have had to stump up for tuition fees, school uniform, PE kit and the rest, in the hope that a year later I'd pass the scholarship and their financial worries would be eased. It was a gamble they cheerfully accepted.

There were about sixty of us, all day boys (boarders having been repelled) in Everest House, a detached house of red sandstone within the main school grounds. One of the first things I noticed about the teachers was that they weren't women. Messrs Keating and Cashell were strict but fair, enjoyed their work and were good teachers, each with a sense of humour. And then there was Brother Cummings. He would have been quite old by then, tall, thin, white-haired with eccentricity bordering on mild insanity. He used to smoke chalk, for instance. By that I don't mean that he would put a stick of chalk in his mouth, light up and puff away contentedly. I mean that he would suck on the chalk as if it were a cigarette. I don't know whether or not he inhaled, but it was a peculiar habit, not to mention the peculiar habit that he wore as an Irish Christian Brother, which was always covered in a fine white dust. Although he could be fierce, it was mainly pretence, and I think we were all quite fond of him.

He was certainly quite fond of me. We came in to school one Monday morning to discover that all the paths around our particular neck of the school grounds had been covered over with tiny pebbles and limestone chippings. 'On no account,' we were warned, 'are you to grab handfuls of pebbles and throw them.' Grab handfuls of pebbles and throw them? Hey, what a great idea. Why hadn't we thought of that? At break time it rained loose chippings with the result that in less than five minutes the pathways were muddy tracks and the lawns were pebble-dashed.

Cummo stormed into the classroom: 'Hands up all those boys who threw pebbles?' Nobody put their hands up. As ever in situations like this I would feel guilty, even if innocent, and consumed with the need to confess. Why? To be a sacrificial lamb? To assuage the shame of those too cowardly to own up? To nobly take the rap on behalf of my compadres? Or simply to bring closure? For whatever reason, I put my hand up.

'McGough, I'm surprised at you.'

'I didn't actually throw them, sir . . . I just picked a few up and, er . . . threw them back in the same place.'

'In exactly the same place?'

'Yes, sir.'

'Do you think I'm stupid, boy? You stand outside in the corridor and I'll deal with you in a minute.'

So I waited outside the classroom. I had never seen the infamous strap at close quarters. I'd heard of it. I'd heard it. But I'd never been on the receiving end of it.

Clearly, it was make-or-break time (or possibly, make a break for it time? But three intense Hail Marys kept me bravely in check). One by one, the other sinners emerged until finally there were seven of us all lined up. Where was Potter, though? He who had cast the first stone? Well, he was a Protestant so maybe he didn't have to own up. Without further ado, Brother Cummings weighed into the miscreants, arms flailing, strap slapping. Everybody got four, two on each hand, and then went back inside the classroom. I was the last in line and when the two of us were alone, he leaned forward and, tapping my nose gently with the strap, whispered, 'I don't think you're as guilty as the rest of them, so let this be our little secret.' He then brought the strap down hard on the side of his cassock four times, which to the tricotières listening inside the classroom sounded like the real thing. After that he gave me two, which sounded even more like the real thing. The boys looked at me with some awe as I swaggered jauntily back to my desk. *'Six! And no tears. Phew, that McGough must be tougher than he looks.'*

As well as raising my profile in the eyes of my peer group, Brother Cummings also taught me more than I needed to know about sex. He crept up behind me one morning in his soft Irish brogues and enquired as to whether I was troubled by thoughts.

'Not that I know of, sir.'

'You understand the kind of thoughts I mean?'

I turned my head slightly so that the light streaming in from the window brought a magical softness to my cheeks, producing an effect of childish innocence. 'No, sir.'

Himself protested, 'Is there anything you want to know about sex?'

There was no escape. My brain flicked through a series of possible questions. 'Why all the fuss?' 'What's wrong with watching dogs?' 'Why is the way to hell down the front of your pyjamas?' until I remembered the first line of a schoolboy joke.

'Where do babies come from?' I stammered. He looked at me in silence for what seemed like a moment. Had I gone too far? I wondered. He took a long, unhurried drag on a piece of chalk and walked away.

The very next morning during break he took me to the stockroom. Part of his job was being in charge of selling books, pens and distributing ink, blackboard dusters and boxes of chalk to boys and masters. Boxes of chalk, yes, it must have been like putting Billy Bunter in charge of the tuck shop. He unlocked the door and pushed me gently inside: 'The answer to your question is written down on a slip of paper and hidden under that box of coloured chalks over by the window. I want you to read it and think carefully about the meaning. I'll be back in fifteen minutes.' With that he disappeared, first locking the door behind him.

I remember being more interested in the contents of the stockroom than the words of wisdom and eternal truth waiting to be revealed in the corner. So I played the flute on a pipette, tried on a First Fifteen rugby shirt and measured my head with a board compass. Eventually, remembering what I was in there for, I picked up the box and removed the note. It said simply: 'The baby is a seed.'

As the bell rang for the end of break he unlocked the door

and led me out into the corridor. 'I don't think you'll be troubled any further by thoughts, now remember to say your prayers regularly and give me that piece of paper.' I handed it over. He tore it into little pieces and I'm sure he put them into his mouth and swallowed them. But that could be my imagination playing tricks.

LITTLE MIRACLES

I have always been a year younger than people who are the same age as me. Or to put it another way, my contemporaries are, in the main, older than myself. This may sound strange to anybody with a minimum grasp of mathematics, so let me explain. At the end of my first year at junior school, because I was bright, I leapfrogged the next class, which was Standard Two, and went straight into the third year. It was fairly common practice in those days, but I don't recommend it, as it resulted in my scraping through exams later on by the skin of my milk teeth. At St Mary's when all the class sat for the scholarship exam at the age of eleven, I was only ten and, though bright for a ten-year-old, I was in a class of bright eleven-year-olds.

After the test I felt that I'd not done as well as I should have and waited nervously for the results. As a family we believed in miracles, and a bottle of Lourdes water was always on hand to turn throat cancer into laryngitis and malaria into a nasty cold. On one occasion I was rushed into Waterloo Hospital with appendicitis and spent the night dreading the operation the following morning. But prayer and Mum's last-minute application of the holy water cleared up the symptoms and I was out of hospital in the afternoon. Perhaps this might explain my fondness some years later for medicinal compound and Lily the Pink.

You see, it's no use being a Catholic if you don't take full advantage of the perks on offer, one of which is insurance. So when the scholarship results were due I began making a novena, which involves going to mass and communion for nine consecutive days; before going to school, I'd be in church at seven o'clock, bleary-eyed and praying: 'Please let me pass the scholarship and I'll never commit any sins, especially those involving immodest actions, whatever they are.' Eventually the day of reckoning arrived. It was a Thursday, I remember, the eighth day of the novena, when Mr Keating read out the names of those boys who had passed. My name was not on the list. At four o'clock I dragged myself home, my heart in my satchel, to break the news to my parents. They would have been gutted, but tried not to show their disappointment. 'You can try again next year,' said my dad.

That night I went to bed wondering if I should bother completing the novena. What's the point? I'd made the sacrifice of getting up early and saying prayers that hadn't been answered. 'Perhaps there's no one up there,' I thought, but decided to finish it anyway. 'Maybe my small failure', I thought pompously, 'is part of God's great plan.' So I got up at six again the following morning and went to mass as promised. 'Thanks anyway, but if you could see your way next year . . .' Then I went home. As I was letting myself into the house through the back door, I heard the clunk of the letter box at the front. To this day I can remember the shafts of golden light that filled the hallway, the faint strings of a harp, the distant chorus of seraphim. On the lino lay a brown envelope from the Lancashire Education Department with the news that I had been awarded a scholarship that would come into effect when I reached the age of eleven. Hallelujah!

Whenever my examination results have not been up to scratch I have always excused myself on the grounds that I was a year younger and, deep down, have blamed the fact that I leapfrogged over Standard Two for many of life's failings: not getting that teaching post in Sweden, not being offered the Laureateship, singing off key, premature ejaculation and more, many more. As a matter of strange fact, whenever I'm in a group of people I always think that I'm the youngest, so it becomes a coping mechanism for me, as if my failings will be excused on the grounds of diminished ageing.

At fifteen I sat for the GCE exams in June and failed Latin and Maths, and had to resit them in September. One morning the following month Brother Murray breezed into the classroom, said excuse me to Mr Boggiano who was taking the French lesson and looked around the class. 'I have in my hand the O Level results,' he said, holding up a sheet of paper. 'How many of you scoundrels had to resit the examinations?' Five of us put up our hands nervously. 'Stand up.' We did exactly as we were told. The suspense was palpable and he was revelling in the power he held over us. Adding fuel to the angst, he looked at the paper as if to clarify the results. 'Mmmm . . .' Even Mr Boggiano was shifting nervously in his desk. 'I'll not keep you in suspense any longer, all of you who resat Latin and Mathematics at O level have' – he smiled – 'have failed.' A gasp from us all. Then he said, 'Ah, I was only joking . . . you've all passed.'

We let out a sigh of relief. Brother Murray was as pleased as punch with his little joke which would have been perfect, cruel but perfect, except for one small thing. He looked at Batty – a sad, unattractive youth – and said, almost as an afterthought, 'Except you, Batty.' He nodded to Boggiano and swept out, as Battybus collapsibus on the deskalorum.

At seventeen, I scraped three A levels and went to Hull University, and it goes without saying that had I swanned through Standard Two I would have swanned into Trinity College, Cambridge and ended up with a Double First. Instead of PPE, I followed a joint Honours course in French and Geography, and when the final results were posted I was over the moon with my Pass degree. As fellow graduands fainted and burst into tears because they'd only got a 2.1 instead of a First, I was straight to the bar in the Students Union, buying the drinks. After all, I reasoned, a pass at twenty probably equals a 2.2 at twenty-one. Cheers!

RUNNINGALLTHEWORDSTOGETHER

Michael McCartney said that when we first met I spoke so fast that he could never understand what I was saying, but assumed that because I wore glasses and had been to university it was interesting. By the time he got used to my voice and could understand what I was saying, he realised that it wasn't. I have always spoken too quickly: a garbled rush that ends in a swallowed apologetic mumble. I do find it a constant and pleasant surprise to be employed to present radio programmes and to do voice-overs for TV commercials. Don't they know I gumble and marble? But over the years, and with practice I have learned how to r-e-a-d a-l-o-u-d more slowly, taking my time and breathing properly, but in conversation, when that part of the brain that signals speech receives the impulse to form sounds in the mouth, somehow the words and images all become jumbled up like flotsam on a wave that crashes down on to the beach. The more nervous I am (like in the company of strangers) the higher the wave, the jumblier the flotsam.

Writing, of course, is one way of cleaning up the beach, but even my writing style is staccato. In the words of William Carlos Williams, talking about his poems, 'I found I could not use the long line because of my nervous nature.' And I must confess to being more of a 'red wheelbarrow in the rain' sort of poet than a 'Last night, ah, yesternight, betwixt her lips and mine / There fell thy shadow, Cynara!' kind of one. There is obviously a fault line running through me caused by a lack of confidence, an apologetic sort of 'Get-it-over-with-quickly, because what you're saying isn't original or that interesting, and if you don't hurry up somebody else will butt in.' Even now, at dinner parties I can begin a story and within seconds watch the listeners' eyes glaze over as vowels elide, consonants collide and metaphors trip over themselves in a hurry to get away.

It is probably true to say that I have heard the word 'Pardon?' more than most people. When I was young it would be 'Speak up' and 'Stop mumbling' when having to answer a question in class, and the fact that a black leather strap would be close at hand certainly didn't help. And even though the atmosphere was more liberal by the time I reached the sixth form, I refused to be involved in the debating society for fear of standing up and saying 'This House believes . . .' to be interrupted by cries of 'Pardon?' 'Speak up!' 'Stop mumbling!'

When I was at Hull and studying for the post-graduate certificate in Education, we had lessons in how to project in front of a class: 'Head up high, enunciate slowly and clearly.' And we all stood up and did just that. Except me.

'Mr McGough, the children will not understand a word you're saying. Slow down for goodness sake, or otherwise teach PE. Failing that, become a mime artist.'

Because I gabbled as a child in a Scouse accent, my mother paid for me to have elocution lessons at school, where I learned how to gabble nicer. Sylvia Allen was the teacher and, because she was also in charge of verse-speaking and drama, I was inexorably drawn to both. With three other boys from school I took part in the Waterloo and Crosby Verse-Speaking Festival at the town hall in July 1949. Of the large group of children waiting behind the scenes, I would appear to have been the most nervous, but once on stage I surprised myself by how concentrated and cool I became. Eyes fixed on the back wall above the adjudicators and the audience, I gave 'Jabberwocky' my all. Applause. My first poetry performance.

In those days I wasn't able to command the ludicrously high fees that my agent now charges for my public readings, but I was given a certificate by the Guildhall School of Music and Drama acknowledging that I had passed the Elementary (Grade One) Examination in Speech and Drama. Obviously I would have preferred a gold badge or a medal that I could have worn round my neck when travelling to school, but nevertheless I was immodestly proud of that certificate, and because it says in very small print at the bottom *This certificate must not be used as a teaching qualification* I have never, ever, tried to use it as a teaching qualification, which, you'll agree, says a lot about the man.

MY FIRST STAGE KISS

The Headmaster of St Mary's, when I arrived at the age of nine, was Brother Thompson, a kindly old soul who didn't bother anybody. A literary man with a keen interest in Celtic mythology, he was the author of '*Joysticks*' . . . *A Musical Fantasy*, the first school play in which I appeared. As Gwen Masterton, one of the Mayfair children, whose chum Dorothy is whooshed off to the Caves of Donegal by wicked elves, I wore a black wig and pink taffeta dress, with white ankle socks and dinky patent leather shoes. (And if you're wondering, no, I didn't wear girls' knickers.) And from the sepia photograph before me, very pretty I looked too, even if someone backstage had been a little heavy-handed with the rouge and the lippy. It seems funny now that Brother Thompson, writing a play for an all-boys school, should have included so many parts for girls. The mythic hero Finn McCool strode about with as much mannishness as a sixteen-year-old could muster, but the stage was usually bedecked with doe-eyed Celtic maidens, clasping hands to boyish breasts and cooing. It was all rather unnerving at the time because, to be honest, I used to fancy one or two of them myself, but fortunately, once the drag came off, so did the fancy.

Then there was the short play he wrote about an

imaginary visit to Crosby by Queen Elizabeth the First, which was a once-off performance that took place on the school lawn one beautiful summer's evening. I didn't have the biggest speaking part, but as the Queen I was, dare I say it, the star. Again, I wasn't nervous, remembered all my lines, came in on cue and gabbled loud but clearly. The trouble was, as Miss Allen, the Head of Drama, told me later, that when I wasn't involved in the action I was inclined to fiddle with my brocade neckline, which apparently queens don't do, and became more interested in who was in the audience than what was happening on stage. Also, I corpsed. 'Unforgivable,' said Miss Allen. 'Even for a thirteen-year-old.' I had just sat down on the throne after addressing the good citizens of Crosby when my portly favourite, Lord Scarisbrick, stepped forward, swept the voluminous blue cap from his head and bowed low. Unfortunately, the sweep was over-vigorous and the cap slipped from his fingers. Like a velvet frisbee, it curved above the heads of the groundlings and pancaked into the wall of the gymnasium. My Lord Scarisbrick blushed. I stifled a giggle. A handmaid giggled. A page-boy stifled a blush. My portly lord stifled a corpse. Queen Elizabeth burst out laughing followed loyally by the good people of Crosby.

In 1950 came *Toad of Toad Hall*. I loved the play but rather resented not playing Ratty or Moley or, better still, Mister Toad, running around the stage going 'Poop Poop' all the time. But I was good old Mr Badger, solid and respectable. Perhaps if Brother Thompson had written it instead of Kenneth Grahame, I would have been playing Betty Badger alongside Rosalind Rat and Marcella Mole. Come to think of it, my early acquaintance with the stage play would come in very useful when I found myself locked away in Austerlitz, upper New York state, writing lyrics for *The Wind in the Willows, the New Musical*, which was to hit Broadway in 1987. I use the word 'hit' as in velvet frisbee pancaking into gymnasium wall. But more of that later.

My theatrical swansong was *Richard of Bordeaux*, in which I played Mary, Countess of Derby. By this time I must have been losing interest in school amdram because I can remember almost nothing of the production except for two things: first, that it was staged not in the school hall, but in the larger Alexandra Hall in Crosby, and second, that it starred Laurence Taylor as King Richard. I remember him out of school, tall, dark and handsome, walking down Bridge Road wearing a long black coat, a red scarf thrown carefully round his neck as if he'd stepped straight out of Lautrec's portrait of Aristide Bruant. He quit St Mary's before the sixth form and went on to become Professor of Sociology at York University, and as Laurie Taylor famous as a broadcaster on Radio 4. Back then, though, he was my king and because he loved me desperately (not me personally, you understand, not four-eyes McGough from 4 beta, but the radiant, enigmatic Countess of West Derby), he embraced me on stage and kissed me. On stage; on the lips. We thought nothing of it at the time. No embarrassment in the slightest, but looking back, I bet there were girls in the audience who wished they were in my place. Boys too, I shouldn't wonder.

EVENING IN PARIS

I knew that Joan Taylor fancied me when she switched from the L8 to the L3. She lived in Bootle, a mile or so away, which had a wider choice of buses to take her to Seafield Convent, the school down the road from ours, so when she began to appear on the upper deck with a mate or two in tow, I dared hardly hope that the reason was me. She was lovely. She was a dream. Many of the older boys, those Brylcreem-tongued lotharios of the lower sixth, thought they were in with a chance, but when she crumpled up her bus ticket and threw it at me (if the numbers added up to twenty-one it meant 'I love you') I could have eaten my satchel.

We were fifteen-year-olds, and as our parents knew each other and wouldn't have approved ('There'll be plenty of time for that nonsense when you've passed your exams!') we had to keep our passionate affair clandestine. My sister still recalls to my eternal shame and embarrassment how I would use her as a decoy on Saturday evenings: 'Mum, I'm just going to the pictures with our Brenda.'

'You're taking your little sister? Well, that's very good of you.'

Joan would be waiting outside the Stella or the Regal, and she and I would head for the back row, leaving Brenda to sit on her own down in the front stalls. Sometimes I would give her a threepenny bit to buy one of those waxy cardboard tubs of ice cream with a flat wooden spoon, part-payment, part-bribe, and to her credit she never grassed. It was all unbridled innocence, in fact, and one particular night remains etched into my memory, like . . . like a memorable etching. It was shortly after Christmas and I had bought her a present with the money I'd been saving up for weeks. A tiny bottle of 'Evening in Paris' perfume by 'Bonsoir', which came in a little midnight-blue box with stars and the Eiffel Tower picked out in silver relief.

Cut to a park bench in Bootle: Joan is wearing the perfume and I am sitting with my arm around her. The sky is the colour of the perfume box and the stars stand out in silver relief. We kiss. Five power-lines cross the parchment moon to compose a stave and I half expect nine pigeons to land, C D E, F G F E D C prompting me, on the count of three, to sing: 'By the light, of the silvery moon . . .' We linger over the pause before the next kiss. I become the Eiffel Tower.

Evening in Bootle. Bliss.

Catching the L3 bus meant that Joan and I would walk together through Coronation Park. Past the putting and the bowling greens, the meteorite, fallen and homesick, sited in a bed of flowers, around the boating pond and up the steps into Everest Road. As we were part of a stream of schoolkids there was no holding hands, no kissing, although a good deal of teasing and pushing I shouldn't wonder. As we neared St Mary's school gates I would either walk on ahead or fall back, letting her cross the road to rejoin her friends and carry on to the convent school. One Wednesday morning just as Joan had said goodbye and run on ahead, a hint of Evening in Paris fluttering in her wake, Brother Gibbons leaped out from behind a tree and grabbed me by the ear. Brother Gibbons was the new Headmaster and I wondered if he had been up in the tree all night. Like his primate namesake, swinging from branch to branch through the trees in the park, his long arms extending out from the sleeves of his cassock.

'You're a disgrace, boy, a disgrace.'

'Sir?'

'Horseplay! Wait until I tell your parents about your horseplay . . . with a girl!'

'Sir?'

'Go now straight to Assembly and stand at the front. We'll make an example of you and no mistake.'

So off I slunk to join that small but select band of criminals lined up in the hall. The usual suspects, the late-comers, the no-cappers, the no-hopers, the guttersnipes, and the awful truth was the feeling that I deserved to be among them. Obviously I was puzzled as to what I had done wrong, but it must have been sinful, for wasn't Brother Gibbons the Headmaster and the fount of all wisdom? My parents would surely be outraged at my behaviour, whatever it was. At the end of Assembly Brother Gibbons, having made no mention of horseplay in the park, swept back to his office and the school filed out. Mr McDonald ('Old Jimmy') was in charge of dealing with the day's delinquents. A PE instructor of the old school ('Skip jumping begin'), ex-Army, lean and trim with a toothbrush moustache (blue plastic) he was a decent old fella whose strapping was meant not to hurt. One by one we lined up and mumbled our offence: 'Late, sir.'

'That's the second time this week, Downey.'

'Yes, sir.'

(Whack! Whack!)

'Forgot my cap, sir.'

'McNamara, you'd forget your head if it wasn't screwed on.'

'I know, sir.'

(Whack!) And so on until, last in line, it was my turn.

'Well, McGough?'

'Erhm . . .'

'Late?'

'No, sir. Brother Gibbons told me.'

'Told you what?'

'Told me off, sir.'

'What for?'

'Erhm, walking through Coronation Park, sir.'

'Oh. Well, walk properly next time.'

'Yes, sir.'

(Whack!)

And that was that. Not another word said, neither to me nor to my parents. But it got to me nevertheless. Horseplay one day, rape and pillage the next. I told Joan that maybe we shouldn't walk through the park together again. At least, not until we were married. So what was the point, asked Joan, of her catching the L3 every morning? So she went back to catching the L8 and we stopped seeing each other. Bus journeys were never quite the same after that.

STRAP-HAPPY

When I joined the school in 1947 most of the staff were Irish Christian Brothers, a religious teaching order founded in Ireland by Edmund Rice in 1802: 'To help young people to stand on their own two feet and to change the society that caused and allowed them to be poor'. There were masters, particularly in the upper school, and, apart from the dinner ladies, only two females: a librarian and Miss Allen. The Brothers wore white starched dog collars that irritated their necks, and long black soutanes, or cassocks with wide cummerbund-type sashes. They were imposing, they ruled the roost and there were good Brothers of whom Edmund Rice would have been proud, fine men who worked hard with little reward and no kudos outside the walls of the college. But there were men, too, who answered the siren call of a vocation when they should have left school at fifteen, run away over the potato fields and raised a bevy of copper-haired kids by Mavorneen.

Although the CBs may have invented the long-sharp-shock treatment, I was never subject to sexual abuse at school; nor, as far as I know, were any of my con-temporaries. I've read about dreadful things that happened over the years and watched interviews on television with men who suffered at the hands of paedophiles wearing cassocks, but, thank God, we were never aware of it. What loomed large, however, was the strap. The straps that made a man out of me (nervous, cringing, stammering, but a man nonetheless) came in various weights and sizes. Usually they were about fourteen inches long, one and a quarter inches wide and less than half an inch thick, and consisted of four lengths of leather stitched together. As I write this, I wonder who made them? Catholic convicts, I suppose, or nuns. The Little Sisters of the Good Hiding? And where did the staff buy them? No Internet in those days. Perhaps that old lady in the sweetshop on Crosby Road kept a boxful under the counter?

Some schools had one Brother who was responsible for dishing it out, but at St Mary's all the masters and Brothers had straps, but not all used them. If you were in luck, it would be Mr Donovan who would punish you. He taught English, was a kind and sensitive guy who didn't like corporal punishment, but – 'Well, hey, putting a plastic turd in my desk?' – his strap was light and fluffy, and a beating from him was the equivalent of having your hair ruffled. On the other hand several of the Brothers were practised in the evil art and, although the rumour that some straps had whalebone running through them may not have been true, they were certainly heavier and looked like flattened coshes. And what I hated about the whole scary business was that the strap wasn't used only to punish misbehaviour, but also as a teaching aid.

It's break time and everybody is in the playground. You can tell which class is about to have a French lesson with Brother O'Shea. We are not the ones running around playing tick. We are not the ones heading the tennis ball.

We are the ones huddled against the wall in the corner by the milk crates, pale faces stuck in books, or eyes closed to heaven lisping French declensions. O'Shea's teaching method was so simple and effective that to this day I don't know why his name isn't up there with Piaget, Montessori, A. S. Neill, all the great educationalists. We are told in the previous day's lesson which thirty nouns we must learn by heart, paying particular attention to gender, or which six verbs we must decline in the future tense.

'Morning, boys.'

'Morning, sir.'

'Right, close your books. Connor!' (*Connor stands.*)

'Horse?'

'*Un cheval*, sir.'

'Correct, Batty!' (*Connor sits wiping brow, Batty stands.*)

'Bear?'

'Er . . . er . . .' (*Batty bursts into tears.*)

'Remain standing. McDonnell?'

'*Un ours*, sir?'

'Very good, sit down. Lynch?'

And so on, all round the class. Get it wrong and you remain standing. Get it wrong again and it's two whacks of the strap. As well as being cruel and nerve-racking, it encouraged feelings of guilt and betrayal, because if you knew the answer you sat there hoping that your best mate would get it wrong. Any hint of prompting and you got six. Throughout the whole proceedings he maintained a Bruce Forsyth kind of playfulness, rarely losing his temper, because the O'Shea method was simply the quickest way to get thirty-five lazy boys to learn a foreign language. Or to *think* they are learning a foreign language.

At some point during the late fifties the Irish Christian Brothers became surplus to requirements. They had served a need in providing an education and instilling a sense of worth into working-class Catholic boys at a time when to be Catholic, and Irish at that, was to be discriminated against. Times had changed. Religion became less of an issue and the post-war Education Acts provided better opportunities for the children of poor working-class families. When I was invited back to St Mary's in 1995 to read some of my poems to the sixth form it had changed, but not beyond recognition. In my day it had been a Direct Grant Grammar school, but when they were abolished in the seventies, St Mary's had the choice of either going comprehensive or independent. It chose the latter. The most significant change I noticed was not the absence of the Brothers, and with them the smell of fear and strap oil, but the presence of girls. The sixth form is happily mixed.

The only outsiders ever to visit and address the school when I was there were the Dominican Friars or the Redemptorist Fathers, who came to fire us with tales of martyrdom and missionary zeal. To a twelve- or thirteen-year-old the idea of leaving boring old Liverpool and moving to Africa, converting the black pagans (savage, until you really got to know them) was seductive. As long as they promised not to hurt me, I would offer myself up for martyrdom after a tragically short, but nevertheless meaningful life, bringing lost souls to the bosom of Christ Our Lord. Consequently, I would always join the small queue at the end of the session to put my name down for the seminary and could never understand why so few of my schoolmates (savage, until you really got to know them) signed up as well. Luckily, we would-be Christian martyrs weren't immediately herded into cattle trucks and shipped out to the Congo, but were given leaflets about life in the Order and advised to go away, discuss the matter with our parents and pray. No doubt we meant well, but by the end of the day it became clear that the only conversions we would be making would be leaflets into paper aeroplanes.

Even when I was in the sixth form the idea of a poet being let loose in the school was unthinkable. Not that we had contemporary poets in those days, you understand, they were all dead and safely tucked up in the library. So it was a strange out-of-body experience I felt as I read to these young men and women. In listening to me, would they sense a link with the past? Their past? I chose poems I thought might take on a special significance for them, ones with religious or geographical references that in other schools I might have to explain. But to be honest, even though they seemed to enjoy the reading, I don't think it was particularly special for them. If they were poetry pagans, I don't believe I converted them.

THE BATTLE OF THE POTATOES

During one memorable spring term the last two periods of Friday afternoon were given over to 'Horticultural Studies', a startling innovation in the curriculum but too good to last. Our form would single-file out to a small allotment at the rear of the school overlooking Coronation Park, where Mr Dickinson would pretend to await us eagerly. With his flat cap, rust-coloured tweed suit and cheeks like wrinkled tomatoes, he was straight out of Ambridge via Thomas Hardy. He spoke in a broad, twinkly Lancashire accent that we all mimicked even when talking to him. I assume that we were meant to learn about gardening and about the growing of vegetables. To develop a sense of wonder at the rhythm of the seasons, the richness of the soil and a respect for the earth and all the treasures therein. Unfortunately, Mr Dickinson may have been a dab hand at the milking of cows and the cutting of corn, but he couldn't cope with thirty-five Scousers let loose in a field, last thing on a Friday afternoon. Soon wheelbarrows were being pushed at breakneck speed in chariot races, hoes and rakes had become spears hurtling through the air. Fallon picked up a sickle and with great skill pinged it all of twenty yards into a tree trunk beyond the park railings. Then came the Battle of the Potatoes which, although our finest hour, was ultimately to end in defeat.

Mick Cullen spotted a potato in the soil, pulled it out and threw it at Terry Cannon, knocking off his glasses. Potatoes in the ground? This was news to us; until that moment we all thought they grew in sacks. Soon everybody joined in and the sky was fizzing, black with soil and spuds. Friday afternoons had never been so much fun. An organic, GM-free potato in my hand, I was looking around for a soft target when I saw the Angel of Death, Brother Murray, his face the colour of raw liver, flying towards us like something out of *The Matrix*.

Unfortunately Mick was facing the wrong way and didn't see Brother Murray pick up a shovel and slam it into his back. The lad went down, dare I say it, like a sack of potatoes. Mr Dickinson was nowhere to be seen. We were screamed at and sent back to class to await the strapping of a lifetime. We helped Cullen to his feet, bruised and shaken (and lucky not to have been seriously injured) and trooped like a defeated army back to the classroom.

We were kept waiting for half an hour, time for the fear to build, the faces to pale and Batty, who would always cry, to cry. Eventually Murray came in, his anger somewhat subsided, but deadly nonetheless. We all lined up and received four strokes each. Lucky, he told us, not to be bent over the desk and beaten till we couldn't sit down for a week. When it was Cullen's turn we wondered if Murray, out of a sense of guilt (and the fear surely, that Mick would tell his parents about the assault) would ease up on the lad. Even try and make light of the abuse, which they sometimes did. But no. Four of the best. 'Let that be a lesson,' he said.

And it was. A lesson in mindful violence.

ALONG THE CANAL BANK

I wanted to tell you about the canal a hundred yards away from where I grew up and I began with my walking along the bridle path, but I typed in 'bridal path', which I thought was the correct spelling when I was a boy. Where brides went walking, I had assumed. Where they were led by their husbands in the olden days, still clasping a bouquet, perhaps, a pink satin halter round the neck. Silly me. But strolling along that bridle path, with not a sprinkling of confetti in sight, was what I did a lot of. If you headed away from Liverpool in the direction of Leeds and kept on going it was like being in the countryside. And that's what I did one afternoon in late summer with George, a mate from school.

Except for the occasional cyclist or someone taking their dog for a walk, it was always quiet, and we walked and talked, ate our butties and drank our pop. We kept an eye out for water rats and tried to put a name to all the birds we spotted: ('Jimmy', 'Alan', 'Margaret', 'Francesca'). We'd walked for miles and it was early evening when we turned to retrace our steps home, and we'd just rounded a bend in the canal when suddenly, towering in front of us like a stink-bomb factory blocking out the sun, was our friendless neighbourhood psychopath, Puggy Lewis.

Even though we outnumbered him by two to one, or a

hundred per cent, it wasn't enough, and besides, he was hopeless at maths. We could turn tail, of course, and leg it back down the towpath, but that would have been cowardly. Sensible, but cowardly. (Towpath! Yes that's better than bridle path.) So there he was, barring our way, piggy eyes dull and unblinking in a big, fat suet pudding. 'Hello Piggy,' I said brightly, then regretted it immediately. 'I mean Puggy.' Luckily for my nose he had disappeared behind some bushes to re-emerge with a heavy sack. Instinctively, George and I knew that it wasn't filled with presents for the poor children of the neighbourhood. Whatever it was filled with, it filled us with dread.

'You're just in time', grunted Puggy, 'to witness the great disappearing act.'

A bird swooped low across the surface of the water and disappeared into the trees beyond, and I wished I could follow it.

'Did you see that chaffinch?' I said in the vain hope that a conversation about bird classification might follow during which Puggy would forget why he'd come to the canal.

'Shut it,' he said and swung at me with the sack. It caught me on the shoulder and had it not been for my superb balancing skills and magical powers I would have toppled into the slimy blackness.

'Not a word to anybody about this, d'ye hear?' We nodded. 'Now stand well back while I give this lot the heave ho.' We did just that as Puggy swung the weighted sack round his head a few times before letting it go. It swung in an arc over the setting sun before hitting the water like a smack in the face. There were a few outraged bubbles followed by silence.

We watched the ripples unravel for a moment until George broke the spell: 'What's in it?'

'Mind yer own business, and don't forget what I told yiz. Breathe a word about it to anyone and you're dead.' As if to underline the threat, he grabbed George's nose between thumb and forefinger and squeezed until the poor lad's eyes watered.

Using my superb balancing skills and magical powers, I backed away. 'We won't tell anyone,' I promised, 'especially not the NSPCC or the RSPCA, or the CID.'

Confused by the acronymous jumble of letters, Puggy frowned. 'Just don't.' And wiping his moist fingers down the front of my shirt he swaggered off down the towpath. George and I watched him disappear before dawdling home. On the way we saw a 'Swimming prohibited' sign floating face down in the water and wondered what the fish made of it.

The canal bank was also where my dad used to take me for walks on a Sunday afternoon. He had big docker's hands and being tiny I would cling to one of his fingers as he relived his days in the Merchant Navy before the war. Storms at sea and men drowning. He talked of faraway places, the delights of Rio de Janeiro and of the spell that Auckland had cast on him. (I was later to learn that he'd filled in the immigration forms and booked our passage to New Zealand, but Mum had cried off at the last minute.) I think he often regretted not settling out there and of course it gave me food for thought. How different would my life have been? Would I still have written poetry? I assume so. Would I have had a number one in the charts? I don't think so. Would I be writing an autobiography? I doubt it. Would

I have been happier? Ah, who can say? If Dad's stories filled me with a sense of adventure and a restless desire to grow up and see the world, Mother's stories, usually at bedtime, were designed to make me feel peaceful and secure, and sleepy.

One of my biggest regrets in life is that my own books weren't around when I was a child. I would have identified with the characters in the stories, laughed at all the jokes, and as for the poems, they would have been so much fun to recite, and easy to learn by heart. But as we all know, things don't always work out the way we would have planned. Because I write for children, visit schools and perform in theatres to huge crowds of the little blighters, you would imagine that I would be an enthusiastic and gifted reader of bedtime stories to my own children. People often tell me how lucky and grateful my kids must feel to have me for a dad.

'How I envy the McGough children. Night after night of magical word-juggling at the hands of a consummate craftsman!' Well, er, not quite. More often than not my wife would be shouting upstairs, 'Now go to sleep, otherwise your father will come up and read some of his poems.'

You could hear them groaning, 'Oh no, not the consummate craftsman . . .' Then silence. I don't know why, but I always found it hard work reading even the stories that I'd loved as a child, Grimm's fairy tales, Aesop's fables and the rest. I would get bored very quickly and embellish, do silly accents and leave out great chunks. My daughter Isabel would always insist on my going back, although none of the boys seemed to mind, or notice. My eyes on the big, smiling Thomas the Tank-Engine clock. 'Gosh, is that the quality time? Must fly. Goodnight, God bless.' Kiss, kiss. Exit.

I am back on the canal bank, but it is late in the evening and the moon is reflected in the inky black water. I am not with a mate this time but with a girl, and if it weren't for the end of the chapter looming up, I would furnish you with gratuitous and explicit detail of our encounter. However, there is only enough room left for me to say thank you to Maureen. Thank you, Maureen.

RAILINGS

All the McGough boys had been good footballers, Frank had been on Everton's books and if it hadn't been for the war, Andy and Ted might have turned professional, so I must have been something of a disappointment to my dad, who had represented Liverpool as a schoolboy. He was pleased, though, when I made the school cricket team and in a poem called 'The Railings' I describe him standing outside the school sports field at Manor Road, Crosby, one Saturday afternoon watching me playing against Wallasey Grammar School. I remember seeing him there and wishing that he would come in and sit with the other fathers outside the pavilion. But he was too shy, and I suppose because he worked on the docks he felt like an outsider, and assumed that the other dads would be posh and snooty.

> *Third ball, a wicket, and three more followed.*
> *When we came in at the end of the innings*
> *the other dads applauded and joined us for tea.*
> *Of course, you'd gone by then. Later*
> *you said you'd found yourself there by accident.*
> *Just passing. Spotted me through the railings.*

The image of railings also serves to illustrate a feeling of separateness, how some men of his generation found it difficult to express themselves emotionally, and when writing the poem I visualised myself as a teenager in need of a fatherly hug. Like many poems it is honest but not necessarily true. Certainly he felt out of place in college halls and libraries where p's and q's had to be watched, but now I wonder if it was the teenage me that put up the railings and not him. I notice with my youngest son, Matt, sixteen at the time of writing, that when I try to give him a big hug he withers a little, embarrassed by this sudden burst of paternal bonding. My grown-up sons lift me off my feet every time we see each other, great bear-hugs. Perhaps it's an adolescent boy thing.

I have never written poems, though, about my mother and this has puzzled me. Was writing about my father, who died before we'd had a chance really to know each other, a way of finding out more about him? Was I bringing into focus a figure who was important and loved, but nevertheless on the touchline, looking in? Perhaps the poems arose out of a sense of guilt, that I never quite became the son he had imagined. He was proud of the fact that I made it to university, for hadn't he worked hard enough all his life to get me there? (Holidays had meant a day out somewhere, usually the beach at New Brighton or Southport, but we never stayed overnight. For him, a week off work meant the chance to give another bedroom a new coat of paint.) But I remained a puzzle to him and had he lived long enough to see me have a book published or appear on *Top of the Pops* he might have said to his mates, '*Our Roger, a real chip off the old block.*' Well, perhaps not, but my subsequent career might have explained some of those traits and characteristics that irked and confused him:

The inability to hammer in a nail straight
The inability to mend a puncture
The nose stuck in a book when it's a nice day outside
The head in the clouds
The four-eyes, the self-obsession, the nervous tic
The verge of tears, the dandification
The lack of interest in motor-cars, boxing
The lack, in fact, of manliness.

My mother, though, was at the centre of my little universe and in some ways, of course, still is. It is on a Sunday that it usually happens, I'm in my room, not working but procrastinating, when I want to ring her. A sudden urge to telephone and tell her something trivial, about the kids, perhaps, or about what Hilary and I are planning for Easter. Nothing important, just chat. But she is long gone, my mother, and the number I pretend to ring, WATerloo 6017, no longer exists. At university on a dull Sunday such as this, part out of duty, part homesickness, I would go to the telephone box outside the Junior Common Room and build a leaning tower of pennies on top of the black metal box, before lifting the handset, warm and heavy still with conversation, and ring home. It was invariably she who answered, although occasionally it would be my sister, barely able to hide her disappointment that I wasn't Robby or Bill or whoever, ringing to retrieve her weekend. My father felt uneasy about them (telephones, that is, not the boyfriends, although he was never too keen on them either). And when I wrote letters home from university, 'Dear Mum and Dad', I knew she would be reading them. The occasional letter from him, written in neat capitals, I treasured because I understood the effort that he'd put into it, but the majority, signed off with 'Look after yourself, lots of love, mum and dad', were from her. Hugo Williams has written that his poems are short pieces of writing that he posts in the hope that one day a reply will be waiting for him in a blue envelope, propped up on the mantelpiece. I suspect that because I communicated effortlessly with my mother during her lifetime there is nothing left unsaid. She lived long enough to see my first books published and to keep a scrapbook of newspaper cuttings about the Scaffold, and I hope that she has received all the poems written after her death (with the possible exception of the sequence 'Holiday on Death Row', which would have embarrassed her. For as she used to say: 'There's no need for that sort of language, Roger. It's not clever.').

The sixties began for me with incense, flowers and candles. In the parlour the heavy curtains are drawn, even though it is a hot Thursday morning in July, and the dancing flames are reflected in the brass fittings and on the polished oak. Outside, the queue of men waiting to pay their last respects runs halfway down the street. Silent and ill-at-ease in heavy three-piece suits and ties, they melt and wipe their brows with dazzling white handkerchiefs. Inside, like railings made out of wax, a row of candles is melting. Everything is melting: my mother, my sister. The smell of incense, wax and severed lilies is overpowering. I am melting into my father.

Requiescat in pace.

THE LURE OF HULL

Going to university was a huge adventure, not only for me but for the other half-dozen sixth formers from my year who had chosen Hull. Why Hull? At first I had considered Liverpool. (To be near me mam? Not quite, but applying there to study Geography might indicate the lack of an adventurous spirit.) Luckily, my home team turned me down, which was just as well because I had no feel for the subject apart from a certain painstaking skill at drawing maps, and suspect I would have been kicked out at the end of my first year and ended up on the dole. Alternatively, I might have learned to play the drums and teamed up with John, Paul and George to form a group called Roger and the Silver Beatles, who knows. Hardly anybody at school chose to move down south, except a train-spotter in the upper sixth, who went to Exeter to study Maths and was never heard of again. I went for an interview at Leicester, who offered me a place, but I discovered on the train going down there that it was in the Midlands, so turned it down. Leeds had a crappy green-and-maroon scarf, whereas Hull's blue and gold I found quite attractive, and Kevin McNamara, later a Labour MP, had gone to Hull two years previously from St Mary's and not only survived but positively enthused about it. Yin and yang, if Liverpool was the right ear on the face of Britain, then Hull was the left one, and that symmetry appealed. Also, it was easy to get into and so, in 1954, I went there to study for a Joint Honours degree in French and Geography, and within days knew exactly where Paris was.

It wasn't until I got to university that I discovered there were courses in Philosophy, Psychology, Sociology (there wasn't a drama course at the time), which I might have found more fulfilling, but my choice of subjects was defined purely by the fact that I'd got my least worst marks in French and Geography. Many people assume that being a poet, I studied English at university, and perhaps I would have, had I not failed O level English Literature two years previously. Having enjoyed the nuts and bolts of language, parsing and sentence construction, as well as the smattering of linguistics on offer, I had passed the English Language exam without difficulty, but when it came to Literature I was shamefully found wanting. Joan Taylor must shoulder some of the blame, as well as Maureen, Nancy and Rita. However, my failure to read the set books may also have contributed to my downfall.

It was the headmaster at Brian Patten's secondary modern school who recognised the lad's burning genius and encouraged him to write poems, and there are many writers who will testify to one particular teacher who spotted the seed of potential talent and helped it flower. But in my case? Well, the seed must have been there but it was to lie undernourished and undiscovered for a few years yet. I would occasionally write a decent essay, but my propensity for puns, irony and irreverence was frowned upon. Throughout my schooldays I never wrote a poem and, to my knowledge, neither did any of my contemporaries. Poetry was what girls and dead people wrote. Years later this propensity for puns, irony and irreverence brought me to poetry, and enabled me to break taboos and poke fun at authority, although my preferred image was that of a goddess with Pre-Raphaelite golden ringlets leading me by the hand to a curtained-off bedchamber.

Every week, when I receive wonderful little poems written by five-, six- and seven-year-olds I marvel at their talent, knowing that I couldn't have written so well at their age. It's probably the result of enthusiastic parents and teachers, of course. (Oh, and by the way, if you're a teacher, please don't send me all your class's literary efforts with a kind note saying that they'd love a reply from their favourite poet. I'm touched and thrilled but Time and Energy, alas, sit on each shoulder like a pair of ragged epaulettes.)

The other occasions when I get to read young poems are when I'm judging a competition. It's great fun, but less so now than it used to be. In the olden days (pre-1999 approximately) all the poems by the infants and first-year juniors would be handwritten and usually illustrated; in fact, drawing and writing were part of the same impulse. There was something special and unique about each entry, from the bold or spidery handwriting to the creative misspellings. But now, of course, thanks to the dreaded computer, every poem has been spell-checked, and is laid out on the page as if it were ready to go off to *The Times Literary Supplement*. Nothing has been gained, I believe, and much has been lost.

When the Magnificent Seven Old Maricolians arrived at Hull we were divided up. Five were billeted in what was known as Camp Hall (nothing pansy about it, quite the opposite, in fact, for this vast sprawl of tarted-up Nissen huts was formerly an army camp) and two of us, Tom Downey and I, were allocated rooms in the much plusher Needler Hall. Whereas Camp housed hundreds of hoary male students, Needler, a bijou residence by comparison, catered for only sixty and, with it's white-stucco Palladian exterior and landscaped grounds with lawns that could be walked upon and trees that could be sat beneath, it seemed like a four-star hotel.

Many of the students, particularly the ones who had done National Service and the better-off ones, couldn't wait to get out and set up on their own, but I had never known the luxury of central heating, unlimited hot water, indoor toilets, chambermaids, three-course dinners with coffee served afterwards in the Junior Common Room, and took to it like a duke to claret.

Unlike a four-star hotel, though, we weren't allowed to 'entertain' lady guests in our rooms except between the hours of 4 p.m. and 9 p.m. on Saturdays and Sundays, which put a lot of pressure on a young chap. It was all right for those who had steady girlfriends in Goole or Beverley who could travel over for quick nookie, but for those of us who were novices at seduction, and Catholic into the bargain, these licensed occasions of sin were initially terrifying. Of all the girlfriends I took back home to meet the folks Mary, a student at Endsleigh Teacher Training College in Hull, was my dad's favourite, mainly because she played hockey for Yorkshire and knew more about football than I did. By 7.45 that first Sunday evening in my room at Needler, I had talked Mary out of the armchair to sit next to me on the bed and, emboldened, had put my arm round her shoulder. Had I been content to leave it at that, to feel her warmth next to me, to inhale the heady perfume of her womanliness while we talked hockey or geography, everything would have been all right and she might have ended up marrying me instead of Michael Parkinson. But, overcome by curiosity as much as lust, I attached my left hand to her right breast, and a Catholic one at that. Before too long, about three-fifths of a second, she swung a right hook that knocked me off the bed and across the floor. Later, as she was applying a cold-water compress to the venial bruise on my forehead, she confessed that she hadn't meant to hit me so hard, but was doing weight training, and anyway, nice girls don't.

Male students normally stayed in Hall during their first year, sometimes for a second year, but were only admitted for a third if they were elected on to the House Committee, and as I was loath to give up the good life and pig out in a student flat along the Albany Road, I stood for election as Hall Librarian and was duly elected. And my new duties brought me into close contact with Hull's most famous librarian, the poet Philip Larkin.

LARKIN

Philip Larkin became the university librarian in 1955, the same year as his third volume of poetry, *The Less Deceived*, was published, and there was the merest hint of celebrity about him, in the sense that he was probably the only member of staff who was known to the general public outside the East Riding. He would have taken up residence at Needler Hall at the same time as myself, for he was the newly appointed sub-warden, presumably a temporary arrangement providing him with accommodation until he found his own. As sub-warden his only duty seemed to involve saying grace before the evening meal whenever the warden, Peter Coveney, was in absentia. Like a toppling church steeple he would stand and intone darkly '*Benedictus Benedicat*', as graceless a grace as any heathen could wish for. As soon as the meal was over he would disappear in a huff of tweed, avoiding all contact with students. We never exchanged a word in the year that we were in residence together because: (a) I was too fledgling a poet to have approached him: '*Excuse me, Mr Larkin, how many lines does a sonnet have exactly?*' and (b) he was scary.

A friend of mine at the time was Neville Smith, who went on to earn his living as a scriptwriter (*Gumshoe* starring Albert Finney and *The Golden Vision*, a TV film based on the life of Alex Young, the legendary Everton centre forward, were two of my favourites) and Neville told me of the time he was standing at a bus stop in the pouring rain waiting for a number 24 bus to take him to the university, when Larkin, beneath the black dome of a capacious umbrella, walked up and stood about two yards away. The rain came down even heavier and there was no shelter. Eventually, Neville plucked up courage and moved closer to the bone-dry poet: 'I did enjoy "The North Ship"'. Larkin stared down at him and said, 'If you think you can begin a conversation in order to share my umbrella you've got another think coming.' And with that he pressed the catch on his umbrella so that it folded close around his head.

Except for choral verse and poetry as drama I had never been particularly interested in poetry at school. Poets were male, middle-class, Protestant, probably gay and certainly dead, and suddenly here, within touching distance, was a published poet who was probably only three of those things. Most people who have been to university will agree that the most stimulating and affecting life changes occurred not in the lecture room, but in the bar, in the Common Room, or during a coffee-fuelled discussion late at night in somebody's flat. My own life until then had been narrow and I had brought with me all the prejudices of my class and religious upbringing. For the first couple of terms we Scousers had stuck firmly together, ring-fenced against posh accents, suede desert boots, wine drinkers and southerners. But, inevitably, holes began to appear in the fence and within the year we would be toasting our southern friends with raised desert boots filled with wine: 'Chars!' I was introduced to Dylan Thomas late one night in a student room, not the bard himself, but the LP of *Under Milk Wood* featuring Richard Burton, and I was hooked. The rhythms and the images awakened within me something I didn't know was there and I began reading poetry as if for the first time.

Boring old lectures in French literature suddenly became interesting when we began to study the poets. François Villon, troubadour, womaniser and petty thief, caught my imagination and my first attempts at verse were ballades in the French medieval style, resplendent with 'thees' and 'thous'. When the class moved on to the Symbolists – Verlaine, Rimbaud, Baudelaire, de Nerval – so did I, and opened my arms to the promise of decadence and a trip down the rue Morgue. Like Arthur Rimbaud I longed for a '*dérangement de sens*' but as I was on a student grant provided by Lancashire Education Committee I thought I'd better wait until I'd graduated. However, I read the *Meditations of St John of the Cross* and fasted for several days with a view to achieving a mystical experience, which in some ways I did, although not a religious one. One weekend I went without sleep and wrote continuously for eighteen hours. The result was a long poem influenced by Eliot, Rimbaud and Nietzsche about the poet leading mankind across the swamp of indifference and cruelty to some sort of paradise. On the Richter scale of juvenilia it doesn't register, but the experience of writing it filled me with such certainty of my new calling that my life was changed from then on. At nineteen I was a poet.

I knew students in the English department who wrote poems because they desperately wanted to become poets and who published their pieces in the college poetry magazine in the belief that this would anoint them. I have been to poetry events, book launches and prize givings, and met writers who, having decided to become poets, started writing poems and made a career out of it. Often, though, it seemed as if they were writing poems that mirrored other poems, as if the urge was fuelled by the desire to be a poet rather than to write poetry. But in my case I had never considered a life in poetry. Until I wrote my first poem, that is. Having written the Miltonesque poem that would lead mankind to safety (Milton as in Keynes, that is, not John), I knew with an unshakeable belief that whatever I did in life, whatever profession I fell into, poetry was to be my vocation.

From an early age I had been pretty good at art and had I been allowed to pursue my interest at secondary school would happily have gone to art college. I could draw reasonably well and assumed that, with practice and good teaching, my skills would improve. I could paint and the more I painted the better I would become. Obvious. But would I ever become an artist? Perhaps with luck and dedication, given time I would. With poetry it's different. Write a poem and right away you're a poet. Bingo! What kind, of course, remains to be seen and heard.

Questionnaire:

(1) Do you agree that the spirit of the poet craves spectators – even if only buffaloes? (Nietzsche)

(2) Is your utmost ambition to lodge a few poems where they will be hard to get rid of? (R. Frost)

(3) Is the writing of poetry a learning process or a description of the already known? (G. Stein)

(4) Can you see resemblances between apparently incongruous things? (Aristotle)

(5) Will your book serve as an axe for the frozen sea within us? (Kafka)

(6) As a poet are you willing to be overheard rather than heard? (Hume)

Over lunch at the *Observer* one judgement day (i.e. a small group of poets assembled to judge a competition sponsored by the newspaper), Ted Hughes said that when he went up to Pembroke College, Cambridge in the fifties, of the two hundred or so students who were in his year on the English course, most had high hopes of becoming novelists, poets, dramatists, and yet he could think of only three or four of his contemporaries who were still making a living as full-time writers. Not including critics, he added with some feeling. For the year was 1989 and his fourteenth collection of poems, *Wolfwatching*, had just appeared. He looked at the plate before him and waved his knife and fork over it as if they were twitching talons. 'It's like you've been around for a long time, and this young critic gets your book to review, and hungry to make a reputation for himself, he puts it down in front of him like this plate of cold meat and tears into it.'

So there I was in Kingston-upon-Hull in the fifties with a small pile of poems upon my plate, wondering whether or not they were edible. Had I been in the English department I might have been tempted to risk all and show them to one of the younger lecturers. So I did the next-best thing. Along the corridor from my room was a lad from Newcastle doing an MA in English. Geordies, I thought, salt of the earth. So one evening I selected a few of my tastiest cold cuts and knocked on his door: 'A mate of mine in Liverpool has written some poems and sent them to me. He's desperate to know if they're any good or not.'

He invited me into his room, pulled up an empty crate of Newcastle Brown and bade me sit down while he read the poems. This didn't take long. Eventually he said, 'Tell your mate not to give up his day job just yet.'

(That's not true, actually, for that expression wasn't common parlance in those days.) But the gist of what he said was that my mate should consider writing for the theatre, because he had written dramatic monologues rather than poems. Although the criticism was not unkind, and he probably saw through my cunning alter ego ruse, it was not what I wanted to hear. What every unknown writer wants is the immediate recognition of genius. Unformed, as yet unborn, but genius nonetheless.

I am always being asked to pass an opinion on somebody's poem, perhaps at a book signing where the unpublished poet grabs the chance to nab me while I'm pretending to be approachable and friendly. *'What do you think of this? You can be perfectly honest . . . Thank you. Oh, well . . . er.'*

And off I go, knowing that whatever I say, however encouraging, will not be what the listener wants to hear. I will not leap up and announce to the milling crowds: *'Can I have everybody's attention for a moment, please. I want you all to take a good look at this person standing modestly at my side, for he/she will be the next William Blake/Emily Dickinson as sure as eggs is eggs. Genius, ladies and gentlemen, a round of applause, please, for a new star in the poetic firmament.'*

At least in that sort of situation the pain of rejection, for that's what it ultimately is, can be softened by a warm smile and a firm handshake, or kiss if I'm still fired up after the performance. But when I open a large brown envelope at home and take out the manuscript and the accompanying letter: '*Dear Mr McGough (may I call you Roger, I seem to know you so well even though we have never met?), I enclose a selection of poems that I have written, which friends tell me deserve a wider audience. As a published poet you are in a position . . . etc.*' my heart doth sink a little. Not because it's a bother – because, in fact, I've always regarded it as a privilege that comes with the job of being a professional poet – but rather because of my inability to be of any real help. I haven't the time to offer detailed criticism of the poems, nor can I publish them. All I can do is to give vague encouragement and tell the writer to get in touch with the Poetry Society (www.poetrysociety.org.uk). There, I've saved you the price of the stamps and the large brown envelope.

I will confess, though, to having been smart-arsed on occasion, but only when I believed the writer was thick-skinned enough to take it: '*Thank you for sending me your poems, which I enjoyed reading. However, even though your heart is in the right place, I fear that your words aren't . . .*' That conceit of beginning the letter with a thank you to the sender I borrowed from Philip Larkin, for when I was in my post-graduate year studying for my teaching certificate, I decided to throw caution to the wind that bullies in from the North Sea and show my poems to the man himself. I still lacked the confidence to approach him in person, so I opted for the large-brown-envelope ploy.

A week or so later he replied with a very kind letter in which he thanked me for having sent him the poems, which he had enjoyed reading. At the heart of it he believed that I was walking an impressionistic tightrope which, although exhilarating, meant that on occasion I fell off. Had I published any of the poems, he wanted to know, and if not, suggested I send a few to *Torch*, the university's literary magazine.

There was no further contact between us until 1980 when he wrote to me in Liverpool with a request for my manuscripts to add to the archive collection he was developing. In the ensuing correspondence I mentioned how grateful I had been to have received that letter from him in the fifties and he wrote saying how surprised he was to learn of a former self that encouraged young talent. '*I must have been a very different me in those days,*' he wrote. I wasn't over-enthusiastic about parting with my notebooks because I like to have them on hand, but it was for my alma mater after all, and I was by this time a Larkin fan (not to mention my gratitude to him for having included me in his *Oxford Book of Twentieth-Century English Verse*, 1973) so I sent an exercise book containing early versions of poems featuring PC Plod, which must have thrilled him no end. However, in his reply of 27 March he thanks me and, referring to copies of my books in the university library, says ruefully, '*I was certainly impressed by the condition of our copies of your books: they show signs of a good deal more wear and tear than mine do. Congratulations!*'

The following year, when I had moved down to London and was living in a small flat on the Fulham Road, I sent him a copy of a small booklet of poems entitled *Unlucky for Some*, published by Bernard Stone of Turret Books, and he sent a thank-you note dated 9 March, which ended alarmingly: '*Many thanks for your kind thought in sending me the book, which I found splendidly depressing.*'

In fact, I never did take Larkin's advice about submitting my poems to *Torch*, not from fear that they would be torched, but rather because mine seemed so different from those published in the magazine that I wondered if mine were poems at all. Perhaps 'Taxidermy' would have been a more accurate name for a magazine full of objects which at first glance appeared to breathe, but which on closer examination were stuffed and lifeless. Someone described a certain kind of poem as a room in which the poet has arranged the furniture of his erudition to be admired and *Torch* was very much a furniture showroom. In comparison, my rooms seemed a tad MFI, practical but comfortable. Instead, I sent my poems off to *Torchlight*, which was the student newspaper of the time, and they were happy to include them.

Thrilled as I was to see my poems in print, I was even more pleased to have my cartoons accepted regularly by *Hullaballoo*, the student rag mag. So pleased, in fact, that I was encouraged to send a batch off to *Punch* with a view to a possible career as a staff cartoonist. (I didn't suggest as much in my letter of submission, of course, but I rather hoped their reply would include the offer of a little flat near Bedford Square and the promise of untold wealth.) What the editor did say was '*Weak in ideas and drawing, I'm afraid*'. End of career as famous cartoonist.

WORKING AS AN ARTIST
ON THE LEFT BANK

If you are travelling to Litherland from Liverpool city centre along Linacre Road, you will pass under a railway bridge; on the right-hand side there is a bus depot and opposite, just past the Palladium Cinema, is Langton Road leading down the hill to Seaforth, beyond which you may be lucky enough to spot a ship moving slowly out to sea. A hundred yards down you will see a sign saying 'Litherland Boxing Club' and on the top floor of the building you'll find an artist's studio. You're welcome to come in and have a look around.

I would have been eighteen or nineteen, and when home from university would go to various dance halls with my mates. The big ones in town like the Locarno and the Grafton were intimidating and a bit rough for us fey students, so we favoured venues like the Moulin Rouge in upmarket Birkdale. It was on the dance floor there that I met the girl who was to become my Giaconda, my Venus, my Aphrodite, my own, my very own, nude.

During a slow foxtrot she asked me what I did for a living. The trick, of course, was never to tell the truth. 'I'm a student,' would not be the velvet key to a fumble in the car park later. Student equals no money, no car, no chance. So

I would ring the changes. 'Soldier on leave'. 'Plumber'. 'Airline pilot'. 'Journalist'. 'Hair stylist'. Whatever my reply, the girl would invariably snort, 'Liar, yer a student.' This time, however, because my new pal Norris really was an artist and knowing that I was keen to hone my painterly skills, had offered me the use of his studio, I said modestly, 'I'm an artist.'

'An artist?'

'Yes, I paint. I've got my own studio.'

'What do you paint?'

'Oh, the usual. Still life. Flowers.'

'Naked ladies?'

'Sometimes.' (Lies! Lies!)

'Would you like me to pose for you?'

Let me make it clear right away that Barbara was no scrubber, but a well-spoken middle-class girl from Formby.

'Do you mean without any clothes on?'

Suddenly the foxtrot had turned into a pack of hounds galloping in hot pursuit of something hairy and inedible.

'Yes please!'

We had arranged the sitting for 2 p.m. the following Saturday afternoon. Enough time for a few thumb-nail squiggles, hot sex and then church in time for confession at 6.30. I let myself into the studio just after midday, having first checked with Norris that he would stay away. I fluffed up the brushes in the jam jar to create a surreal flower arrangement, then hung his best unsigned painting on the easel, the canvas I would be working on when Barbara arrived. If Barbara arrived, that is (surely she'd have more sense than to trek across town on a wet Saturday afternoon to take her clothes off for a second-year geography student?

I mean, artist). It was January. It was dark and it was cold. I switched on the only heating, a one-bar electric fire, uncorked the flagon of Hirondelle white wine (at least that was warm) and sat listening to the cream of Litherland youth beating shit out of each other two floors below.

Barbara eventually did arrive and, to her credit, modestly undressed; then, with rather less modesty, posed naked. In the nude. To my credit I didn't make a pass at her. On the debit side, I hadn't brought along a sketchbook, assuming that there would be one of Norris's lying around, so my lightning charcoal sketches were made on wrapping paper and on the backs of boxing-match posters. The poor girl kept shivering and I was struck dumb at the sight of her unbridled goose bumps. After twenty minutes or so she asked to see how I was doing. The bold iconography of my work puzzled her (although not as much as it puzzled me).

'It's charcoal,' I explained.

'It's certainly not me,' she said.

'Just preliminary sketches before I begin painting in oils,' I proffered, watching her get dressed. 'Would you like a glass of wine? It's what artists drink.'

It was still raining as I walked her to the bus stop.

WORK EXPERIENCE

When I was student, the long summer vacations were usually spent in Greece, either sailing between the islands or just simply lying on a beach sipping retsina and reading the latest Robbe-Grillet novel. No they weren't. They were spent earning money and gaining work experience, which in my case amounted to having bad experiences at work.

The Toy Factory

I had always fondly imagined toy factories to be bright, primary-coloured places full of rosy-cheeked craftspersons whistling while they worked, but the one I spent a miserable two and a half months in was a large shed of Dickensian squalor beneath the railway bridge, where workers who still had ten fingers were regarded as cissies. We made money boxes out of metal sheets and I was part of a production line that pressed out the various shapes on a machine with an iron bar on the right-hand side that you pulled across, remembering to lean backwards as it swung both ways in front of you. The small metal pieces were Stanley-knife sharp and at the end of my first day my fingertips were like arterial road maps. Because of the smoke-blackened windows, even in August the place was dark, and the smell of oil and sweat made me pine for the taste of retsina.

My part in the metal-money-box-making process was to take the small sheet of pressed metal from the worker next to me, secure it on to the anvil-shaped base of my machine and punch out the coin slot. On my right sat a young man not much older than me with a cleft palate and severe learning difficulties, and one morning during my second week he managed to leave his thumb on the 'anvil' as the heavy press descended. 'Ugh ugh . . .' I believe is what he said, as he held up what appeared to be a large raspberry lollipop. When it exploded he slipped off his stool to the floor in a dead faint. The machine was hosed down and the worker replaced. I never saw the lad again but it was rumoured that he was hitch-hiking around Europe and having no difficulty getting lifts.

The Bakery

Now I am in a large, airy, sun-filled room the size of an aircraft hangar, proud to wear the brown overall of this well-respected Merseyside bakery. The mistake that was always made in those days (and perhaps still is) by workers who were put in charge of students was the assumption that because they were at college they must be intelligent. So, inevitably, the horny-handed son of the toil would explain the rudiments of the job and then skive off, leaving the student to carry on. In my case a big mistake. Lenny's job was to lift the freshly baked tin loaves off the conveyor belt and put them into a tray, and when the tray was full take out another and carry on. Every fifteen minutes or so a driver would come and remove the trays steaming with the bakery's delicious, factory-fresh tin loaves and deliver them to shops in the area. Lenny showed me what to do and disappeared. I was suddenly alone in the airy, sun-filled room the size of an aircraft hangar as the loaves, the bastards, trundled towards me like enemy tanks. Lenny was not horny-handed without reason and had failed to point out that the loaves were pipingly, excruciatingly, painfully hot, and after placing a few loaves gingerly in the tray my hands burst into flames. That's an exaggeration, but my palms were red raw with the heat. (Gloves? Now that would have been a good idea. Hygienic as well as more comfortable for the worker at the loaf-face.)

While bending down to pick up the loaves I had dropped, the steaming convoy would trundle past on the moving belt above, and while I was attempting to retrieve them more would be swept on to the floor. And so on. Within minutes my main concern was not to fill the trays, but to prevent the loaves from travelling twenty yards along the track before disappearing through a black, rubber-flapped door into an ominously large machine. I knew I was failing when the Heath Robinson contraption started to make groaning noises, followed by a sustained hiss. Next thing, squashed loaves began to issue forth from the top of the machine, and it became a volcano erupting floury lava. Like the Roman soldier at the gates of the burning city, I remained steadfastly at my post until one of the drivers arrived to collect the trays and pushed the stop button on the conveyor belt. That afternoon the good soldier was posted to the tray-scrubbing shed.

The Sugar Factory

I don't know what it is about me and machines, but we just don't get on, which is surprising considering my infant bonding with that mechanical cheese. Tate & Lyle had a huge factory on the Dock road and employed an army of students during the summer vacations. One day I would be part of a gang humping bags of sugar on to the back of lorries and the next I would be stacking boxes in the stacking-box shed. For a month I worked the night shift in the Char House, or Charcoal House, a Victorian building on three floors where raw sugar was filtered through charcoal as part of the cleansing process. I enjoyed working through the night and watching the sun rise each morning over the river, and I liked the company of the men I worked with. The constant breaks for tea and toast and roll–ups in the furnace room with a group of surreal Scouse philosophers, who shared with the dockers an aptitude for bestowing colourful names on their colleagues – the Balloon foreman: '*Don't let me down, lads*'; the Sheriff foreman: '*Where's the hold-up?*'; 'Lino': '*He's always on the floor*'; 'Phil the Cot: '*He's got fourteen kids*'.

Instead of loaves, it was charcoal dust that did for me this time when the chargehand left me on my own at 2 a.m. on the third floor. The huge space with its tiled walls and clanking metal pipes was like the engine room on some abandoned liner: 'All you've gorra do is stand by this big pipe here, and when the noise changes hit that button there.'

'What about these dials?' I asked, pointing to a handful of quivering fingers.

'Take no notice. See yer, lad.'

So I pulled up a chair and sat down in front of what looked like a small ship's funnel and waited for the noise to change. What noise? I couldn't hear anything. Oh, yes I could. Did he mean that faint sifting noise, like the sound of icing sugar passing gently through a sieve? Or did he mean the ticking noise coming from one of the dials? No, he'd told me to forget about the dials. Could he have meant the scuffling noise coming from the far corner? No, that's a rat, take no notice. It's amazing the sounds you can hear when you're cast adrift in an ocean liner above the rooftops of a sleeping city. Foghorns, of course, out on the river. A baby crying in a tenement block? Two lovers giggling in Paradise Street? In the empty jazz cellar, the pianist plays a final blues. Eyes closed now, I feel myself drifting into a sweet aural reverie. Drifting . . . drifting . . .

Suddenly, what's that noise? Snoring? The sound of somebody snoring? When I realised that I'd been asleep but not snoring, it was time to panic. The noise, and it was increasingly deafening, was coming from the blasted funnel and it was time for me to spring into action as I'd been trained to do. I hit the button. The trouble is that five minutes is a long time for charcoal to be pumped along lengths of piping and the eruption, though lacking the glorious yeasty smell of the bakery volcano, was a good deal more volatile and disruptive. Black clouds billowed around the room and the charcoal dust settled to a depth of several feet. It was like a satanic snowstorm. My Al Jolson impersonation failed to impress the chargehand when he arrived, but at least he helped me shovel out the dust and hose down the room. The next day the good soldier was transferred to humping bags of sugar on to the backs of lorries.

The Holiday Rep

Before I took up my first teaching post, an advert in the *Liverpool Echo* caught my eye. It was from a holiday firm seeking a suitably qualified person to act as a courier and take a group of holidaymakers to Italy. I'm not suitably qualified, I thought, so it sounds just the job for me. In retrospect, I should have been suspicious of Mr Gerovski from the moment I walked into his tiny office in the city centre and confessed, 'I'm afraid I don't speak Italian.'

He waved my concerns away: 'Schno matter, schno matter.'

'I do have a degree in French and Geography, though.'

'Schit down, schit down.' So I schat down.

As he passed over bundles of tickets, passports, visas, dockets and forms, he explained that it was to Rimini on Italy's Adriatic coast that I was to lead the charge of thirty-six Scousers. No charter flights in those days, but ferries and trains, and on arrival in Milan I had strict instructions to ring him and find out which hotels we would be staying at. And it was there, on the vast, marble concourse of Milan Central Station, eighteen hours after setting off from Liverpool, that he confided we weren't actually going to Rimini, but to Cesanatico, a few miles up the coast. 'You needn't tell them,' he assured me, 'they won't know the difference.'

By the grand central station I sat down and wept.

On the Monday morning I was arrested and taken to the

police station at Forli. I wish I had been tortured. Obviously it wouldn't have been very nice at the time, but now I could describe to you in sickening detail how the *carabinieri* had attached electrodes to my genitals and beaten me with grissini sticks . . . '*No, I won't tell you his name, not in a million years . . . Oh, all right then, it was Mr Gerovski.*'

Apparently, his scam had been to book English holiday-makers into various resorts along the coast and, when the bills came in, to move them along to the next town. He had invested all the money he'd received at the beginning of the season in the hope that by the end of it he'd be in profit, but it had all collapsed and he was in jail awaiting trial in Liverpool. This was not good news and even though I was released without charge, I was concerned for the group. Would it be warm enough at night on the beach, and would there be enough lilos for them to sleep on? To their great credit, the hotel owners let them all stay on, providing full board even though they knew they wouldn't be getting paid.

'*Un saluto agli albergatori del Adriatico.*'

GROUNDHOG DAY

In 1999, Sarah-Jane Hall from BBC Radio 4's travel department invited me to take part in *Sentimental Journey*, a series about retracing your steps, revisiting a favourite holiday haunt in the genial company of Arthur Smith, so I chose to return to Cesanatico in the hope of finding some of those generous hotel owners and thanking them. Unsurprisingly, we didn't take the train there via Milan, but flew direct from Gatwick. Although, as it turned out the train might have been quicker. Our cunning plan was that Sarah-Jane, Arthur and I would take the 11 a.m. flight to Bologna and meet up with some of the staff from Penguin Children's Books who were over there for the Book Fair. A leisurely lunch followed by a stroll around that beautiful city and a car to Cesanatico in time for a light supper, a grappa or two and an early night. We arrived at the airport in good time to check in and were told that there would be an hour's delay before take-off. Not a huge problem.

In the sad sequence of events that was to follow, I would like to make it clear that Sarah-Jane was in no way to blame, for she is one of those women who work for the BBC for whom you would cross croc-infested rivers, car-congested motorways and even, as I did, risk death by rucksack in the Grand Canyon.

Let us say, for the sake of argument, that it was Arthur who said, 'As we've got bags of time let's jump on one of those little trains and have a coffee in the other terminal.' Which we did and, returning to the departure gate forty minutes later, were told that the plane had left on time.

'But you said . . .' we chorused.

The next flight was at 8 p.m., to Florence, where we could take a train to Rimini and a car from there, which we did.

Have you ever spent eight hours at Gatwick Airport? Obviously, the people who work there do it every day, but as a transit passenger there are only so many aftershave lotions you can spray on in duty-free. We arrived at our hotel in Cesanatico in the middle of the night and I was sure the grumpy old night porter had been a handsome young waiter there forty years before. In my best Italian I asked him, and in reply he said how overwhelming my aftershave was. Even though Sarah-Jane turned down my suggestion to revisit the torture chamber in Forli, we did manage to get a decent thirty-minute programme, thanks mainly to Arthur, and I learned that Leonardo da Vinci designed the canal and that the original inhabitants were Celts, but I never did find anyone who remembered a visit by thirty-six desperate Scousers back in 1959.

I suppose I should pick up on that 'death by rucksack' allusion, mainly because it opens with another tedium-packed incident at the same aerodrome. An old friend of mine, the writer and broadcaster Pete McCarthy, had sold the idea to Sarah-Jane of a series of radio programmes called *American Beauty*, in which he and I would travel around the States, talking to people, describing what we saw and generally having a good time at the Corporation's expense.

For the first programme we would fly to Las Vegas and spend a few days there, before driving on to the Grand Canyon, where we would attempt a death-defying descent, camp in the valley (on our own, in the dark) and then at first light climb back up again.

At 8.30 a.m. on 15 June 1994, a silver Mercedes called to collect me, and an hour and fifteen minutes later we were at Gatwick, where Sarah-Jane was already waiting at check-in at the North West Airlines desk. She picked me out from the crowd very easily because I had chosen to wear an apricot suit, which I'd been too embarrassed to wear at home but which I thought might blend into the pastel-coloured heartland of US kitsch. Bloody typical, no sign of Pete, who always leaves things to the last minute. But he arrived, cool as ever, and we checked in. At least, Pete and Sarah-Jane checked in.

'Is your wife travelling with you today?' asked Bill Murray at the desk.

'Er, no.'

'Then why have you given me her passport, sir?'

'Er, pardon?'

Within minutes, the BBC's rescue and retrieval operation was called into force and I rang home to tell Hilary that a motorcyclist was on his way to pick up my passport. I think it was a couple of lamb chops that Hilary was buying at the time, although it might have been a rail for the new curtains in Isabel's bedroom; wherever she was, she wasn't at home when I rang, nor when Evel Knievel scorched the gravel in front of the house. I wished Pete and Sarah-Jane a good flight and they wished me a safe journey as I took the tube back to Hammersmith.

The next day it was Groundhog Day, because at 8.30 a.m. the same silver Mercedes arrived with the same driver, who dropped me off at the same entrance, and as I made my way to the same check-in desk and saw Bill Murray, looking straight through me as if he'd never seen me before, I thought if I see Sarah-Jane now I'll be condemned to spend eternity checking-in at Gatwick. I did escape the loop, however, and, after the eight-and-a-half-hour flight to Minneapolis, plus a five-hour wait for the connection to Las Vegas, was met at the airport by Pete, who had really enjoyed his day off lying by the pool.

THE RATTLESNAKES

People interested in the skiffle craze that swept across the country in the fifties will readily refer to Lonnie Donegan, The Vipers, Nancy Whiskey, and rightly so, but one band that escaped the attention of the media at the time was Tinhorn Timmons and the Rattlesnakes. The reason this ballsy outfit never made it on a global scale was that the Rattlesnakes, indigenous to the desert of East Riding, were content to play locally in small venues, and had offers been made to tempt them to the Big Smoke and a career in the music industry, they would have refused. For they knew they were crap. Or, to be painfully precise, *we* knew *we* were crap. The university was very small when I arrived, with less than a thousand students, which meant that there were fewer choices to be made when signing up to join a society or club. In the absence of surfing, hang-gliding and bungee-jumping clubs, I opted to join the cricket club, the table-tennis club and the Catholic Society. My reasons for joining the last were far from spiritual because, quite simply, Cath Soc had the best-looking women on campus, attracting French mistresses, señoritas and a bevy of sad-eyed Polish girls. Atheistic sexual predators and agnostic ne'er-do-wells would also sign up so they could attend our social nights and cop off with the convent-educated girls that by rights should have been ours. It just wasn't fair.

The Jazz Club attracted a sassy crowd and I'd occasionally go to their dances, where the jazz was cool and modern. Unlike me, unfortunately. I did have a sort of Buddy Holly resemblance and we were both born in towns beginning with the letter L, but whereas he exuded sexuality, I merely exuded. The Saturday night raves featured 'Norris Walker and the All Stars', who played the sort of dance music our parents would have quickstepped to. I never listened to music that much, unlike my pals who tuned in to Radio Luxembourg and AFN, but when two of them started up a skiffle group and invited me to learn bass and join them, how would I have known that it would be the first small step on the road to musical glory? (Ahem . . .) The bass that I mastered, needless to say was not a double, nor an electric, but a tea chest. Take a large plywood chest, empty the tea leaves and tie a length of string from one corner to the top of a broom handle, affix Elastoplast to index and middle finger, and bom–bom, bum–bum off you go: '*Ladies and Gentlemen, put your hands together, please, and give a warm Hessle working-men's club welcome to Tinhorn Timmons and the Rattlesnakes.*'

The skills I acquired on stage with the Rattlesnakes were to stand me in good stead many years later, particularly the ability to carry on playing or singing while the audience ignores you, and not to take it personally when they come backstage and scream abuse. I am thinking with particular fondness of the Garrick Club in Leigh one wet Friday night in February 1975. Part of the Scaffold's schedule at the time involved the dreaded northern cabaret circuit, which meant doing two hour-long sets at two different venues for a week. For instance, in 1970 we appeared at the New Monk Bretton Club at 9 p.m. and then we'd shoot over to the bigger club, the Cavendish in Sheffield, for the eleven o'clock slot. Occasionally we would use the house band, but more often than not we travelled with our own group. At the time of our Cavendish days we were still bubbling along in the public's consciousness with 'Lily the Pink' and 'Thank U Very Much', but by the time we got to Leigh, outside Manchester, the consciousness bubbles had popped.

I have before me a folded yellow card, which was the supper menu of the Garrick Club, and for 10p you could have kicked off with a bowl of soup, then tucked into scampi and chips in a basket for 70p, or if you wanted to go mad, a sirloin steak with chips and bread and butter would have set you back all of 95p. On the back of the menu is the running order I'd written out for the show, which includes three of our minor hits, 'Do You Remember', 'The Leaving of Liverpool' and 'Liverpool Lou', as well as 'Lily' and 'Thank U Very Much', the other thirty-five minutes consisting of poems and revue sketches.

The week had not gone well for us in terms of audience numbers but the Friday night was pretty busy and we hoped at least to finish on a high note (in our case probably flat). After the show we were in the dressing room hanging up our stage suits in the fridge when there was a knock on the door. Without waiting for a reply, two women high-heeled in, bold and brassy. Automatically John, Mike and I reached for our pens to sign the autographs, or the photographs, or the thighs, whatever was on offer. The ladies introduced themselves: 'I'm Mel and this is Dot.'

'Hi, girls.'

'How long have we been comin' here, Dot?'

'Five years.'

'Every Friday night for five years and that were the worst show we've ever seen, weren't it, Dot?'

'It were shite.'

'Hardly any songs, no proper jokes and we couldn't believe our ears, friggin' poems. What were it like, Dot?'

'It were shite.'

It goes without saying (or, rather, it would have gone without saying if I hadn't said it) that they didn't want our autographs, even though Mike kindly offered.

Another advantage of a small campus was the proximity of events that were on hand. Would I regularly have attended Union debates, I wonder, if they were held half a mile away? Whereas the weekly debate took place in the mixed Common Room (yes, that's when we had Men's and Women's Common Rooms for folk of similar sex who wanted to be with each other). The men's was smoke-filled, noisy and full of card players, whereas the women's was serene, chintzy and full of women reading poetry and knitting. Or so my girlfriends insisted. 'Mass debates', as they were hilariously known at school, were held when I was in the sixth form, but I never took part, being unable to follow a single train of thought when speaking in an upright position, and so at Hull I was mightily impressed with the fluency and wit that was part of our weekly diet. It may not have been the Oxford Union. In fact, it wasn't, it was Hull Union, but it had Roy Hattersley who was a star performer: 'My learned friend is a self-made man . . . who worships his creator . . .' as well as Kevin McNamara, Bob Cryer and a number of others who went on to a life in politics. I never marshalled the courage to stand up and speak, but on occasion I'd be moved to write a poem about a topic under discussion (the war in Cyprus, the standard of food in the refectory) and have it published in *Torchlight*, copies of which change hands today for one pound fifty. Change hands?

   'Hey, I like your hands.'

   'Thank you.'

   'Would you like to change them?'

   'What for?'

   'Well, I'll swap you this tea-chest bass for them.'

   'OK, it's a deal.'

   'Good, let's shake on it.'

   . . . *'What with?'*

SUPERPOET!

National Service was one of the bogeymen that lurked in the bushes when I was growing up, waiting to leap out and grab any callow youth on his eighteenth birthday, put him in uniform and shout at him. School friends of mine who didn't go into the sixth form were conscripted and sent away. A few of them seemed to have enjoyed the experience, especially the ones press-ganged into the Navy, who came home on leave from the Med all tanned and manly. Those in khaki and Air Force blue, however, mainly resented the two years spent in Catterick, or Mildenhall, or wherever it was that they painted grass green and pretended to be invisible. Having no wish to join them I went directly to university, hoping that by the time I'd completed my course, National Service would have been abolished. Unfortunately it wasn't, but I had another throw of the dice: stay on at university for another year and keep the sergeant majors at bay. Having already decided to go into teaching, I enrolled on the post-graduate teaching course that would enable me to become a schoolmaster and one day the Shadow Minister for Education.

In retrospect, I was lucky to have graduated at all. It had become clear to me (and my tutors) fairly rapidly that my interest in Geography was limited. I always contrived to go down with flu whenever a geological field trip was in prospect, and the various poetic musings and witty asides I worked into my essays on ocean currents and seismic plates were cruelly ignored. While sitting my Finals I wrote one of my better poems about the pressures of city life (borrowing freely from my epic about leading mankind out of the marsh) during the three-hour Regional Geography paper. Because I hadn't done the required reading around the subject, my poem was probably an act of desperation rather than one of defiance, but even so I was disappointed to learn some time later that for my efforts I had been awarded 'Nul points'.

I assume that I failed Geography completely, and that it was the French side of my degree that saved me from public scorn and my parents from bitter disappointment. Although my enthusiasm for poetry and ideas had taken hold in time for me to produce some decent essays, I did have an Achilles heel. Some weeks before I was due to sit Finals, one of the lecturers, more by way of filling in time, asked the group to read aloud a passage from the French text we were studying. When it was my turn I gave a Gallic shrug to get me in the mood and dived in. After half a dozen lines, as I was getting into the swing of things, he butted in, rather rudely I thought, and asked to see me at the end of the period. He led me outside the building into one of the forecourts where nobody was about. He was breathing shallowly and his face had paled as he leaned towards me. He's going to kiss me, I thought. But no.

'Mr McGough, how has the department arrived at a situation where you are about to sit for your final examinations, which include a viva conducted in French, a language of which you are unable to speak a word?'

'I don't know, sir.'

'You don't know? Didn't you spend the required term in France during your second year?'

'Er . . . no, sir, my grandmother was ill, sir.'

'But you must have spoken French in class?'

'No, sir.'

'Why not?'

'Nobody asked me to, sir.'

All of which was obviously quite worrying for the teaching staff. The prospect of an external examiner discovering a third-year language student who mumbled French in a Liverpool-Irish accent might prove a costly embarrassment, and so arrangements were made for my grandmother to go poorly again at the time of my viva and my Achilles heel remained undetected. (Except for the arrowhead embedded in it, which causes me to limp from time to time.)

My Education year was a doddle compared with my three years as an undergraduate because I was interested in most aspects of the course, particularly educational and child psychology, and rather fancied the idea of pursuing a career in it after a few years' teaching. I was also going steady with a second-year Sociology student from St Helens called Josephine Twist, whom I'd met at a Cath Soc hop, a honeyed blonde, whose overarm smash on the tennis court would have had Sir John Betjeman keeling over with apoplectic lust. But all too soon our courtship was put to the test when I was allocated a school in Cleethorpes for my winter term's teaching practice, which meant sad, rain-soaked goodbyes each Sunday night before boarding the ferry across the Humber (Gerry Marsden would never have had a hit song with that) and glad, rain-soaked hellos on Friday evenings.

I have never visited Cleethorpes *in* season, if it has one that is, but *out* of season it was a bleak, windswept nightmare. I was billeted along with three other students in Wave Crest, a little B&B run by an elderly couple who were thrilled to have paying guests to moan at and complain about. I particularly remember the breakfasts and the old man, who could have squinted for Lincolnshire, bringing in our bowls of porridge with his thumbs firmly embedded in the grey sludge. 'This'll set you up,' he'd say, wiping his thumbs on the seat of his trousers.

Nor do I have fond memories of the Humberstone Foundation School, a grammar school with a proud tradition of being traditional. The boys were fine, but it was the staff who got up my nose. With a few exceptions they totally ignored me, even resenting my presence in the staffroom: 'You can't sit there, it's History.' 'Not that mug, it's Physics.' And in general they were dismissive of boys who weren't in the top stream. But I was there to learn and learn I did, so much so that when it came time for me to leave and the Headmaster, whom I'd met only once, handed me the reference I could use when applying for a teaching post, I was delighted to read that I was a pleasant, shy young man who, with further experience should develop into a teacher of average ability.

The term I spent there wasn't completely wasted, however, for I was interested in teacher–pupil relationships and how to achieve an easygoing atmosphere in the classroom and yet maintain a reasonable standard of discipline, so I was advised to sit in on one of Mr Gould's English lessons with 4 beta, 'a particularly unruly crowd'. I got to the classroom before the teacher and sat down at the back, pen and notebook in hand. All the boys were chatting away but there was no shouting or fighting or throwing missiles, and when Mr Gould entered and took his place at the head of the class, the noise subsided even though some of the boys were still talking and fiddling with their books. I shall never forget Mr Gould's strategy for creating order out of chaos, for it was to stand me in good stead later in my career as I strove to develop into a teacher of average ability. He picked up a pencil (Faber-Castell HB, I made a note of it, for such little details can make all the difference) and began tapping quietly on the desktop. Gradually the chatter ebbed away into silence. 'Thank you, gentlemen, now let us begin the lesson . . .' Magic.

That was March 1959 and the following September, stiffened with missionary zeal, I strode into the classroom of 3N at St Kevin's Comprehensive School for Boys in Kirkby, stood behind the table and took out my Faber-Castell HB pencil. The lads took not a blind bit of notice and if it hadn't been for the scream from Delaney when I stuck it in his ear I would be there to this day, tapping away with my little pencil stub.

In the fifties, when the old back-to-backs along Scotland Road and south to the Dingle were pulled down, families who had lived in the city for generations were offered the opportunity to relocate to the countryside. It may have sounded appealing, the intentions may even have been of the best, but it was a disaster. New houses and tenement blocks were thrown up and thousands of people were transported to Kirkby, fifteen miles outside Liverpool. When I arrived to take up my post, there were a few mobile shops and a church but no pubs, clubs, shopping centres, cafés, sports centres, or any ingredients vital to nourishing a community.

There were two mixed comprehensive schools, Ruffwood and Brookfield, and two Catholic single-sex comps, St Kevin's and St Gregory's, huge schools, so newly built the cement was still drying, and all within walking distance of each other. Except for the heads of department, all the teachers were, like myself, straight out of college, wide-eyed and enthusiastic, and the staffroom was a buzzy, happy place, such a contrast to the chill of Humberstone: 'Not that urinal, it's Latin.'

Because the boys were streamed according to ability it had been decided not to go down the tried and mistrusted A B C D route, because with an eight-stream intake and the likelihood of it getting even bigger, the fear was that boys in the lower streams would identify themselves as being losers and behave accordingly. So the Head came up with *Pax Dominum Vobiscum* (The peace of the Lord be with you) and the boys were streamed thus: P A X D O M I N and it worked a treat. At least until the end of the first week, by which time the lads in the top stream had worked it out and told everybody else. As young Delaney said on that first morning, handing me back my waxy pencil, 'This is 3N, sir, it stands for Nutters.'

I like to think I was a decent teacher in that I enjoyed being with the boys and tried hard to encourage them, especially the ones who were unlovely and unloved. It's always easy for a teacher to get the bright ones to respond, and then to glide along with them in tow, but it's the ones at the back of the class, surly and unresponsive, who were the challenge. Being a teacher-of-all-trades and master of none, I taught English as well as everything other than science, and one of the set books was *Palgrave's Golden Treasury of Verse*, from which I'd had to learn great chunks at school. Except for the odd narrative verse, usually involving heroics on the battlefield, most of Palgrave went in one ear and out of the other (rather like that Faber-Castell HB pencil), so I didn't have high hopes for the poetry lessons.

What I began to do, of course, was to read my own poems in class. By my second year at St Kevin's I was leading a double life: schoolmaster by day and Beat poet by night.

After much soul-searching and busloads of guilt, I had broken off my engagement to the beautiful Josephine, much to the disappointment of the folks at home who thought she'd make an ideal Mrs McGough. In those days it was customary to settle down in your early twenties and nearly all my friends were getting hitched, so it took some courage to go against the flow and swim into the unknown. I was possessed of the romantic idea of the poet as an outsider, a lonely figure wrestling with his demons, for whom marriage and the conventional life would be stultifying. And so, being fancy free, I had begun to develop a taste for the city's subterranean nightlife, which involved my carrying to school a brown canvas bag containing my poetry survival kit: tight jeans, a black roll-neck sweater, a packet of Gauloises and a notebook filled with poems about lost love. Rumour has it that at least two nights a week after school I would take the bus into town, go into the nearest telephone box and emerge as *Superpoet*.

But as well as my lost-boy, come-hither poems I had quite a number of funny ones about football and grannies and about Liverpool that appealed to the kids I was teaching: 'Arr aye, sir, don't do the dead oncs, give us some of your pomes.' After worrying at university about whether what I was writing was indeed poetry and, more important, whether anybody would be interested in it, suddenly the question didn't seem relevant. Here was my audience, not only those lads in Kirkby, but my fellow teachers, relatives and friends, as well as the crowd listening at the bar and that girl, particularly that girl at the table in the corner, the one with the dark eyes and long brown hair, wearing paint-stained jeans and a black leather jacket.

TODAY, A REAL LIVE POET WILL
BE VISITING THE SCHOOL

A few months ago I was at a large country house hotel for a conference on creativity in schools, organised by a local Education Authority, my sort of gig, really. I find myself being engaged more and more in this sort of crusade, firing up those who work in education about the importance and power of poetry. Of course, most of the delegates are well aware of the message, but so much of their time is spent on administration and finance that it easily gets lost: *'We'd do a lot more poetry if it weren't for the league tables, or the curriculum, or Ofsted, or the weather.'* I read poems and usually include a prose piece based on my experiences of visiting schools as a keen young poet. It was in May 1978 when I was invited to spend a week visiting schools in the Doncaster and Scunthorpe area, ten schools in five days. It sounded like a tough assignment but I was game. The Monday morning couldn't have been easier, a warm welcome from the Head of English, who took me along to the library and introduced me to the sixth form, all of whom, he explained, were eager to explore the jewel-encrusted caverns of my soul. They were shy and unforthcoming at first, but after I'd read a few poems and we'd talked, they opened up and the morning flew by. My initial misgivings about the project began to ebb away and I looked forward to the afternoon session at another school.

The ebb tide began to turn as I walked up the driveway to witness all the staff leaving. Perhaps I've come on the wrong day, I thought. Wrongly, as it happened. The teaching staff had indeed been given the afternoon off, because some poet or other had volunteered to look after all the kids for the rest of the day. Even the soporific English teacher nipped off to the staffroom after introducing me to the baying mob ('Got a pile of books to mark,' he yawned. 'I'll pop back at four o'clock.').

I was in the school hall faced with 600 kids of mixed age and ability, holding my little green folder containing poems for a performance that would last roughly thirty minutes. I had to think on my feet, so I stood up. I suppose I could read every poem twice; they were making so much noise they wouldn't notice anyway. Or I could take out my trusty Faber-Castell HB, or, better still, I could make a run for it. What I did, in fact, was open the book and read to them and, to be fair, once I'd started they listened. Not all the kids, of course, but you know what it's like, when there are ones who want to listen they will make the others keep the noise down. After half an hour, I said, 'Any questions?'

'Sir, where do you get your ideas from?'

'Sir, why do poems always stop just as they're getting interesting?'

'Sir, where did you get your shoes from?'

'Sir, how much money do you get?'

'Sir, what's the longest/shortest/funniest/best poem you've ever written?'

Having given them my all, or at least, bits of it, I said,

'Thank you for all those interesting questions, and now we'll take a short break during which time I want you to write a poem called "Skiving off" and give it to your English teacher when he wakes up.' I left the stage, picked up my coat from outside the staffroom and got the hell out of it.

Whenever I walk into a classroom for the first time, there will always be two girls sitting on the right-hand side who will stop chewing, turn to each other and look up at the ceiling with a 'God, the state of him' kind of expression. One gets used to it and my mission is always to try to win them over. Headmasters don't help, sometimes, and I'm thinking of the one on the following Thursday morning who introduced me to the class by misquoting a poem I wish I'd never written followed by one of Mike Rosen's, then placing his chair behind me so that he could keep a beady eye on the class.

Nowadays schools are normally pleased to welcome poets, artists and musicians into their midst, but in those days there was often resentment: '*The Upper Sixth are great fans of your work, but they're far too busy studying English Literature to see you, but rather than waste your time I've arranged a visit to 4n, just follow the noise and the bloodstains along the corridor and you can't miss them.*'

After my session in the hotel conference room, I was approached by a well-turned-out lady in her middle years who asked me if I remembered her. It was a rhetorical question from this former schools inspector, and Gillian Roxburgh reminded me of our last meeting. It was Christmas Eve 1968 and this is what happened. 'Thank U Very Much' had reached number four in the charts and the Scaffold were busy rushing around doing radio and television. One of the most popular shows on ITV at the time was the *Eamon Andrews Show* and we'd driven down from Liverpool to the studios in London. The show was pre-recorded at five o'clock and was to be screened at eleven, so as soon as we had the all-clear, we leaped into the car and Mike drove us back, hoping to be in time to see the show at home. However, as we arrived at the outskirts of Birmingham it became obvious that we weren't going to make it. There were no video recorders in those days, or pubs with TV sets still open at 10.45 at night. So when we reached Sutton Coldfield we decided to put ourselves at the mercy of the locals, stop at the nearest house and ask if we could watch ourselves on the set in their living room. Unfortunately the old Punjabi gentleman, getting ready for bed at the first house we called at, didn't recognise us, nor did he own a TV set. But the second house . . . Bingo!

'Luddy 'ell,' said the young man as he opened the door. 'It's the Scaffold, I'm just watching you on telly, come in, come in.' We barged past him in time to see the three of us wearing white suits run on to the set and burst into song. 'Gillian,' the young man was shouting upstairs. 'It's my wife, she's in the bath and she's one of your biggest fans, Gillian!' As soon as the Scaffold had finished we joined in the audience applause and made our way to the door. 'You can't go yet, Gillian's just taking her curlers out, she'll never believe you were here.' So we stayed for a swift Scotch, said hello to the newly-wed as she swept into the lounge all coiffed and lovely, and disappeared into the night. Mrs Roxburgh told me how she and her husband had dined out on that story for years, but never really knew if anybody believed them.

BUS STOPS

I believe I may have been the inspiration for a poem written by Wendy Cope called 'Tumps', which stands for Typically Useless Male Poets, a sociological grouping of sad sacks who can't mend things, can't do-it-themselves, can't drive. I must say that I'm proud to belong to this small but ineffectual elite, for on the plus side we can make a decent curry and, being tigers under the duvet, are consequently much in demand at parties and registry offices. The result of not being able to drive, however, has meant that much of my life has been spent on railway platforms and, more especially, waiting at bus stops.

The bus stop outside St Philip's Church Hall on Linacre Road in Litherland, where I caught a red Ribble bus six mornings a week going to grammar school in Crosby, and where, on the top deck, I experienced calf love for the first time at the sight of Joan Taylor's calves.

The bus stop on Rice Lane, where I used to catch the number 19c green Corpy (Liverpool Corporation bus) to Kirkby when I was teaching at St Kevin's. It was coming home on that bus after four o'clock that I occasionally saw Adrian Henri. I had no idea who this strange man was, but he always sat upstairs at the very front and, being huge, had two seats to himself, which enabled him to turn and face his pals in the seat behind. They were all teachers too, I gleaned, from a secondary modern in Netherley, but what I found fascinating was the conversation of the big, fat, black-bearded guy. Although less of a conversation than a lecture. It was as if he was addressing the whole of the top deck on Mayakovsky, Charlie Mingus, Kurt Schwitters and other heroes of his that I had never heard of.

The bus stop on Paradise Street, where I waited for the cream and green Crossville bus to take me out to St Helens to visit my fiancée – a long and boring journey that gave me too much time to think about our future together. It was returning to Liverpool one winter's night that I was gripped by the fear that once I boarded the marriage bus there would be no getting off. I would only have been twenty-two at the time and although Jo, to whom I'd got engaged at university, was beautiful and bright and all things right, I was too young. There were other buses. (And here's a thought: perhaps if Jo had lived nearer to Liverpool there would have been less time to brood and we might be married today.)

The bus stop in Princes Avenue, Liverpool 8, nineteen years, two sons, a stepson and one divorce later, where I struck up a conversation with the only other person in the city who didn't know that there was a bus strike. Hilary Clough was a lecturer at the Polytechnic and had a Ph.D. in microbial biochemistry, so we had lots to talk about. Blonde and blue-eyed, she laughed in a Yorkshire accent as we walked together to the Philharmonic pub. We had both arranged to meet friends there and, as often happens in coincidences of the heart, they were late arriving. In the meantime I bought Hilary a drink. She bought me one. We decided to get married, have two children called Matthew and Isabel, and live first in Notting Hill before moving to Barnes. Which we did.

Not bad for a Tump.

Truly Unique Mind-boggling Punster.

Tired Untidy Miserable Plonker.

Tasty Unsalted Mashed Potato.

CINDERS

In the late lunch of my life (I prefer that to 'the twilight of my days') a small miracle occurred. I had known all along that Hilary was pregnant, because not only had she told me so, but she had begun to look pregnant, attend ante-natal classes and acquire a cot, a pushchair and all the usual infantanalia. However, part of me remained unconvinced – perhaps it was simply a dress rehearsal to test my reaction. Would I panic and make a run for it? In my fiftieth year was God pulling my leg? Why news of Matthew's birth on 29 April 1987 didn't make the evening newspapers I will never know and why a push-by-push account of the delivery wasn't made into a TV special I can only put down to the fact that a miracle ceases to be a miracle when it happens all the time (but isn't that even more miraculous?). Even to this day I can't see a woman in the street with a baby without wanting to stop and applaud. Women who can't drive, who know nothing about football, do it. Women of every shape and size do it. Peel themselves back and push out another life.

'The waters have broken,' Hilary calmly announced at 6.30 that bright spring morning, an expression that always had me puzzled. The idea of water being breakable. Waves break, not water, it leaks, it spreads, it spatters, but break?

Anyway, as morning broke, so did the waters, leaving little time for a discussion about linguistics. A firm believer in natural childbirth, she went through the whole routine as if it were her hobby and she had been doing it for years, while I busied myself with cold flannels and cooling water sprays feeling as useful as a synchronised swimmer stranded on Ayers Rock.

> *The contractions are coming faster now.*
> *Every ten minutes or so*
> *A crush of pain made bearable*
> *Only by the certainty of its passing.*
>
> *Midwives come and go.*
> *At nine forty-five, a show.*
> *It must go on. The floodgates open,*
> *A universe implodes.*

Although I joked, after Matthew was born, that the main drawback to late fatherhood was that it prevented my wife and me from going out to the cinema or to restaurants in the evening, its effect was to provoke an intensity of feeling that otherwise I might not have experienced. In the period that followed I looked again at the relationship I'd had with my father and writing about it helped me to face up to the role that I'd suddenly been given. When Finn and Tom were babies I was young enough to be optimistic and selfish. Of course, there had been football in the park and bedtime stories and family holidays, and although they wouldn't have nominated me for one of the Great Fathers of our Time awards, they knew that I would always be there for them, but I was cocooned by poems, cut off from their real world by my need to daydream. Now, however, being equally selfish but older and therefore less optimistic, I worried deeply about my new responsibilities. Spike Milligan didn't help either, when he telephoned one morning only days after Matthew had been born. He began by congratulating Hilary and me, then started off about there being too many people in the world already, and about there not being enough resources, and about how the food was going to run out very soon, and what with the ozone layer and global warming we were all going to die. Doomed, do you hear, we're all doomed! It was not Spike at his best.

My father died of a coronary thrombosis at the age of fifty-three. So many of his workmates on the docks died too at his age that it seemed like a plague, a contagious disease with an appetite for big, strong men just past their prime. They weren't all smokers either, like my dad, nor were they heavy drinkers, so perhaps it was the stress of the war taking its toll all those years later. He came out of hospital after his first attack, gave up smoking and went on a diet and, hardest of all, gave up going each week to Goodison Park to cheer on his beloved Everton. He hated the idea of being ill, a state synonymous with weakness and he'd always been tough. Hadn't he come home from the dentist that time, after having all his teeth pulled out and eaten an apple? Well, that was his story and I wanted to believe it. But tough or not, the new regime didn't work and within the year he was back in Walton General. He was fond of Jo and I dreaded telling him about wanting to break off the engagement, especially when we visited him together on the ward and he seemed so dispirited, despite the news that he would be let out at the end of the week. At five o'clock in the morning two days later the phone in the hall rang. You know, don't you? The way the incessant ring grips you by the heart, stops you breathing. Brenda and I let Mum rush downstairs to answer it because we knew it was for her.

And then, there's Dad, laid out in a coffin in the parlour, and Grandma McGarry saying how peaceful he looked, almost smiling as if that's how he'd passed away. And us saying yes, and me thinking, no, Grandma, for I'd disposed of the pyjamas he'd been wearing and they were still wringing wet, and he'd died alone and in agony.

But thanks for the kind thought anyway.

Thirty-odd years later when I was fifty-three I realised just how young he had been. At the time it had seemed the age that most men died, unlike the women who appeared to go on and on. And here I was at the same age and how was I feeling? For someone who had decided pretty early on not to get married and settle down and have children for fear of disturbing the Muse, I was a complete failure. There had been two marriages and three sons, and now, at fifty-three, the age that my father died, Isabel was born. My father had died not only before knowing any of his grandchildren, but before reading a poem of mine or seeing me on telly. I was a son who'd gone away to university and never really come back.

And so, looking at Isabel I was beset with complex emotions. Would I live long enough to see her learn to walk? Hear her first words? Lend her money? Hilary's family are from Knaresborough and one Christmas we took Matthew and Isabel to Harrogate theatre to see the pantomime *Cinderella*. The next day, thinking of Prince Charmings and happy endings, of ashes and golden carriages turning into pumpkins, I sat down to write 'Cinders':

> *After the pantomime, carrying you back to the car*
> *On the coldest night of the year*
> *My coat, black leather, cracking in the wind.*
>
> *Through the darkness we are guided by a star*
> *It is the one the Good Fairy gave you*
> *You clutch it tightly, your magic wand.*
>
> *And I clutch you tightly for fear you blow away*
> *For fear you grow up too soon and – suddenly,*
> *I almost slip, so take it steady down the hill.*
>
> *Hunched against the wind and hobbling*
> *I could be mistaken for your grandfather*
> *And sensing this, I hold you tighter still.*
>
> *Knowing that I will never see you dressed for the Ball*
> *Be on hand to warn you against Prince Charmings*
> *And the happy ever afters of pantomime.*

I have this theory that all children are poets before they go to school, where they are taught how to see the world in a rational and adult way. Making links between seemingly unconnected objects, they can animate the inanimate with ease, but formal education very often succeeds at the expense of the imagination. I'm thinking of examples from my own kids: Finn on watching a lighted candle on the table, the wax melting and running down the side, 'Ah, the candle's crying.' Tom, looking up at the new moon, 'Look, a bit's fallen off the moon.' Matt in pain, charging into the house with a splinter in his finger, 'Daddy, daddy, the wood's bit me.' I wish Isabel had been the girl on the train at Didcot who had pointed at the huge cooling towers and cried, 'Ooh, look, a cloud factory.' Poetry everywhere, but inevitably the well-meaning parent or teacher will say, 'The candle isn't crying, silly, it's the energy caused by the agitation of the molecules resulting in the change from a solid to a liquid state.'

When education marches in with its book of rules, its right and wrong answers, all too often the poetry, that way of seeing the world and describing it in unusual ways, goes out of the classroom window. Poetry, music, art, drama, dance have been seen by successive governments as the icing on the curriculum cake, whereas if they were at the core, with the academic disciplines radiating from them, schools might well turn out more imaginative young adults, able to respond to the fast-changing world. Montessori and Steiner are not central defenders in Chelsea's midfield, but educationists whose visionary ideas could be incorporated into the state system.

And while I'm holding forth as the new Minister for Education, might I just add that every school will be garnished with playing fields and sports facilities to include tennis courts and swimming pools. Home Economics and Cookery for all, the handling of personal finances and relaxation techniques would be par for the coursework. And if you are worried about Physics or Geography, have a word with my secretary and we'll sort something out.

'The Way Things Are' is a poem that I very often read when I'm at one of those conferences for Headmasters and English specialists, because it encourages teachers to foster and maintain in their young charges a fresh, childlike view of the world, as if making sense of it for the first time, as well as warning them against the dangers that lurk in the darkness. It's a poem that I wouldn't have written had I not had children, so perhaps the Muse was less disturbed than I had imagined all those years ago.

No, the candle is not crying, it cannot feel pain.
Even telescopes, like the rest of us, grow bored.
Bubblegum will not make the hair soft and shiny.
The duller the imagination, the faster the car,
I am your father and this is the way things are.

No, old people do not walk slowly
because they have plenty of time.
Gardening books, when buried will not flower.
Though lightly worn, a crown may leave a scar,
I am your father and this is the way things are.

GOODBYE KEVIN, HELLO MABEL

At various times in my life, friends have tried to instil into me their passion for driving and all have failed. I actually held a provisional licence for a while, which was exciting, but that was as far as I got, because I just wasn't interested. Perhaps if I'd passed my test and bought a car I might have stayed longer than two years at St Kevin's, but because the bus journey was so long and tedious I decided to find a job nearer the centre of town. The one advertised in *The Times Educational Supplement* looked too good to be true: 'Assistant Lecturer in Catering French at the Mabel Fletcher Technical College, Liverpool'. Catering French? *Qu'est-ce que c'est que ça?*' I asked myself (in a Cork accent). The Principal, Miss Odell, took a shine to me at the interview even though I suspect I was the least qualified and experienced applicant, and to my surprise she offered me the post. And so goodbye Kevin, hello Mabel.

As teaching jobs go my new one was a cracker, and if Bella Fortuna hadn't eloped with me two years later, I'd happily have served my time there. The Mabel was a technical college with courses in millinery, nursery nursing, shop assisting and, of course, catering, and as you might have guessed, ninety per cent of the students were female and all over sixteen. As there were only two other men on the staff when I arrived, one of whom was gay the other badly crippled and nearing retirement, when it came to '*Hands up, girls, which male member of staff do we fancy?*' it was a one-horse race. Not that I took advantage of my position, by the way – I was a good Catholic boy, remember – but I did enjoy my mornings with cadet nurses on day release from Walton Hospital, some of whom were the same age as me, and I did thrill to Tania, a saucy sixteen-year-old milliner when she surprised me in the storeroom. (*The door clicks shut behind him, he turns: 'Tania, I really don't think . . .'*)

My main duties involved teaching menu French to would-be chefs, and although at the time I couldn't boil an *oeuf*, at least I could spell one and I soon became a fount of culinary knowledge that was useless except when faced with the menu in a fancy restaurant. Do you know what Potage Robespierre is? Beetroot soup, actually, and although the students could make it, they didn't know about the bloodthirsty Robespierre who inspired it. Do you know why a *chinois*, used in the kitchen for sifting, is so called? Because it is shaped like a Chinese conical hat. Do you know where Crème Brûlée gets its name from? A famous chef created the dish for Napoleon to celebrate his defeat of the Austrian Army at Brûlée in 1803. I could go on for hours.

One of the perks of my new job was that I didn't have to bring cheese sandwiches and an apple to work every day, but instead could saunter along to the Staff Restaurant and tuck into the five-course gourmet lunches cooked and served, free of charge, by the catering students. And there was another perk. As well as teaching English to the nurses and to those on the salesmanship course, and because I was the only male member of staff who could run in a straight line, I was put in charge of the PE department. This involved playing footy with the lads and a spot of netball with the girls, as well as providing me with my own changing room in the PE block where I could lie down after one of those hefty lunches. (*The door clicks shut behind him, he turns*: 'Tania, I really don't think . . .')

The actual college itself wasn't built when I was appointed and for the first eighteen months I was peripatetic, visiting the various sites all over the city. My brown canvas bag came into its own now as I would stay in town after college, and meet up with friends in the pubs and clubs of Liverpool 8.

The El Cabala, a glass-fronted, airy café on Bold Street, was where I sipped my first cappuccino from a see-through Perspex cup and saucer, and learned from the menu about the coffee-coloured habits of the Capuchin monks. Although it failed to mention the short black habits of the Espress monks. The most exciting coffee bars, though, were the ones that stayed open late and catered for students, artists and the beatniks who were appearing on the scene, the Masque, the Picasso, the Basement, run by a local painter, Yenkel Feather, and best of all, Streates. This was the time, of course, when pubs closed at ten o'clock and even though there were shebeens and after-hours drinking clubs, most young people were content to sit around late into the night nursing coffee-flavoured drinks and listening to jazz. Here was an audience waiting to be entertained.

Listening to that Dylan Thomas record at university had been an ear opener for me, as had the visit by the poet Vernon Watkins, to read and talk about his friend Thomas, but it was a reading given by Christopher Logue that really fired me up. Looking like he'd come straight from Montmartre, dressed all in black and sinister, he read his political and hard-hitting poems in that crackling theatrical voice of his. Though a little shocked, I was hooked. An EP record called *Redbird*, Logue reading the poems of Pablo Neruda to the jazz accompaniment of the Tony Kinsey Quintet, would be passed around and wowed over by the young Beats in the city's coffee bars. As was Allen Ginsberg's rendition of 'Howl'.

If you couldn't be in San Francisco with Ferlinghetti, or in New York with Ginsberg, or on the road with Kerouac, then London was where it all seemed to be happening with the poetry and jazz concerts organised by Jeremy Robson, and featuring Logue and Adrian Mitchell, as well as Laurie Lee and Dannie Abse. Michael Horovitz and Pete Brown were travelling up and down the country with their free-form poetry and jazz collaboration *Blues for the Hitch-hiking Dead*, and I was stuck in Liverpool where nothing was happening.

At the time I used to envy those writers who lived in such exotic places where the very pavements must have emitted psychic poetic energy. What lyrics I would write if I lived on the Lower East Side. (As a matter of fact, it was quite common for some of our local Beat poets to write about yellow cabs, and walking along 52nd Street, because this was the hip furniture you could bring into your verses to appear cool. A year or two later when I began to set poems in a Liverpool landscape, as did Adrian and to a lesser extent Brian, they seemed unnervingly surreal and non-poetical.) Since those days, of course, young poets have whined to me,

'Oh, it must have been easy for you to write poetry, living in Liverpool at such an exciting time.' But a writer struggles to dignify his particular time and place, 'No easier, mate, than it is for you right now, right here.'

I was still living at home and envying those free spirits around me with flats in town, so when Jane Cook, a lecturer in the art department at college, offered me the use of a room above the garage at the back of her house in Sefton Park I was over the moon . . . I mean garage. There were wooden stairs on the outside of the building leading up to a space that was dark and unheated, but it was dry and it was mine, and I pretended that it would become a second home. It never did, of course, because one mattress on the floor does not a fully furnished bijou apartment make, but I fondly remember that Siberian winter, like the time I offered Pete Brown a bed for the night. He and Mike Horovitz had been reading in town, after which we'd all got roaring drunk, ending up with Pete, hairy-black and bearlike in his tartan lumberjacket, looking every inch the 'Back Cricklewoodsman', skating on the icy pavements and sliding down the wooden stairs as I tried to get him into the room. Luckily we were too drunk to die of hypothermia, and I like to think that he drew heavily from the experience when writing lyrics for Cream in the years that followed.

The point of the bolthole, though, as you may have guessed, was not to offer shelter to itinerant drunken poets, but a place to which I could lure suspecting females. To be painfully honest, I had more success providing for passed-out poets than I did with the females, although I did notch up one notable victory. I refer to 'Comeclose and Sleepnow', a poem whose style echoes Wilfred Owen and e e cummings. The true inspiration, of course, was the girl, but I can't recall her name. One of the lines, 'Shoes with broken high ideals', is a clumsy play on words, but I was so thrilled with it at the time that I never had the heart to change it. Brian Patten published the poem in *Underdog*, his little magazine, and it would appear at the beginning of my section in *The Mersey Sound*. So, as Lennon and McCartney would have it, 'Thank you, girl.'

I heard my first Beatles record while walking down the corridor at the Mabel, when it was being played on a gramophone in the Student Common Room. Later in the week, when I heard 'Love Me Do' being played on the wireless, it was exciting in a way that few people would understand today. Pop songs were American (yes, I know we had Dickie Valentine, Dennis Lotus and Tommy Steele, but really?) and here was a record by four lads from the town where I lived. What was going on?

The Philharmonic Hotel, lying midway between the two cathedrals on Hope Street, became my favourite pub once I had gravitated towards the centre of town. With its crystal chandeliers, copper panels and ornate wooden mahogany friezes carved by craftsmen who had worked on the Cunard liners, it remains a magnificent example of Edwardian flamboyance. Most evenings, after a pleasant day with the nurses and would-be chefs at college, I would meet up there with a group of teachers and artists, plumbers and sparks including my new pal John Gorman, and John Hewson, known as 'Hewo', the pub jester, who was to become the Scaffold's stage and road manager. And it was at the Kardomah Café in Clayton Street where we used to gather on Saturday afternoons to chat up the girls and plan our big night out. The reason most of the girls were there was not to be chatted up by the likes of us, but by the likes of Faron and the Flamingos, Rory Storm and the Hurricanes, the Undertakers, the Whatevers. Ringo was a regular and even before leaving Rory to join that other group, he looked a million dollars in his suede overcoat and leather jacket. Yes, you could say we were jealous, just a teeny bit.

It was in the Kardomah one Saturday afternoon in 1963 that we heard about rehearsals that were about to start at the Playhouse Theatre for John Osborne's new play *Luther*, and there were job opportunities for young men who could sing Gregorian chant. So Gorman and Hewo, myself and another teacher, Mike Collins, who, having been educated by the Christian Brothers, had the Latin and were afraid of nothing, downed our coffee and nipped round the corner to offer our professional services. I think the director, Bernard Hepton, would have been well within his rights to have opted to hear a few bars of Gregorian chant before taking us on, but he didn't, and perhaps was to regret it in the weeks that followed.

Our main task during the performance was to slip on stage during the blackout between scenes and move furniture around. Dressed as monks, we would carry on a heavy refectory table and a couple of benches while singing 'Veni Creator Spiritus' in County Cork accents, and when the lights came up be sitting silently at table pretending to eat polystyrene bread while proper actors acted. Luther was played by a young actor with dark, brooding good looks called Inigo Jackson, and other cast members included Barry Jackson, Noel Davis and a comely but snooty young actress who kept a pet hamster in her dressing room. The Assistant Stage Manager, who had the unenviable task of trying to keep us in order backstage, was Jean Boht, who went on to fame as a television actress and more besides. I enjoyed the whole experience, which was a universe away from my day job at the Mabel Fletcher, but sadly, darling, as a group we could perhaps be accused, darling, of not taking the whole theatre thing seriously enough, darling. And we got into big trouble because of it.

I am not referring to the occasion when John whispered into the ear of the snooty young actress as she was about to go on stage, 'Your hamster's just died.' But to the strange business of the fan letters. After a successful opening night and once the show was up and running, letters would arrive at the theatre from fans in the audience, which would be posted on a noticeboard outside the Green Room.

'What a stunning production . . . Bernard Hepton fully deserves . . .'
'Inigo Jackson is star quality . . .'
'Noel Davis again thrilled us with . . .'

One afternoon before the Saturday matinée Gorman brought along sheets of headed notepaper purloined from various furniture removal firms, and the four of us composed paeans of praise to ourselves, signed them as if by the owner of the firm and pinned them to the noticeboard.

'The acting was very good and so was the direction, but for me the play really came to life during the blackouts . . .'
'. . . the table humping was pure poetry . . .'

'Forget Inigo Jackson, for me the star was the monk who carried off one of the benches single-handedly . . . etc.

On the Monday evening we were told to report to the Theatre Manager, Mr Willard Stoker, on the third floor who, having reminded us that the Playhouse, founded in 1866, was the oldest repertory theatre in the country, tore into us for our lack of respect and our philistine attitude to long-established theatrical traditions, and if it weren't for the fact that Gregorian chanters were hard to come by, we'd be out on our ears. Good-day, darlings.

BEATNIK HORROR!

Streates Coffee Bar on Mount Pleasant, a candlelit, white-washed basement that wore a duffel coat and echoed to the sounds of modern jazz, was to poetry what the Cavern was to rock'n'roll. Johnny Byrne, novelist and screenwriter, was then a mischievous young Dubliner with an encyclopaedic knowledge of the American Beats who took up semi-residence there and began to organise regular poetry readings featuring Pete Brown and Spike Hawkins, a wild, charismatic southerner with an ambition to be an eccentric genius. Local poets then started to perform: Phil Tasker, who battled against his inner demons using the audience as a punchbag; and 'Tonk', faux anarchist whose Beat rantings seemed to have come straight out of Greenwich Village.

Thom Keyes was a public schoolboy pretending to be a cool, hip poet before going up to Oxford, where he wrote a novel called *All Night Stand* imaginatively based on the antics of a Liverpool rock band, which brought him a lot of attention and a huge advance for a follow-up. Although Thom enjoyed the idea of being a writer, he found the writing part interfered with his life as a literary figure, so he approached me one night at the Round House in Chalk Farm, quite pissed, and asked if I'd write the first chapter of his next novel for fifty quid. 'What's it about?'

I asked. He shrugged, 'I don't know, you're the fucking writer.'

Thom eventually spent his time between Bolivia and Hollywood, where he lived exceedingly well off the advances for a screenplay he'd written about airships, selling and reselling the film rights. He must have been in his fifties when I saw him hunched over the bar at the Chelsea Arts Club, looking miserable and nursing a large brandy.

'What's the matter, Thom?' I asked.

'My goose is cooked, Roge,' he said, 'no more golden eggs. Someone's making the fucking film.' Sadly, he was right and the film released the following year proved to be not so much an airship as a lead balloon.

Halfway through a reading one night in November 1961 Pete Brown told me there was a journalist there I should meet, a guy from the *Bootle Times*, so I went upstairs expecting a hard-bitten forty-year-old who'd come along to write the usual 'Beatnik Horror!' piece, and instead met this hard-bitten fifteen-year-old who'd come along to read his poems. Brian Patten was soon to acquire a reputation as a wunderkind, as much for the passion and intensity of his calling as for the poems themselves. Whereas I seemed to have stumbled upon poetry in my late teens and was still weaving it into my life, poetry appeared to have taken hold of Brian as a boy and it was already his whole life. It was this purity of vision, the sense of his own talent that drew me to him. Not that we became mates, for the age difference meant that we moved in different circles.

I still have a yellowing copy of the *Bootle Times*, price threepence, dated 10 January 1962, in which Brian plays devil's advocate in an article which begins:

When poetry was first recited to jazz in the cellars and coffee clubs of 'beat land', many people thought that it had reached its nerve-racking climax. But now it's been taken one step further, and as Shakespeare is turning over in his grave, the modern poets are reciting poetry to PAINTING. And it's being taken seriously!

'And why shouldn't it be taken seriously?' asks bearded Roger McGough, a Litherland poet [Brian unwittingly pigeon-holing me and pre-empting all the other tags, Pop, Beat, Liverpool, Performance, Children's etc.].

Speaking to Roger, an assistant lecturer at the Mabel Fletcher Tech. College in Wavertree, at a recent poetry recital in a Liverpool 'Cellar' club, I asked him: 'As a published poet, what is your answer to those who scoff at modern poetry?'

'People', he said, 'object to "modern" poetry on the grounds that it is not beautiful in the "nice flowers and pink clouds" kind of way.' Looking across to one of the weird paintings on the cellar wall, he added: 'Today poets are more concerned with the sadness of life and convey it in terms of the social settings that we live in.'

Brian then goes on to tell the reader that Adrian Henri will be '"Translating" the poetry to canvas', and that we will be joined on stage by 'Pete Brown who is the foremost "beat" poet in England, and Adrian Mitchell (well-known at many London recitals)'. And casting aside his devil's advocate guise, he lists the necessary information regarding the gig at the Crane Theatre, exhorting his readers to get along there.

Being at the Mabel allowed me far greater freedom and mobility, and because of my father's death, or despite it, I felt the need to move away from home and became increasingly drawn to Liverpool 8, an area of faded grandeur inhabited by artists, students, college lecturers and prostitutes. The flat at 64 Canning Street that Adrian shared with his wife Joyce was a cultural revelation with its polished bare floorboards and white walls covered with his paintings. No instant coffee in the Henri household, but coffee beans that Adrian would polish and then grind ceremoniously, singing along to Cannonball Adderley, and the first time I ate wholemeal, pebble-dashed bread was in his kitchen served up with salami, haloumi and houmous, foods that just weren't on the menu at the Mabel Fletcher College.

The first Merseyside Arts Festival took place in August 1962 and its prime mover was John Gorman. I had seen John around town, you couldn't really miss him, in a dog-tooth check suit, occasional bowler hat and, more often than not, odd socks. A prankster, a performance artist ahead of his time, he was also a visionary wheeler-dealer whose enthusiasm for poetry and the arts was totally infectious, and he put together a band of helpers to organise the events, including the sculptor Arthur Dooley, a photographer, a couple of painters, a poet (and assistant lecturer), an artist's model and two ladies' hairstylists, one of whom was tall, skinny and good-looking and wore tall, skinny, good-looking clothes. His name was Michael McCartney and rumour had it that his brother was in a group called the Beatles who were bound to be famous one day. To keep the idea of an arts festival in the public conscience, John and I organised weekly events at the Hope Hall, a club beneath the Everyman Cinema and Theatre, soon to be joined by Adrian Henri and occasionally by Brian, although he was kept busy running his own poetry nights at the Green Moose.

The evenings consisted of satirical sketches and surreal dialogues, interspersed with a poet and perhaps a folksinger or guitarist. At first John would read his own poems and together we did most of the scriptwriting, but it soon became obvious that his talent was as a comic performer. With an expressive face and a body seemingly made of rubber, he was both mime artist and clown. He had a range of funny voices, perfect timing and an addiction to improvising that could be either exhilarating or terrifying for his fellow performers. But what made him unique was the strange mix of the cuddly and the threatening that at times had the audience in two minds as to whether to stay and laugh or run for cover. Imagine Tommy Cooper coming at you with a chainsaw. We were soon drawing large crowds and, this being Liverpool, half the audience wanted to be up on stage and involved in the action, so the sketches were expanded to include more performers. But for the Scaffold, Michael McCartney might well have had a successful career as a graphic artist or as a photographer, and his initial involvement with the group was at the blunt end of a camera, but he couldn't resist the siren call of maidenly applause and was soon up on stage, script in hand.

The good thing about not having to learn lines and rehearse was that I could just turn up on the evening with the new scripts, hand them out to whoever fancied taking part, we would read them through over a pint in the corner, then get up on stage and perform. We liked to pretend that there was something more immediate and pure about reading from a script, and we were not to be confused with *actors*, darling, like the ones down the road at the Playhouse.

I never kept any sort of diary until 1967, when there were so many things going on that I bought an appointments diary to get myself organised, but sifting through newspaper cuttings, theatre programmes and advertising flyers of the year before that *annus mirabilis*, I wonder how I managed to hold down a teaching post as well as performing nightly at various clubs around the town. For success at Hope Hall had led to Monday poetry nights with Brian and Adrian in the basement of a restaurant on the London Road called Sampson & Barlow's, and late-night comedy sketch shows at the Blue Angel Club on the Friday. I was still living with my mother in Litherland, and feeling guilty about spending so much time away – and feeling guilty, too, about breaking off my engagement to Jo.

The frenetic writing became a way of keeping the demons at bay, and after a day's teaching I would head into town and spend a couple of hours at the Picton Central Library before meeting up with John or Adrian. Most of the sketches and poems were written in exercise books nicked from the college storeroom (*The door clicks shut behind him, he turns: 'Tania, I really don't think . . .'*) and contain lots of half-formed lyrics with crossings-out and rewrites scribbled alongside. One poem, however, appears to have been composed in one sitting with hardly any revisions. 'Live fast, die young' was my motto, and although I failed to live up to it on both counts, I remember writing 'Let me die a young-man's death' at a table within the vast, ornate Victorian bell jar, and thinking about the front room of my grandmother's house in Seaforth when I looked upon the face of death for the first time.

> *Let me die a youngman's death*
> *not a free from sin, tiptoe in*
> *candle wax and waning death*
> *not a curtains drawn, by angels borne.*
> *'What a nice way to go' death.*

I am in the parlour and so small that I have to stand on tiptoe to peer into my grandfather's coffin. I don't know what time of day or night it is because the heavy curtains are closed and the only light is from the flickering candles, which reflect on the coffin's white satin interior and cast shadows that move across his face like black fingers. Everything is made of wax, the lilies, the candles, the body, the mourners silently filling the room. Everything is melting into everything else as the smell overpowers me. *Requiescat in pace.* 'What a nice way to go.'

US AND THEM

Whereas the shows at Hope Hall tended to be just that, 'Shows', with music and comedy as well as poetry, the readings in Sampson & Barlow's tended to be more experimentally poetic, where Adrian in particular would involve the audience in Dadaesque word games like Exquisite Corpses, or simply get everybody to write down a word or a sentence, to be collected during the interval and read out at the end. His series of 'Silent Poems' consisted of him holding up to the crowd a number of empty picture frames for them to gape at in awe and wonder (or, chuckle, as they usually did). To a first-time visitor, some of these ideas may have seemed arty-farty, but humour and self-mockery were very much part of it. Audience involvement was an essential element of what we were all trying to do at the time, to break down the barrier between them and us.

These early experiments led Adrian to be the prime mover in organising a series of 'Events' or 'Happenings' using mime, dance, poetry, painting and music, inspired by similar events taking place in small art galleries in New York, where artists such as Jim Dine and Robert Rauschenberg assembled intrinsically worthless junk as material for painting and sculpture. In 1962, when Adrian was a tutor at the Manchester College of Art, he set up an

'Event' at the Whitworth Institute in Openshaw, where a critic (art? drama? football?) dropped by and, puzzled by the whole affair, wrote a two-column review for the *Guardian* dated 12 December:

> In a room hung with advertising posters, among the bus tickets, the mangled prams and step ladders there was poetry, spoken by Mr McGough, a Liverpool teacher in corduroy jacket and jeans, the first five minutes of which were intentionally inaudible beneath the tape-recorded jazz. The spotlight fixed on a girl in a black sweat-suit, immobile beneath the step ladder. 'Manchester,' read Mr McGough, 'the city with the soft centre.' The girl got up and did a snaky dance.

As a result of this rave review we were invited into BBC TV studios in Manchester the next day to film a three-minute excerpt that Cliff Michelmore introduced from the London studio during the six o'clock news the same evening. 'Look what the bearded weirdos are up to now . . .' sort of thing. Our filmed insert consisted of me perched on top of a stepladder reading inaudibly, while Carole Mason writhed and snaked beneath, Mike Evans played a saxophone and Adrian threw paint all over us. It was truly ground-breaking.

John Willett, the biographer of Bertolt Brecht and a distinguished art historian, however, was more impressed by our forays into the theatre of the absurd. He was working in Liverpool at the time, researching his subsequent book *Art in the City* and during a visit to the upstairs theatre in the Hope Hall in 1963 he witnessed *Nightblues*: 'It was spontaneous, unpretentious, I thought, and above all, indigenous. It seemed to meet the demands of a young and attractive audience, who later packed out the club downstairs.'

As John Willett observed, our audiences, comprised mainly of sixth-form schoolgirls and art students, was indeed a young and attractive one, which, in retrospect, may go some way towards explaining our mission to break down the barriers between 'them' and 'us'. 'Us' being very keen to get in there among 'them'.

He also observed that McG, now beardless and devoid of corduroy, might have a career outside the classroom and very kindly recommended me to his own literary agent, Hope Leresche. Three weeks later I was having lunch at Choy's restaurant on the King's Road in Chelsea with my new agent, and if the moon is one of those round paper Chinese lampshades, I was over it.

BEAT INTERNATIONALE

With the growing success of the readings in the Everyman Theatre basement, with audiences pretty well guaranteed, the British Council and other arts organisations began to use it as a venue for poets visiting from overseas. An evening of Canadian poetry went down particularly well, featuring the then granddaddy of them all, Earle Birney, and a young, good-looking man called Michael Ondaatje with whom I swapped my latest book for his. I still have my signed copy of *Rat Jelly* and wonder if he still has my *Summer with Monika*. Or did he do what I used to do (shame on me) when travelling across Australia where every other person I met seemed to have published a small book of poems? Leave *Gleanings from Life's Highway* and *The Silence of Stones* on the bedside table for the housemaid in lieu of a tip.

One of the greatest international names we had, and the one that was the most difficult to spell, was Yevgeny Alexandrovich Yevtushenko. Unfortunately I was out of town and missed his reading, which was so popular that it was held upstairs in the main theatre and sold out. A friend of mine, Clare Manifold, was studying Literature at the university and Yevtushenko was her hero, and because no books of his were on sale after the reading, she was first in the queue next morning when the bookshop on Hardman

Street opened its doors at 9.30 for a book signing. When her hero arrived she was wide-eyed, ready and waiting.

'What is your name?' he asked, pen poised magnificently.

'Clare.'

The poet fixed those steel-blue eyes directly into hers. 'Clare.' He savoured the chime of it. 'Clare, my last day in England, and I meet the most beautiful girl in the world!' He signed with a flourish, handed her the book and turned his attention to whoever was next in line.

Clare, weak at the knees, made her way past the waiting fans and hurried up the hill to attend her first lecture. Halfway there she changed her mind, the lecture was not important and she was in too much of a tizzy to concentrate, and besides, why hadn't she bought a copy of *Bratsk Station* for Valerie whose birthday was coming up? So Clare hurried back down the hill and joined the tail end of the queue still snaking down Hardman Street. Half an hour later and now last in line she came face to face with her hero once more. 'What is your name?' he asked, pen poised magnificently.

'It's for Valerie.'

The poet fixed those steel-blue eyes directly into hers. 'Valerie.' He savoured the chime of it. 'Valerie, my last day in England, and I meet the most beautiful girl in the world!'

I opted not to tell Yevtushenko that story when my wife and I were having supper with him in a little town outside Venice in 1996. Some months previously I had received a fax from Georgio and Marcellino inviting me to participate in the 'Beat Internationale' to be held in their home town of Conegliano in honour of Allen Ginsberg. Not only was Ginsberg reading but he would be joined by Gregory Corso and Lawrence Ferlinghetti, who would be coming over from the States, as well as a host of leading European poets including Enzensberger, Yves Bonnefoy, Yevtushenko, Voznesensky, myself and numerous Italian poets. When I talked to Georgio on the phone he confided that not only would Leonard Cohen be there but that Lou Reed and Bob Dylan, who were touring Italy, had also promised to perform. There would be no fee, unfortunately, explained Georgio, but I would be welcome to bring my wife, and all costs would be covered.

He was there to welcome Hilary and me at the Marco Polo *aeroporto* and on the drive to our hotel explained that sadly, it looked as if Bob Dylan wouldn't be able to make it after all.

'But Leonard Cohen and Lou Reed will be there then?' I asked.

He shook his head. 'Sadly, no.' The nearer we got to the Canon d'Oro Hotel, the more sadly Georgio became.

'Enzensberger?'

'Sadly, no.'

'Bonnefoy?

'Sadly no.'

'At least it will be great having Ginsberg on stage with Corso and Ferlinghetti,' I ventured, fingers crossed. 'Or is it . . . sadly?'

'*Si*' said Georgio. 'Sadly, Corso could not get a visa and Ferlinghetti, his heart is not strong at this moment.'

Worse was to come. It had become painfully obvious that only Brits and Russians will go anywhere for a freebie, and, although Voznesensky had arrived, he was staying, for reasons unknown, in a different hotel. During supper, when

Hilary and I were sitting with Yevtushenko and Marsha, his new young wife, Georgio and Marcellino, each with a mobile phone, were pacing up and down the restaurant in heated conversation. Why phone each other, I thought, when they're in the same room?

Eventually Georgio came over. 'Roger, you are a friend of Allen, *si*?'

'Well, not a friend, exactly, I've met him once or twice . . .'

He held out his mobile. 'Please talk to him, he is staying in Milan and refusing to come for the performances in his honour.'

I took the phone. 'Hello, Allen, Roger McGough here, I don't know if you remember . . .'

Ginsberg cut through, 'Listen, my publishers have fixed up some readings in Milan. I told those guys three fu★king months ago.'

'But Allen, they've gone to a lot of trouble . . .'

'*Ciao* Roger.'

I handed the phone back to Georgio. 'Sadly, Ginsberg can't make it either.'

Despite this little setback, the 'Beat Internationale' went ahead in a 700-seater auditorium packed to the gunwales with respectable middle-class Italians. Disconcertingly, it didn't start until almost past my bedtime, and the show opened with a homage to William Burroughs featuring a harpist and a belly dancer, and included a reading by someone who had worked in City Lights Bookshop in the sixties, as well as a 'Famous American singer-songwriter' whom nobody had ever heard of, and after the first two songs we all knew why.

Actually, it is often a feature of reading in a country where English is not the spoken language that sharing the platform will be a 'popular and distinguished British poet' of whom I've never heard. And the more far flung the country, the more popular and distinguished the poet will be. Years ago there was a poet called Brian Thomas who lived outside Birmingham and billed himself as 'the well-known Black Country poet'. A few years later, after moving to Wales, he became Bryn Thomas 'the well-known Welsh poet'. Driven out of Wales by arts centre audiences, he emigrated to Australia and I met him in Melbourne where he had become B. S. Thomas 'the well-known British poet'. Any day now I expect to come across him at a festival in Edinburgh or Cheltenham and be introduced to Bazzer Thomas the 'well-known outback poet'.

On stage now is Voznesensky wearing a white tuxedo and looking like a Russian Bob Hope. His reading is accompanied by slides and his voice, both powerful and tremulous, speaks of loss and sadness. Yevtushenko tonight is sporting his pearly king outfit. The Russian poets grow into the size of the room, forty people in a bookshop or 2,000 in a football stadium, Russian poets seem to adjust perfectly to the cubic dimension.

Allen Ginsberg, too, had this shape-changing ability, although having witnessed in 1965 his serene, intimate reading at a small bookshop in Hardman Street, Liverpool, followed some months later by a rant in front of 7,000 at the Albert Hall, I decided his trick was not to grow into the size of the venue, but to reduce the capacity of the hall to suit him.

Ginsberg spent some time in Merseyside in search of the

Beatles' aura and got on famously with Adrian Henri, his scouse doppelganger, who put him up in his flat, and was delighted to come across his hero at the kitchen sink one morning washing the dishes and singing a Buddhist chant. Exhilarated by his visit, Ginsberg proclaimed, 'Liverpool is at the present moment the centre of the consciousness of the human universe,' which, depending on who you talked to in the pubs and clubs around town, was either quoting the bleeding obvious or going just a teeny-weeny bit over the top.

THE LIVERPOOL ONE FAT LADY
ALL-ELECTRIC SHOW

Although students from the art college formed a high percentage of our audiences at the Hope Hall, there was a small clique of painters who regarded poetry and performance as poncy-woncy, and one evening they turned up trying to look like hard cases in their paint-spattered denims to interrupt a reading. Unfortunately for them, the poet they chose to heckle not only had a psychopathic hatred of Jackson Pollock, but worked nights as a club bouncer and, although manuscripts and beer were sent flying, the scuffle was short-lived.

At the time, although the Beatles were the most popular group on Merseyside, they hadn't yet achieved stratospheric superstardom and could walk the streets unmolested, and so Paul McCartney would occasionally turn up with George Harrison, smile, applaud, give his younger brother the thumbs-up and leave before the end. Lennon, however, never showed, which at the time surprised us. But it shouldn't have done for had John still been at college he would have been one of the paint-spattered Liverpool School of Hard Cases, for whom it wasn't art if it didn't make you sweat. Paul told me much later that, although as a schoolboy he would hang around Phillip, Son &

Nephews, the bookshop on Renshaw Street, surreptitiously reading the poems of Auden and Louis MacNeice, he and Lennon agreed that it was all very well being artistic, but poetry was going just that bit too far.

In fact, it was all fairly straightforward, the art forms that were acceptable to working-class youth at the time. Hollywood films, New York painting and sculpture, popular music (as on disc, Radio Luxembourg and American Forces Network): OK. Poetry, opera, ballet, foreign films, classical music and theatre: sorry, not for us. It was partly a class thing, of course, but also 'sensitivity' was construed as weakness and intelligence as attention-seeking. It was an attitude that we three poets felt as well and had to deal with in our differing ways. Adrian would turn up to read his poems wearing paint-stained denims, thus straddling both worlds, whereas for Brian it was sensitivity writ hard. The reason so many of my early poems began seriously and ended with the rug being pulled from underneath the reader stems from that insecurity. It is the poet saying, 'Don't worry, I'm not trying to be clever, I'm really just one of the lads.'

Thelma Monaghan was one of the lads too, in a paint-stained jeans and leather-jacket, womanly sort of way. We met at a dance at the art college where she was in her final year painting large geometric Op Art canvases, and I persuaded her to give the Hope Hall a try. She'd been with John Lennon at the Art High School, as well as going through college with him, and initially shared some of his prejudices about poetry, but needless to say, a couple of unarmed stanzas from me and she was a changed woman. Divorced, she lived in a small flat on Princes Avenue in the

My mother aged 16

My father in Sweden aged 17

Flaunting the silverware with
Mother and Grandma McGough

Brenda and I; and (*below*) at
New Brighton Pool

...post *Lily the Pink*

heart of Toxteth, with her son Nathan, a bright, attractive three-year-old, unaware that one day he would manage the Happy Mondays. John would pop in occasionally for some art college gossip with Thelma, as did Paul, who had been out with her a couple of times, but I have to confess that, being somewhat jealous of these handsome guys wearing expensive clobber they'd bought in Hamburg, I didn't make them welcome, and besides, Posterity was parked in the street outside, the engine running. One night I stayed over. The following week I stayed over and over, and within a couple of months I had moved in.

Prior to this I was still living at home in Litherland and commuting daily to the Mabel, although spending more and more time on the mattress above the garage and on sofas in hidey-holes all over Liverpool 8, and so the move was both exciting and liberating. It was also cheap, because as I didn't own any furniture there was no removal firm involved, just a suitcase, a brown canvas bag and the number 28 bus. But there was something else that I moved into the ground floor flat of number 26 Princes Avenue, which we could never get rid of, and that was guilt. As the family saw it, I had broken off an engagement to a lovely Catholic girl to go and live in some crummy flat in a downtrodden area of Liverpool with a woman who was not only divorced, but had a child. I had brought shame on us all. This was unfair on Thelma, whose flat was studiedly bohemian and, except for spots of oil paint everywhere, spotless. One of three children brought up by a single mother, she had not had an easy life, and although street-wise and tough, she was insecure and in need of constant reassurance. Above all, she was an artist and something of a rebel, which appealed to me no end, and her belief in me as a poet fuelled my fantasies of the misunderstood outsider. Although in a relationship that was doomed to fail, I felt a huge release that enabled me to concentrate on being a writer, not a teacher who wrote in his spare time.

Liverpool has always been a city that needed to be loved, that need, perhaps, forged out of a sense of shame for having grown wealthy on the back of the slave trade. Not that we had seen the wealth, of course, except in the once-gracious houses now turned into flats, and when I reached my teens and the docks were closing down and the river had become a ghost highway, it seemed suddenly old, shabby and unlovable.

> *A city with bags under its eyes*
> *Its river a wiped grin*
>
> *The only liners now it sees*
> *Are bin.*

The city had always been proud of its comedians, Robb Wilton, Ted Ray, Arthur Askey, Ken Dodd, as well as its boxers and soccer players, but away from the music hall and the sports arena who could we look up to? We would claim as heroes anybody, even slightly famous, who had links with the city.

'*That John Gregson was born here.*'

'*So was Rex Harrison.*'

'*Rex Harrison? Are you sure? He doesn't sound like a Scouser.*'

'*Yes, he was born in Huyton, and Frankie Vaughan definitely is, and Michael Holliday.*'

If success was achieved by those born within the sound of

waves lapping the cast-iron shore, they didn't exactly boast about it and we'd all be miffed when non-Liverpudlians were cast as Scousers in films and on telly.

'*Billie Whitelaw was great in* No Trams to Lime Street, *but you can tell she's not from round here, can't you?*'

'Z Cars, *with Stratford Johns and Frank Windsor, they're just cockneys pretending.*'

And then along came the Beatles. Suddenly, from having no media attention at all, the city was saturated with it. Television crews would be filmed filming television crews filming television reporters reporting on the next big thing to come out of Merseyside. Who would be the next Beatles? they wanted to know, as if the Fab Four were the tip of the iceberg rather than the iceberg itself, drifting south and slowly starting to melt. In 1963 ABC television were planning a series of late-night chat shows with music and comedy, to be recorded live in their Manchester studios. The producers came to see one of our performances at Hope Hall, the enticingly entitled *The Liverpool One Fat Lady All-Electric Show* and invited five of the gang to audition. Adrian Henri and Jennifer Beattie, our leading lady, failed to cut the mustard on the casting couch and so the producers went for the writer, the comic and the Beatle brother. Michael McCartney handed in his notice at André Bernard's hairdressing salon, I packed in teaching and John Gorman packed in being unemployed.

A SHORT CUT TO PARADISE

Although television programmes like the *Johnny Carson Show* were popular in the States, the chat show format was relatively new in this country when James Lloyd was signed up by ABC to host a live Saturday night show called *Gazette*. Among the day's celebrities who talked and walked were *The Avengers'* Patrick Macnee, Barry Humphries looking like a young Charles Baudelaire, Spike Milligan and Jonathan Miller, and there was a music spot featuring one of the up-and-coming bands of the day: 'Them', fronted by a baby-faced Van Morrison, Lulu and the Lovers, the Kinks, Spencer Davis and Manfred Mann, many of whom were making their first appearance on television.

As were the Scaffold, of course. We had decided on the name at a time when we considered ourselves mainly satirists, with the idea of heads rolling and reputations left hanging. We dressed all in black, with cotton gloves, so that we wouldn't be mistaken for guitarists. One of my favourite quotations, which I failed to work into our publicity material, was from the Victorian murderer Charlie Peace, whose last words with the rope round his neck were: 'What is the scaffold but a short cut to paradise?' As the act evolved we dropped the sinister gallows element to embrace the word's more common usage, as in building construction, which gave rise to a glut of photographs of us draped around rusty pipes making jokes about scaffold erections.

Which segues neatly but coarsely into Sheila Fearn, a young actress in the Barbara Windsor mould whom the company brought in to add glamour, and some professionalism, to the resident 'trio of lively wacker wits'. We were also assigned a director, Clive Goodwin, to work with us during the week, helping choose and rehearse material for the show. Clive was a left-wing, right-on Londoner, cultured, suave and handsome, obviously someone we just had to take the piss out of. He was wary of us, of course, as well as being outnumbered, and saddled initially with prejudices about life oop north, although after a few nights clubbing around Liverpool's hotspots we unsaddled him and a strong friendship was forged on the anvil of improvisation.

'Improv', as it was to become known, arrived at ABC's Didsbury studios via Chicago, where a group known as Second City performed improvised comedy on television. Obviously, charades and similar parlour games that involve people taking it in turns, most of them reluctantly, to make fools of themselves, were invented by show-offs, so I've never been a fan of actors or comics competing with each other on stage to grab the punchline, for not only does it encourage limelight theft, but it puts the writer out of a job. However, as the first comedy group in this country to improvise weekly on live television were the Scaffold, I may have to take some of the blame for its popularity twenty-odd years later.

What happened was this: on taking their seats in the studio, the audience would be given a selection of the week's newspapers and asked to choose the headlines that caught their eye. Before the commercial break, James Lloyd would read out half a dozen of the most popular and say that we'd be back after the adverts to perform some improvised sketches based on those headlines. So while the nation was being sold the virtues of 'Strand' cigarettes or 'Murraymints, Murraymints, the too good to hurry mints', Clive would be sifting through the headlines in the hope of finding ones that we'd picked out during the week and rehearsed. Just as we did, the audience would pass over headlines such as HAROLD WILSON TO MEET BREZHNEV IN MOSCOW and HOTEL BURNED DOWN IN MANILA, MANY LIVES LOST in favour of LARGE DANES TOLD TO HAVE COATS TRIMMED and US FLIES IN HAMBURGERS, which we would improvise in the relative safety of ABC's rehearsal rooms in Teddington, and perform live to camera on Saturday, punchlines guaranteed. With a couple of sure-fire sketches under our belt, we could then improvise around the unseen headlines until time ran out. (And it's no use all you purists out there muttering, 'Hey, that's cheating.' Because it wasn't. Not really. And anyway, we hadn't been to drama college or anything. So there.)

As the average age of studio audiences tended to be in the lower seventies and the show went out well after their bedtime at 11.05 p.m., the producers came up with the idea of transporting our fans from Liverpool to Didsbury to laugh loudly and scream politely (thankfully, nobody whooped in those days). When the transmission was over they all piled into the coaches and the night swallowed them up. Meanwhile we all piled into the Hospitality Room and swallowed up the night.

These days, after a chat show, guests are encouraged to rush straight home or, on special occasions (like the producer's just been sacked) they may be invited upstairs to toy with a crisp and a glass of wine. But this was the golden age of post-show bacchanalia, so imagine a bar on the *Titanic* when news got around that the ship was safe and it was the iceberg that had gone down. Nothing beats a pint of shandy in the cricket pavilion after a day in the outfield, or the frosted flute of champagne that welcomes you into the reception, but nothing quite matches the first triple Scotch and Coke that winks at you from the bar when you've just come off the set after a live TV performance. Except, perhaps, the second. Or, possibly, the third.

'A man is never happy for the present, but when he is drunk,' Dr Johnson once dictated, and yesterday I was in Laugharne (pronounced 'Larn', as in 'If you pass me the yaugharne, I'll daugharne your socks after I've milked the cows in the baugharne') recording a *Poetry Please* programme, which we called *Booze and the Muse*, about poets and their relationship with alcohol. Brown's Hotel on the high street of this lovely coastal village in south-west Wales is where Dylan Thomas drank, with or without Caitlin, and, according to legend, eavesdropped on bar room conversations to provide him with lines and characters for *Under Milk Wood*. Mind you, this seems a bit too good to be true unless you can imagine the scene in the snug on a wet Wednesday evening.

LANDLORD Well, here comes Dai the Fish. Had a good day, boyo?
DAI Aye, I've been out on the sloeblack, slow, black, crowblack, fishingboat-bobbing sea, and I've

got a thirst like a dredger, so give me a pint of stout, will you. It's quiet in here tonight.

LANDLORD   Aye, you can hear the houses sleeping in the streets in the slow deep salt and silent black, bandaged night. That will be one shilling and fourpence.

DAI   I see Dylan the Eavesdrop is up to his old tricks, pretending to be so busy doing the crossword he can't hear us. Watch this. Good evening, Mr Thomas, Caitlin still in London, is she?

DYLAN   Yes, Dai, she'll be back home tomorrow.

DAI   I bet you can't wait, eh? Whacking-thighed and piping hot, thunderbolt-brass'd and barnacle-breasted, flailing up the cockles with eyes like blowlamps and scooping low over her lonely hotwaterbottled body.

DYLAN   That's right, Dai, yes. 'Barnacle-breasted', that's one word, is it?

LANDLORD   And here comes Back-to-front Binyon. Good evening Back-to-front, and what have you been doing all day?

BINYON   Me? Oh, Llareggub.

As part of the programme I talked to Tommy Watts, who had been the publican for over thirty-five years, and he reckoned that it was the morphine that doctors gave him in the New York hospital that did for Dylan, rather than the nineteen straight whiskeys. According to Tommy he was a diabetic, and in Brown's he always drank halves and only pretended to be drunk because that's what people expected of him. Personally, I think that only a drunk would pretend to be drunk, halves or no halves, but I agree that people's misconceptions of 'The Poet' can lead to fiction skewing dangerously towards reality.

In February 1976 I was invited to launch a newly built library in south London, where I was to read my poems for thirty minutes before officially declaring the building open. The chief librarian proudly showed me around, then took me into his office where I could relax and prepare myself for the performance. 'I know what you poets are like,' he said, and opened a cupboard to reveal six crates of Guinness. As far as I know, the reading went OK but I don't remember getting back to Liverpool.

One Saturday night after *Gazette* we were celebrating the sinking of yet another iceberg in the Hospitality Suite when three of the guests, Jonathan Miller, Willie Rushton – then starring in *That Was the Week that Was* – and ace war photographer and Steve McQueen lookalike Don McCullin, all expressed the desire to sample the delights of Liverpool's clubland, so we quickly downed our drinks in time to catch the magical mystery fan-packed coach. On the East Lancs road on the outskirts of Liverpool we were forced to a halt by the flashing blue light of a police patrol car. From the vantage point of the high coach windows we could see an upturned Mini and a crowd of people on the grass verge beside the road. I was first off the bus, 'Let me through, let me through,' I cried, 'I'm a poet.' But as the onlookers stood back it was the qualified doctor, Jonathan Miller, who was first at the scene. Kneeling on the grass and sobbing hysterically was a young woman cradling to her breast a young man who appeared to be unconscious and bleeding from a head wound. Dr Miller knelt beside the couple and spoke softly. The girl looked at him, still dazed but comforted by his presence, then she looked over his shoulder and saw through her tears Mike standing there. She dropped the young man's head into her lap as she brought her hands to her mouth: 'Mike McCartney! Wake up, Jimmy, wake up. It's Paul McCartney's brother!'

MACCA'S TWENTY-FIRST

On 18 June 1963 it was Mike's brother's twenty-first birthday and we were invited to the party at Aunty Jin's house in Huyton. It was only a matter of months since 'Please Please Me' had been number one in the charts and Beatlemania was limbering up on the touchline. The top act of the day was still the Shadows and Paul was dead chuffed that they'd made the effort to turn up, although their Cecil Gee outfits and Brylcreemed quiffs seemed slightly dated. Brian Epstein, a born circulator, circulated with ease from group to group, a word here, a hand on the shoulder there, and there was already a sense of rivalry between those signed to NEMS and those still playing in hope. Although there were other agents and managers on Merseyside, and some notable groups like the Searchers and the Swinging Blue Jeans who achieved success outside Epstein's empire, there was a growing sense that if the Nemsmobile didn't stop to pick you up you'd be doomed to a life on the hard shoulder, and it wasn't endearing to watch butch guitarists and tattooed drummers flirting with Eppy.

One of the Beatles' favourite bands was the Fourmost, who were later to have hits with 'Hello Little Girl' and 'I'm in Love', written especially for them by John and Paul. They performed in Aunty Jin's lounge and it must have been while watching them playing that I missed the punch-up between Lennon and the popular DJ Bob Wooler, who may or may not have insinuated that John had enjoyed a holiday fling with Mr Epstein. Nowadays half of Liverpool appears to have witnessed the fight, especially musicians too young to have been there, but at least my claim to fame is that I *was* there and still missed the action. However, I did see Bob Wooler wandering around with what looked like a butcher's apron clutched to his nose, muttering darkly about people not being able to take a joke.

I was in the kitchen with Thelma and Billy Hatton, the bass player with the Fourmost, looking at a reproduction of Breughel's painting *The Fall of Icarus* and so was not witness to the other talking point of the evening, when John touched a girl called Rose in an inappropriate place. The marquee in the back garden. Her response was a good old-fashioned slap in the face, to which he replied with an equally old-fashioned right hook to the consternation of everyone on the dance floor. While Billy J. Kramer was helping Rose to her feet and John was apologising, we were still in the kitchen, discussing W. H. Auden's response to Breughel's painting in his poem 'La Musée des Beaux Arts', in which he notes how ordinary life goes on while, unobserved in the background, 'miraculous births' and disasters take place.

This morning I attended a service at the Brompton Oratory where my youngest son's school choir sang the mass in Latin and sang it beautifully. Matthew is no chorister himself, but many of his friends are and I was struck by how these teenage boys, whom in 'real life' I know to be as slovenly, lazy and sullen as one could wish for, could suddenly be transformed into a choir of angels, able to touch the congregation with a sense of the divine. I don't know if

John Lennon was in the choir when he was at school, and I'm pretty certain he never sang the mass in Latin, but to hear him sing or watch him on stage, even then, was to witness a kind of transformation into something other-worldly. As a young man he seemed to be a seethe of contradictions, the insecure, piss-taking bully on the one hand and the fallen angel with aspirations to be a spiritual leader on the other. But it goes without saying that if John had been as well-balanced, easygoing and charming as Paul, the velvet glove of the Beatles would have lacked the iron fist. He was the chilli to Paul's jam, the knuckle to his duster, the pole to his lap-dancer, the 'sod-off' to his 'nice-to-meet-you', the hallucinogenic icing to Paul's birthday cake.

As all I'd ever wanted to be was a poet, I had never really planned a career and was quite content to go along with the forces that propelled me, which in those days were Mike and John. Although I was perfectly happy with Hope Leresche, who continued to look after my literary interests well into the eighties, they were impatient for the kind of success they believed only Epstein could bring. He had never seen us perform, but as a favour to Paul agreed to take us on, so in 1965 the Scaffold climbed aboard the Nemsmobile. Having been three big fish in a small pond, we were now three small lobsters in a big pan of boiling water, for not only did the NEMS menu feature the Beatles, Gerry and the Pacemakers, Cilla Black and so on, but it had expanded to include American dishes such as the Supremes and Johnny Mathis. I've no idea where this restaurant analogy is headed, but it hints at the sense of confusion that overwhelmed us almost immediately. Where were we going? Why had our bodies turned bright red?

I don't recall ever having a conversation with Brian Epstein and, although he would greet Mike warmly, I think he remained puzzled as to what John and I actually did. On the rare occasions I visited the NEMS office in Soho I felt like an impostor.

GIRL BEHIND DESK Hi.

ME Hello, I've come to see Mr Epstein.

GBD And you are?

ME Er . . . Roger McGough.'

GBD I'm sorry?

ME I'm one of the Scaffold.

GBD Scaffold?

ME Yes, with Paul McCartney's brother, Michael, I'm with him. We've got a meeting, you see, and I'm early . . .

GBD If you'd just take a seat, Rodney . . .

However, if we were going to topple the Beatles off their perch we had to start by making a record. Eppy had no problem in getting us a recording deal and, more important, in persuading George Martin to produce our first single. As well as having the obvious Beatles connections, George had worked with the Goons, and the Peter Sellers album he produced, *Songs for Swingin' Sellers*, was a comedy classic. As un-rock'n'roll as you could get, he would not have looked out of place behind a desk in the Foreign Office, but he was kind, patient and determined to give us a leg-up into the charts. However, it would have taken more than genius to transform the pair of pig's ears that we brought into the studio that morning, and 'Today's Monday' and 'Three

Blind Jellyfish' failed to hit the G-spot. Untoppled from their perch, the Beatles went off to conquer the USA while we set off for Stockton-on-Tees and a tour that still gives me nightmares, although mild no doubt, compared to the blind jellyfish whose singing keeps George awake at night.

The Marquee Tour organised by Georgio Gomelski was to be a pop tour with a difference. The difference was that instead of a compère coming on stage between acts and failing to keep the crowd amused, the Scaffold would perform their unique brand of zany humour. (And fail to keep the crowd amused.) The Yardbirds and Manfred Mann topped a bill that included Paul and Barry Ryan and Goldie and the Gingerbreads, and we rehearsed comedy sketches with everybody for a week before setting off. It has to be said that all these teenage idols, particularly Keith Relfe, Jeff Beck and Paul Jones, were more than happy to shed the pop star image and take the mickey out of themselves, and so we couldn't wait to set off and shake the country with this ground-breaking fusion of rock and comedy.

Unfortunately, many of the theatre managers objected on legal grounds (Entertainments Act 1843, whereby props cannot be used on stage during a pop concert, nor will rude jokes or satirical remarks be uttered in front of a teenage audience). And worse still, as soon as Keith, Jeff or Paul appeared on stage with the Scaffold to act out a simple comedy routine the whole place erupted, with 2,000 screaming girls deaf to the insouciant wordplay, the carefully crafted one-liners and the punchlines that would have brought the house down, had the house only taken its hands off its ears for a minute and stopped bloody screaming.

ON THE FRINGE

If you are standing in St Andrews Square bus station in Edinburgh after midnight, and you are alone (which is unlikely, because it is August and Festival time), you might hear the faint wail of a saxophone and ghostly voices reciting quaint, subterranean poems. Could that be Michael Horovitz? Pete Brown? Paul Jones (in those pre-Manfred Mann days, Paul Pond, an Oxford undergrad)? And who's the one with the familiar Liverpool accent? For in 1961, beneath that bus shelter stood a coffee cellar where jazz musicians and poets played, recited, got drunk and slept each and every night of the Festival.

That was my first taste of the Edinburgh Fringe and I had travelled up there with the Liverpool sculptor Arthur Dooley, who had been invited to create a spontaneous sculpture in what was then Binn's department store on Princes Street. He and I would traipse the streets collecting rubbish, which he proceeded to transform into a piece that covered most of the fourth floor, epitomising the workers' struggle against consumerism (or, come to think of it, it might have been one of his stark crucifixions). Whatever the symbolism, it was a huge success. (With Arthur and me that is, the staff and shoppers loathed it.)

Before Mike Horovitz invited me to read at his 'New

Departures' nights in the Cellars Club and we discovered the delights of communal beatnik living, Arthur and I had nowhere to stay, so we slept for three nights on the steps of the Scottish National Gallery. Having been an Irish Guard in a former life, Arthur was an expert in survival skills, and taught me how to stuff newspapers up my trouser legs and cocoon myself in posters for shows at the Lyceum. Although I was a schoolmaster at the time and could have afforded to stay in a B&B, I pretended to be homeless and fiancée-less, and as free as the gulls that swooped over Carlton Hill. 'This is the life,' I thought, 'I'll come back every year and keep an eye on the castle.' And being a man of my word, I did, recently celebrating my fortieth consecutive appearance on the Edinburgh Fringe with a show in the large Music Hall of the Assembly Rooms.

And always the Fringe, never the official Festival. In fact, for the first couple of years I thought that the Fringe *was* the Festival. There was the Tattoo, of course, and there were classical concerts in the Usher Hall and huge theatre companies from Georgia or Nagasaki doing Shakespeare in Polish, but all that was part of the world that belonged to the cultourists who came only once and compared the Festival with Salzburg or Avignon. As a bit player on the Fringe I never felt sidelined, quite the opposite: I always believed I was at the centre of things and it was undoubtedly where I learned my trade. Living in London I'm only an occasional theatregoer, but up there I saw so much that inspired me. The fierce politics of John McGrath's 7.84 company, the sad whimsy of Lindsay Kemp in *Bubbles*, God played by Brian Glover with a Barnsley accent and bald as a billiard ball, ascending into heaven on a giant crane in the *Mystery Plays* on the Mound, 'Finn McCool' at the Haymarket Ice Rink, and the wonderful Kosh Dance company with whom I collaborated on three productions.

When the sand had run out on *Gazette*, the hourglass was not turned back on its head and, although now famous in the streets back home, we were hungry for world domination. To help us achieve our aim Pat Burke, who ran the theatre side of things at the Hope Leresche agency, hired Joan Maitland, a dramaturge, to groom us for success on the West End stage. It was only recently while reading the warm and fulsome obituaries about Pat Burke that I realised what a star she had been, with apparently 'the best pair of legs on stage for two decades'. When she was looking after the Scaffold she had given up her career as an actress, but she was fiercely determined that we would follow in her footsteps. ('*The Scaffold, the three best pairs of legs . . .*') While Pat set up auditions with theatre producers like William Albery and booked us into the Little Theatre in Garrick Yard, St Martin's Lane to showcase our material, Joan Maitland set about turning three mumbling, bumbling promising amateurs into a trio of silken-tongued, balletic thespians.

To help achieve this improbable transformation, she arranged for us to have movement and voice lessons in Liverpool – '*Ning, nang, nong. All together now. Ning, nang . . . John, you're not helping by pulling those silly faces. Ning, nang, nong*' – as well as giving us lessons in stagecraft and sophistication in her large house in North Finchley. At lunchtime her husband, Jack, wearing an apron and monogrammed velvet slippers, would sashay in (they had no children) with a jug of something squashed and a plate of sandwiches: '*No, Michael, the chicken does not taste fishy, those are tuna sandwiches. Tuna? It's a fish. Don't you have tuna up*

there in the north? Oh dear, we do have a lot to learn, don't we?
Like Jack's manners, her theatrical pedigree was impeccable,
although, to be honest, we never recognised any of the
names she dropped except for Lionel Bart, with whom she'd
co-written the musical *Blitz*.

In 1964 the Scaffold took a revue called *Birds, Marriages
and Deaths*, that I'd written and she had directed, up to
Edinburgh, and we opened in the tiny sixty-seater Traverse
Theatre, which was then in St James Terrace on
Lawnmarket. Although we were determinedly amateur, and
our 'alternative' approach challenged the slickly formatted
university revues of the time ('They have succeeded in
breaking the mould which *Beyond the Fringe* had imposed on
its successors' *Scotsman*), the Traverse audience took us
warmly to their hearts, in some cases to their beds, and we
were to become a Fringe fixture there for years to come.
The theatre boasted a small art gallery run by Ricky
Demarco and a very fine restaurant specialising in Scottish
dishes. ('*Good evening, boys. Today's speciality is Herring in
oatmeal*' . . . '*Wha? I'm not eating porridge with kippers*') as well
as a bar that stayed open until midnight.

In those far-off days when pubs closed at ten p.m. and
never opened on Sundays, the bar became a magnet to all the
performing iron filings in town. Nowadays, performers at the
bar in the Gilded Balloon have the haunted look that tells you
they're wondering if the bar at the Pleasance is starrier, or
whether they should be up at the Assembly Rooms. But back
then there was something very reassuring about watching
Peter O'Toole and Bob Hoskins elbowing Larry Adler out of
the way in the rush to get served, knowing that you were
drinking in the only after-hours show in town.

Accommodation was provided by 'Friends of the

Traverse' and was always first class, including the run of an apartment with a balcony overlooking the castle, from where we could watch the Tattoo, drink Scotch and shout silly things at the soldiers. Towards the end of our stay mine host, a kilted barrister, invited a few people round for a musical evening, including *Room at the Top* actor Laurence Harvey and Larry Adler. The former wore monogrammed slippers (without the apron) and crooned, while Larry Adler, still covered in iron filings and bruises from those elbows at the bar, gamely played his mouth organ. You know what it's like when you've drunk six or seven martinis and you're shouting but you think you are whispering? And you're taking the piss out of somebody's monogrammed slippers and you think they haven't noticed? And you're accompanying a famous harmonica player on comb and paper, and you think nobody will hear? Oh dear, one less Friend of the Traverse.

Although I loved many of the shows I saw on the Fringe in the early sixties, the main excitement was to be found in the Traverse bar in the afternoons, where Hamish Henderson, poet and professor of all things Scottish, would introduce Hugh MacDiarmid and Robert Garioch to read their poems in Gaelic. A highland shepherd would sing, a piper play a pibroch and every day local poets like Brian McCabe and Alan Jackson would entertain:

> *nae hat,*
> *and the cauld rain fallin*
> *dearie me*

Alan Jackson

I loved the surrealism of Norman MacCaig and Edwin Morgan and, because the link between folk music and poetry was so vital, I felt closer to the Scottish poets than to their English counterparts. When the Traverse moved down the hill to larger premises in the Grassmarket, the afternoon sessions became more organised and attracted large crowds, and many more fine poets including Pete Morgan and a young art student from Glasgow called Liz Lochhead. By the late sixties it was very much Edinburgh-on-Mersey with Adrian Henri, Brian Patten and myself performing, with Andy Roberts accompanying us on guitar. I had met Andy when the Scaffold first played the Traverse and he was a sixth-former working as a musician in *Stewed Irish*, a clever late-night revue from Trinity College Dublin. He had become so taken with the three of us and with the poetry of Brian and Adrian that he decided then and there to enrol at Liverpool University and study law. Despite graduating, he chose not to become a sharp lawyer in favour of writing music and playing guitar, for which we all remain grateful.

When the Scaffold hit the national charts with 'Thank U Very Much' in 1968 our venue during the Festival was a week at the Palladium Theatre. Although a great success, it distanced us from our Traverse audience, and there would be no going back to homely sixty-seaters. There would be a different show every year in a different venue and with different people.

I'm writing this surrounded by press cuttings, diary entries, programmes and letters, both loving and threatening, to do with a short lifetime in Edinburgh. On the wall are framed posters of some of the shows I've done there: *Wordplay*, a revue starring the comparatively unknown Victoria Wood; *Lifeswappers*, adapted for stage from a play I had written for television; *McGough & McCarthy*, Pete McCarthy as the hard-nosed comic pitted against the stand-up poet; *Words on the Run* with Willy Russell; *Mouthtrap*, a play that Brian Patten and I concocted about a pair of poets trapped in a dressing room and visited by the angel of death, played by Helen Atkinson Wood; and to tell the truth, I'm getting bogged down with detail. However, when you realise that I've played the Fringe every year since 1961 for an average of, say, two weeks at a time, that adds up to eighty-eight weeks, which means that I've spent over a year and a half of my entire life in Edinburgh. Och, I'm practically Scottish.

And to prove it, here is a spooky but heart-warming story, in a three-generational sort of way. When I was in Edinburgh in 2002, performing at the Book Festival in Charlotte Square, I went to have lunch in Henderson's, a favourite old haunt on Hanover Street, and was making short work of an alfalfa sprout lasagne when I fell head over heels in love. What happened was that I looked up and saw a girl of about eighteen and my heart, as the poets say, skipped a beat. It was love at first sight and yet it couldn't be, I'm too old for that sort of thing. Then, to add to my confusion and before the twang of Cupid's arrow had died away, the girl was joined by an equally beautiful lady who was obviously her mother, and twang! I was in love again. A double dose of delicious déjà vu. I was on the point of forsaking my alfalfa in favour of going over and introducing myself when they were joined by a third lady. I hesitated and looked closely at this attractive sixty-year-old when, bang, it hit me. Not love, but the realisation that it was not Cupid's arrow that had pierced me but Time's arrow. The OAP was once the eighteen-year-old I'd fallen for forty Festivals ago and engaged in a brief Highland fling. She recognised me:

'Och, you've not changed at all.'

'But I'm bald and wrinkly.'

'Like I said, you've not changed at all.'

I joined them for tea, and while we chatted the years fell away until, miraculously, grandmother, mother and daughter all became the same girl.

And what takes me back there year after year? Certainly not the deep-fried pizzas with herring in oatmeal topping, nor the hope that I might be the first poet to win a Perrier award. It's partly to do with meeting old friends, but it's mainly to do with the city. We have been having a drawn-out love affair for most of my adult life and my going to perform at the Festival each year provides the excuse to meet up with an old flame. Although I have aged, she hasn't, and when I try to rekindle the old excitement, that first flush of youthful passion, I can't, but the good thing is that she doesn't seem to mind.

One sunny morning I went to the Royal Botanic Gardens and sat on a bench overlooking the city spread out below, with Arthur's Seat and the Firth of Forth neatly in frame, and I wrote this:

> *The best show in town*
> *Is the one down there*
> *Edinburgh.*
> *Starring: The Castle,*
> *The sun, and the firth-fresh air.*

It's not a piece of verse I'd normally wish to publish or read in public, because it's private. A billet-doux for an old and faithful lover.

LETTER TO MONIKA

Dear Monika,

I know it's unlikely, but did you by any chance listen to *Summer with Monika*, the dramatisation of the poems that went out on Radio 4 in April 1998? Of course, if I had an address I could send you a cassette or CD. It is so long since I saw you, can it really be over forty years? A lifetime.

In fact, it's so long ago that people who weren't born then ask me what Liverpool was really like in the sixties. As if I should know better than anybody else of my age. And to be honest, I don't, for memory is so selective, isn't it? Except, of course, that it was always sunny in those days, and that people were always smiling and being nice to one another. All right, I jest, but the fifties were so dully retrospective and conformist that things could only get better. They did away with National Service for a start, just in time to save me from a fate worse than jankers, and that gift of two years really made a difference to young men of my generation. Would John, Paul, George and Ringo, while serving in the King's Own Liverpool Light Infantry, have got together one night in a Nissen hut and formed the Beatles? I doubt it. Billy J. Kramer and the Royal Corps of Signals? The Swinging Khaki Trousers? Gerry and the Squarebashers? Suddenly there were alternatives – art colleges, universities, all available for working-class kids. A generation of teenagers with hope and energy and time on their hands, who didn't want to dress like their parents or listen to their kind of music. Was it the same where you were?

And do you know what else they ask? They say, Monika, was she a hippy? Can you believe that? When Flower Power drifted across the Atlantic from California in the late sixties many young people grasped the ideals of freedom and gentleness that it seemed to enshrine, but I was old enough to be cynical. What may have begun as a peace movement initially, an antidote to the horrors of Vietnam, had become a fashion show. It was fun, but essentially mindless. If I sound slightly jaundiced, it's not because I've got jaundice, or because I believe that as a decade it is often misconceived, so powerful are the images of the period, but rather that I regret the false sense of nostalgia that passed into the tribal consciousness of young people. They inherited, many of them, a sense of loss, an 'if only I'd been there' sort of yearning. What was exciting about the sixties for me was that I was young, and there's never a better time to be young than when you're young. The summer I wrote about was early sixties, pre-pill, pre-psychedelia, CND not LSD. And as for the Permissive Society, it may have sashayed on to Merseyside years later, but if it ever went to parties, then it arrived just after I had left.

Decade

We never wore kaftans or put flowers in our hair
Never made the hippy trail to San Francisco
Our Love-ins were a blushing, tame affair
Friday evenings at the local church-hall disco

Heard it on the grapevine about Carnaby Street
Looked for Lucy in the sky, danced to the Mersey Beat
There were protests on the streets and footprints on the moon
Times they were a changin', but the changin' came too soon

Those were the days my friend, there was something in the air
Though we never wore kaftans or put flowers in our hair.

Just across the road from the huge building site that was to become the Catholic Cathedral (or Paddy's Wigwam as the wits would have it) was a former evangelical church called Hope Hall, and before it became a music and poetry venue, and long before it became the Everyman Theatre, it was a cinema. A sort of art house showing foreign films for intellectuals with a penchant for soft porn, and one evening I was walking past on my way to the Philharmonic (the pub, that is, not the concert hall) when I saw a poster advertising *Summer with Monika*, and I knew it was a foreign film straight away because they'd spelled Monica wrong. I also noted that Ingmar Bergman had directed it, but what struck me most forcibly was the girl in the poster. Without clothes, you were simply beautiful, stretched out on the lake shore at the end of a golden summer's day. (There may have been a boy there too, but he has been erased and replaced with an idealised image of myself.) Monika, long-haired and naked, beside a lake in a pine forest. Very unscouse. An image a million miles from Merseyside. Although I loved the poster and filched the title for my sequence of poems, I never did get to see the film, for which I'm thankful because it left me free to make up my own story.

There had been the love poems I'd written about different girls before meeting Thelma, and those written while living with her. Poems about the pain of loss, about the need to be in a relationship and immediately feeling trapped by it, but there didn't appear to be a thread and the poems seemed like little bleatings in the dark. But having fallen in love with you on the edge of that lake in Sweden, I brought you back to a tiny flat overlooking the Anglican cathedral where we went for long walks round the table and picnicked on the banks of the settee.

I hope you'll be pleased to hear that the poems were published by Michael Joseph in 1967, which turned out to be a very good year for me. It was my first book and I was delighted. The trouble was that the publishers didn't have enough faith in the poems and twinned them with a short novel I'd written called *Frinck*, about a young guy who fancies himself as a singer–songwriter and goes down to London to seek fame and fortune. This was early Scaffold days and the story was partly a warning to myself about the contagion of celebrity. I thought of trying to contact you at the time and sending a copy of the book you helped inspire, but you know what it's like, I was busy and you were . . . you were? I had no idea.

Monika managed to give Frinck the slip in 1978. In other words, a small publisher called Whizzard Press published the poems on their own, with wonderful illustrations by Peter Blake, although the cover, a glorious painting of a girl sunbathing nakedly on a bed, the sandcastle not quite hiding the naughty bit, was to prove too explicit for many High Street bookshops, who declined to put the book on their shelves. Despite this it sold well enough for Penguin to republish in 1990 (with a more decorous cover by Peter).

By the way, Monika, I assume you're familiar with Peter

Blake because he's been world famous since he designed the sleeve for the Beatles' *Sergeant Pepper* album and was very much involved in designing the set for a production we did at the Lyric Studio in Hammersmith. Directed by Mel Smith with music by Andy Roberts, it starred Alyson Spiro as Monika, Greg Floy as the lover and me as the narrator. Central to the design was a bedroom and Peter was keen to re-create the one from his original painting, which featured on the book and album cover. So while Mel Smith was putting us through our paces in a rehearsal room above a pub in Chiswick, Peter spent the weeks painting tiny pink roses on to a backcloth to represent the wallpaper that extended on three sides around the set.

I would love to be able to say that the show was a huge success and that it transferred to the West End before moving on to Broadway, followed by a round-the-world tour, which included a short season at the National Theatre in Stockholm where Ingmar Bergman, attracted by the title, dropped in and was so enthralled that he insisted on producing and directing the film for Hollywood. (With you playing the lead, of course, Alyson being very decent about handing over the role.) But I can't. The theatre was packed every night and the audiences were enthusiastic. Unfortunately for us, the reviewer on the *Evening Standard* was less so; he put the knife in and that was that. The show never transferred.

(Incidentally, Monika, the reviewer was not a butcher but a sort of drama critic. Do you have them also in Sweden?)

The show closed on Saturday 22 December and I spent until the unearthly hours with Peter and his favourite student, Ian Dury, drinking whisky in my flat on the Fulham

Road. On Monday morning I went down to the theatre on King Street in Hammersmith to collect my things and clear the dressing room. It had also occurred to me, and I'd mentioned it to Peter on the previous morning, that a roll of his painstakingly hand-painted wallpaper might be nice as a keepsake. The thought of cutting the canvas backcloth into rectangles and having them framed, stored and sold over the years had of course never crossed my mind. But too late. On Sunday the backstage crew had dismantled the set and the delicate pink roses had disappeared beneath two coats of black paint.

And so, nearly four decades later, I write a play for radio using some of the poems from the book and I think about you and wonder whether you heard it. And I wonder, too, what became of Monika, that beautiful girl, long-haired and naked, sitting beside a lake on a poster in Hope Street, Liverpool 8.

THE POPPIES

In 1975, in the Beverly Wiltshire Hotel in Los Angeles, a man was observed staggering around the foyer and acting suspiciously. When Security arrived he was incoherent and seemingly abusive, so the police were sent for and he was arrested and charged with drunken behaviour. Hours later, Clive Goodwin died in his cell of a brain haemorrhage. He was forty-five years old. When friends learned of his death, they were surprised and horrified, particularly when it came to light that he had taken only one glass of wine with Warren Beatty and Trevor Griffiths during their meeting about the film *Reds*.

Years earlier Clive, having received an award for bravery in the face of the Scaffold, had gone on to become a highly successful agent. In 1963 he married Pauline Boty after a whirlwind ten-day romance. She was a golden girl who featured alongside Peter Blake, Derek Boshier and Peter Phillips in Ken Russell's film *Pop goes the Easel*. Friends argued about whether she looked more like Brigitte Bardot than Simone Signoret, and about whether she should abandon painting and pursue a career as an actress, for she had already appeared, albeit briefly, with Michael Caine in *Alfie* and only just lost out playing the lead in *Darling* to Julie Christie. Clive seemed to live a charmed life and I must confess to harbouring envious thoughts on returning to Liverpool with Thelma after spending time with the Goodwins in their neoteric flat on the Cromwell Road. 'Why can't you paint like Pauline?' I said to Thelma.

'Why can't you look like Clive?' said she.

While I was improvising a television career with Mike and John, which involved commuting between Liverpool, Manchester and London, Thelma, having forsaken Pauline Boty for Mary Quant, had moved from painting in oils to designing dresses, gone into the posh end of the rag trade with a friend of hers from art college and opened a boutique called, appropriately, Monika. Our un-neoteric flat in Huskisson Street became their sweatshop and for months you couldn't find a chair to sit on without being stuck with pins, or find a length of floor to walk on without stepping on a cut-out paper dress pattern. On the plus side, the place was filled daily with friends of Thelma in various stages of undress. I'd stroll into the kitchen to discover Yvonne wearing nothing but a bra and a reel of cotton, or go into the bathroom and find Vera clad only in knickers and a pair of Courrèges boots. It was a sad day (not only for me, but for all my pals who had suddenly begun dropping in at all hours) when the whole operation was moved downtown.

I was lolling about in the boutique one morning, enjoying my new role as a dress designer's moll, when in came Yvonne, now fully dressed, with three young, beautiful black girls who were so loud and funny that had there been aisles in the shop we would have rolled in them. It transpired that they had not come to buy frocks but to see me, assuming that because I had appeared on television a couple of times I had strong show-business connections.

'We wanna be stars, Roger,' they chorused.

I must admit that I was flattered and interested, and explained that after a few sessions with Joan Maitland and some careful marketing there was no reason why these girls couldn't be a hip, black, British version of the Three Stooges. Strangely, they seemed unimpressed.

'We wanna be the Supremes, Roger,' they chorused.

So I rang up Clive Goodwin, inviting him to join me in a partnership to manage the careers of three sisters who were not only beautiful, had amazing personalities and came from a good home locally, but were happy to sign up for seventy-five per cent. Clive was round within the hour and so the Poppies were born.

If you came out of the boutique on Bold Street and turned left, left and left again, you would find yourself in Seel Street where the Blue Angel Club lorded it over its rivals. It was there one night that Freddie Starr asked me in all seriousness (well, in a James-Cagney-with-a-stammer kind of seriousness) if I would write some comedy material for him. Freddie was popular on the local music scene, but his group the Midnighters had been passed over by Epstein and others, so his future as a recording artist was in the balance. Freddie had loads of talent but was it harnessable? He could sing and tell dodgy jokes, he was a great mimic, he certainly had charisma, but he was dangerous in that unzip-flies-and-wave-it-around kind of way.

'I'm not sure if I'm the right man for the job, Freddie. Don't you think my stuff might be too . . . esoteric?'

'You mean you're not funny?'

'Well, er . . .'

'You doity little rat.'

He produced from nowhere an imaginary tommy-gun and sprayed me with bullets, before leaping up on to the bar. All eyes were now on him as he yelled in triumph, 'Look, Ma, I'm on top of de woild!' and fell backwards into the flames.

Some weeks later I was on the dance floor downstairs, showing the world how to do the twist, when news fluttered through that Bob Dylan had just arrived, arm-in-arm-in-arm with three stunning black girls. When the music stopped I acknowledged the applause and made my way upstairs. As I suspected, there, pinned against the bar by the Poppies, was the living legend. How they had managed to get backstage after his show at the Odeon Theatre and kidnap him I can only guess, but the victim seemed not unpleased. The girls chorused the introductions: 'Bob, this is our manager, Roger McGough, he's a singer-songwriter too.'

'Roger, this is Bob Dylan, he's from America.'

I muttered something suitably humble, which Dylan didn't hear because he was then being introduced to half of Liverpool, so, not being one of nature's hangers-on, I melted away. Ten minutes later a Poppy was tugging at my jacket: 'Roger, we're all going back to the hotel with Bob, and he said to invite you. He's lovely, isn't he?'

So the Poppies, Bob Dylan and I strolled arm-in-arm-in-arm-in-arm-in-arm along Renshaw Street to the Adelphi, and up to his suite, where we were joined by his manager, Al Grossman, the Beatles' first manager and owner of the Blue Angel, Alan Williams, Clive, Mike, and I don't remember who else. What I do remember, though, is sitting quietly in a corner with Dylan and chatting, mainly about what was happening with poetry in the city. He really wasn't interested in talking about himself, it was as if he was already bored with the idea of superstardom. Perhaps it was the Jack Daniels I was drinking, or the overawesomeness of the occasion, but I came away with the impression that when his touring days were over he intended to come back and spend some time hanging out quietly in Liverpool. I'm sure he meant it at the time, although he didn't quite realise how long his touring days were going to be.

Now, I don't want to give the impression that Dylan saw in me a fellow poet, someone with whom he could feel at ease, intellectually and spiritually, someone to whom he could relate on a higher level than the fans, liggers and groupies who constantly surrounded him. No, I don't want to give that impression at all.

Eventually, Clive came over to tell us that the girls wanted to sing for Bob and would he mind. Of course he wouldn't. On the count of three (or, it might have been four or five, even) the Poppies burst into their version of the Crystals' 'Da Doo Ron Ron', a number we had rehearsed many times in the girls' front parlour. They were brimming with confidence, they oozed sensuality, they moved with such style and grace that if it hadn't been for the singing I'm sure Al Grossman would have signed them up on the spot. It struck me at the time that if only we'd brought along a big brass section they might have been able to drown out the voices. But Dylan didn't seem to mind that the girls had sung out of tune (had he even noticed, I wonder?).

Perhaps if Clive and I had persevered with the girls they might have achieved success in the business; after all, with a sympathetic sound engineer and some creative wizardry in the recording studio, who knows what effect a showcasing on *Top of the Pops* might have had on the career of these superb mime artists? However the Goodwin-McGough Management Agency folded even before the notepaper could be letterheaded and we all went back to what we were best at, which in the case of the girls was marrying wisely and living happily.

There was an echo of the way the Poppies introduced me to Dylan in the Blue Angel – 'This is Bob Dylan, he's from America' – that sense of making sure you know who you're encountering to help you avoid making any social gaffes, when many years later, Mike saw Sandy, the youngest and cutest of the sisters. He had just swanned into Stringfellows in Covent Garden, when he heard a joyful shriek from across the room; 'Mike, Mike, come over 'ere.' As he approached the corner table he saw Sandy, seated and cosy with none other than Marlon Brando. Sandy jumped up to do the introductions: 'Marlon, this is Mike McCartney, the brother of Paul, you know, one of the Beatles. Mike, this is Marlon Brando,' adding sotto voce, 'He's an actor.'

THE COMMISSION

I went to Golden Square in Soho this morning to record a voice-over for an insurance firm. I know that some poets have Blakean ideals about the purity of their art, and would never get involved in the corrupt world of finance and industry, and I did, in fact, look deep into my soul but decided to accept on two counts. One, because I already had a pension with the company I would be advertising, I would not be promoting a product I didn't believe in. And two, the money was ridiculous. You also get to meet famous luvvies in reception. This morning it was Alison Steadman whom I first met at the Everyman Theatre in the sixties. She was one of a group of actors including Julie Walters, Anthony Sher, Jonathan Price, Bernard Hill, Pete Postlethwaite, Bill Nighy and George Costigan who lit up the stage, as well as being part of the social life that centred around the Everyman Theatre's bar and bistro. Until then, my experience of grown-up theatre was based on my three-week stint at the Playhouse, down the hill on Williamson Square, an ornate Victorian building, proud of the fact that Noël Coward and Gertrude Lawrence had performed on its stage as children, and catering still for a dwindling middle-class audience. Most of the actors I met while working on *Luther* lived in London, and after each Saturday night's performance couldn't wait to hop into the car and drive back. But a new breed of actor was attracted to Liverpool, not only by the work being done, but by the vibrancy they could sense in the city. With the arrival of young directors like Terry Hands, Chris Bond and Alan Dosser, the Everyman's mission became to bring in new writers (Alan Bleasdale, John McGrath, Willy Russell, Bill Morrison) whose work, usually political and dealing with deeply-felt local issues, involved comedy and music to make it accessible and entertaining to a bright, working-class audience.

My first full-length play was performed in the main theatre in 1967, directed by Peter James. Out of step with current trends, it was neither political, musical, nor dealt with deeply-felt local issues. Called *The Commission*, it was about a writer who had been commissioned to write a play and had failed. Having spent the huge advance, he fears that there could be serious, even fatal, repercussions, for dark forces are hinted at. On stage the author, played by Bill Stewart, addresses the audience directly and illustrates by means of a series of sketches, some funny, others sinister, why he'd not been able to deliver the goods. It turns out in the end that the actors themselves had been the ones to commission the play, and with some balleticism and lots of language they destroy the author. If the play were a wine, there would be flavours of Pirandello and Pinter, black undercurrents of Sartre and a Goonish aftertaste. Best laid down and allowed to mature over the centuries, or opened immediately and poured down the sink.

An article appeared in the *Liverpool Echo and Evening Express* on Wednesday 15 March, five days before the show opened:

The story of Roger's own commission to write this play for the Everyman is quite amusing in itself. 'I received the commission back in November. My first reaction? I laughed. Then I wrote the first act in an old exercise book from St Kevin's Comprehensive School, Kirkby. Then I lost the exercise book. I let it go for a while, then I noticed posters appearing all over the place advertising the play, so I realised it was time to do something. It's all coming along quite nicely although we're still waiting for the permission of the Lord Chamberlain. I've a feeling he may want to make a few cuts.'

And indeed, the Lord High Chamberlain did get his chopper out and we had to lose two whole scenes, one because it included the following innocuous verse:

HIM   You remind me of someone, you know.
HER   Someone I know?
HIM   No, someone I know. Are you . . . Are you?
Are you Modigliani's mistress elongated and pink?
Barbara Hutton in knickers of mink?
Albert Moravia's Woman of Rome?
Sarah somebody staggering home?
Are you Cleopatra in Cinemascope?
Elizabeth Taylor dressed only in soap?
Anne Boleyn when Henry chased her?
Ann Hathaway the poet-taster?
A vicar's missus confessing it's nice?
A geisha girl full of curry and rice?
A woodcutter's daughter carrying logs?

An old lady knitting socks on the bogs?
An airline hostess with no head for heights?
A fat ballerina bursting her tights?
Are you the first lady of the USA
Joining her husband in congress each day?
Are you a Scottish Duchess racked with desire?
Joan of Arc curled up by the fire?

HER   . . . Er, no.

All harmless stuff and although reasons for cuts were never given, the man with the blue pencil could be mistaken for thinking that I was referring to Sarah Churchill and the Duchess of Argyll, who were often in the news at the time.

In the course of my research while writing the play I did discover an interesting and little-known fact about intervals. I had always assumed, as probably you did, that the word interval as used in a stage production was derived from the Latin words 'inter' and 'vallum', meaning literally the space between two ramparts. But I was wrong, and so were you. Alain Terval, the son of a famous Belgian brewer, settled in Paris at the beginning of the seventeenth century, where he set up a brewery. His main interest, however, was the theatre and although he wrote several plays none has survived to this day. At that time theatregoing was in decline, and one of the reasons may have been the fact that it was customary for performances to begin at six in the evening and continue straight through until midnight, or the early hours of the morning. Being French, of course, the dramatists favoured lengthy philosophical discourse and soliloquies would run for an hour or more. People were staying away in droves. Then, in the spring of 1632, Terval had an idea that would revitalise theatre. His success as a brewer had enabled him to purchase several theatres on the Left Bank and it was into these that he introduced a break halfway through the evening, during which ale was sold, as well as beignets, and in some halls snails in garlic butter. The breaks proved so successful that they became longer and longer, and the plays consequently shorter and shorter. This period was regarded by many as the golden age of French drama. '*A quel théâtre allez-vous ce soir?*' someone would ask. '*Alain Terval*' would be the cry. *A l'interval* then became synonymous with having a great night out and a useful weapon in the dramatist's armoury. So now you know.

In the early part of last year I was in a recording studio, this time in Lexington Street, waiting to go into the booth and do my bit for pensions and life insurance. There was a woman already inside reciting one of the poems written especially for the campaign. I didn't recognise her, but she had a lovely voice, rich and northern. Just the sort of voice we need on *Poetry Please*, I thought. Since becoming more confident in my role as the programme's presenter, I was trying to introduce a wider range of voices than some of the overly respectful actorly ones that were sometimes heard. When she came out of the booth to collect her bag from the engineer's room where I was sitting with the advertising people, I told her how beautifully she had read the poem, and perhaps she would be interested in reading occasionally on *Poetry Please*. 'That would be great,' she said, obviously delighted at the prospect of a little radio work, and I felt pleased about being able to give a struggling young actress a step up the ladder.

The copywriters from the agency obviously knew her

better than I did. 'When are you flying out?' they said.

'Friday.'

'Anywhere exciting?' I asked.

'New York, *Bombay Dreams* opens on Broadway next Monday.'

Meera Syal gave us all a cheerful wave and rushed outside to her waiting Daimler.

AT LUNCHTIME

Since taking early retirement from teaching at the age of twenty-four, I've never really had a proper job, so when Sara Davies rang from BBC Bristol forty years later, inviting me to be the new presenter of Radio 4's *Poetry Please*, I suddenly felt very grown-up. Twenty-seven half-hour programmes a year is not too onerous and I get the chance to learn all about the poets whose work passed me by when I was at school, as well as keep up with my contemporaries. In truth, it takes me longer to write the scripts than I had fondly imagined. Turn up at the studio in Bristol with a bagful of poems and listeners' letters and wing it like the DJs do? I'm afraid not. The regular listeners know their poetic onions and will not easily be fobbed off, so, with the help of the producer and an assistant, I wade through literary biogs and critical essays before spending at least a day, possibly two, writing something that hopefully sounds as if I've just arrived in the studio in Bristol with a bagful of poems and listeners' letters and am winging it. Like the DJs do. (Or do they? Perhaps, like me, when not on air they're busily scribbling away for hours on end in order to make the whole thing sound off the cuff. Mmm, perhaps not.)

Occasionally a particularly astute poetry lover will request one of my poems, which puts me in a tricky position as you can imagine. I'd hate to be accused of using my position to feather my own career, further my own nest, flog my own books, but often the producer will cajole, entice, bribe, insist, threaten until I give in. A process that takes an amazingly short time, actually. Last week I read 'At Lunchtime', a poem written in the early sixties when the threat of a worldwide nuclear disaster was uppermost in people's minds. In the poem passengers on a bus, upon hearing that the world is coming to an end in the much publicised four minutes, indulge in a communal bonkfest. Surprisingly (to me) it caused quite a furore in the years following publication, because of its supposed call to permissiveness. When it was used as a school text, concerned housewives would complain to the Head, and then to the local newspaper. MPs were written to, questions were even raised in the House. Amazingly, a copy of the collection it appeared in was denounced in southern California and publicly burned by irate, fundamentally concerned parents in Virginia. The poem ends:

> And the next day
> And everyday
> in everybus
> In everystreet
> in everytown
> In everycountry
>
> People pretended
> that the world was coming to an end at lunchtime.
> It still hasn't.
> Although in a way it has.

The last line says it all. It was a moral tale, for when so many people jumped on the free-loving bandwagon, it was only a matter of time before one of the wheels would fall off, and although I think it's a poem very much of its time, it remains popular, particularly with young actors and drama students, and more particularly, for some reason, with young actors and drama students from Australia. When over there, I've often been genially accosted in a bar or theatre foyer and asked to listen to a rendition of the poem that got someone through their audition and into college. It goes without saying that I'm always bubbly and enthusiastic, and would never in a million years mention that the accent I have just heard belongs to Birmingham and not Liverpool. Although why it needed an accent other than the reciter's own I could never quite fathom.

In February 1981 I was lucky to be in Perth, western Australia, as a guest of the Festival and staying at the Riverside Hotel with members of the Old Vic company including Timothy West, Prunella Scales and Robert Lindsay. At 1 p.m. we were all sitting by the pool toying with oysters and sharing a bottle or two of Houghton's white burgundy when a car horn signalled my lift had arrived. As well as doing evening performances as part of the literary festival, I had been snaffled up to visit schools on a daily basis, occasionally twice daily. Parked outside the hotel was a minibus, dusted with red sand and sporting the inevitable roo-bars. (It hardly needs explaining but roo-bars are large 'don't mess with me' reinforced bumpers that serve to protect the car and its occupants should a kangaroo leap out suddenly from the roadside. When I first heard the locals talking about them I thought they said rhubarb. 'Never drive out into the bush unless you've got rhubarb fitted to your vehicle.' Strange old custom I thought.)

Doug Russell was the English teacher in charge of the day's school visit and as I climbed in there were twelve fifteen- and sixteen-year-olds in a state of high excitement. The drive took longer than I expected with the kids becoming increasingly gigglesome. We were on a dirt track in what seemed like the middle of nowhere, when suddenly from the back came a chorus of screams. As I turned round there was a squeal of brakes, and the minibus screeched to a halt in front of what appeared to be a woman and her daughter. The woman flung herself across the windscreen, no doubt with the aid of the rhubarb, and I saw that it was a boy in drag. The two 'females' climbed aboard, one sporting a pair of balloons up his or her jumper, as everybody began to recite 'At Lunchtime'. They were well rehearsed, knew the poem by heart, and as a piece of dirt-track theatre it took some beating.

And that wasn't the only present I received that day from the kids. After my reading later in the afternoon I was presented with a jar of Vegemite with the lid inscribed 'To Roger McGough with love from Tuart Hill High School'. It was a great day and if any of the kids happen to read this, I just want to let you know that I've still got the jar. Still full of Vegemite, of course.

To Chalk Farm now and the Roundhouse, in the days when it wore flares and waved joss sticks in the summer air. I was taking part in one of those marathon 'Love-ins' that were popular in the sixties. A charity concert to raise money for the people who had organised it. I had done my ten-minute stint and was hanging around at the bar in the hope of being molested, when a tall, skinny youth in white shirt and jeans came on stage and mesmerised the audience with a weird set that included poetry, mime and some existential crooning. Very Left Bank and off-the-wall, he went down a storm (a quiet, puzzled sort of one) and afterwards came over to me at the bar and introduced himself. Those strange eyes, one blue, one grey, and that voice, affected but effective, Mayfair by way of Bromley. David Bowie told me that he had enjoyed my reading and was a big fan. In fact – and he hoped I wouldn't mind – he often included a couple of my poems in his act, his favourite being the one about people making love on the bus. We have never met since, but needless to say, I have waited and waited for the Bowie album (a hit single at least) called simply 'At Lunchtime'.

I met Bernard Wrigley, known as the 'Bolton Bullfrog', in 1977 when the Scaffold recorded the theme tune he'd written for *The Fosdyke Saga* scripted by Alan Plater and based on Bill Tidy's cartoon characters. A likeable, talented performer, he was constantly in and out of Granada TV studios in Manchester, where our paths crossed, and we did a few shows together. One evening at a cabaret club over a pint of Pedigree and a curried cockle pie, Bernard said: 'By the way, Roger, that poem of yours, you know, the one about the people . . .'

'Making love on the bus?'

'Aye, that's the one. Well, I occasionally recite it in my act and come to think of it, I suppose I should pay you for the use of it. But you don't mind, do you?'

'No, Bernard, that's fine. But do you ever mention my name? I mean, do you tell the audience who wrote it?'

'Well, to be honest, Roger, only if it goes down like a sack of cacky.'

SAT'DAY WHILE SUNDAY

What man wears beneath his trousers
Women confide, seldom arouses.

Silken briefs or satin thong
Will make her giggle loud and long

(Of course, you'll never stand a chance
in saggy, Y-front underpants)

Wear boxer shorts, ideally plain
(Not Disney, cartoons are a pain

in the bum) Tartan only for the Scots
No Stars and Stripes, no polka dots

No Union Jacks or football logos
Phallic jokes? Definitely no-noes

Regard your underwear as a friendly go-between
So teach it manners, and above all, keep it clean.

I am just taking a break from transcribing the above on to a pair of boxer shorts using a laundry marker and wondering if I'm pushing the boundaries of poesy too far. At the beginning of the year, a couple of bright sparks at the Chelsea Arts Club came up with a wheeze to raise money for the Artists

Benevolent Fund by inviting sixty artist members to decorate a pair of knickers, which would be modelled, cat-walked and auctioned at the Club on St Valentine's night. The works of art to be tastefully framed.

I joined the CAC in the seventies, put up for membership by Jim Goddard, the television director. In those days the club wasn't the trendy, vibrant place it is today, where there's a two-year waiting list to join; in fact, it was on the bones of its arse. Women weren't allowed into the main bar, the food was indifferent and the elderly members liked it that way, but on the plus side it had two snooker tables, a late, late licence, and huge leather sofas on which the tired and emotional could kip down for the night. After years of pretending to enjoy whooping it up in West End clubs like the Speakeasy and the Scotch of St James, I came to feel more at home in the bohemian ambience of the Chelsea, particularly when the women moved in, and in fact I became so much part of the place that in 1985 I was elected Club Chairman, the first poet to be so, and served on the Council for five years. (No badge, unfortunately.)

At the time I was working with a photographer friend of mine on an arts project to produce a series of typographical images and poster poems, one of which was:

> Out of work, divorced,
> Usually pissed.
> He aimed low in life,
>   . . . And missed.

And my friend suggested the idea of photographing the poem as a piece of graffiti on a gents urinal. But which gents

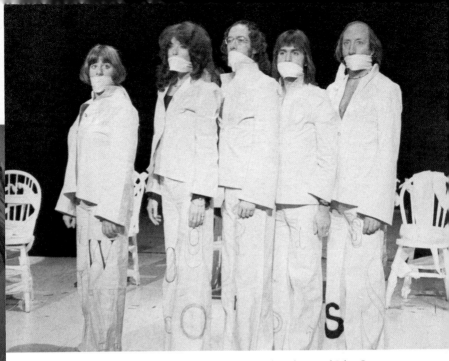

'Wordplay' with Victoria Wood, Lindsay Ingram, Andy Roberts and John Gorman, Edinburgh 1975

On the Circle Line with Adrian Henri

Lost in space, NW3

Clowning about on location
with Tom and Finn

Finn

Tom

The Little Poor Poets
in Edinburgh…

… at Chelsea Arts Club

Bran in Notting Hill

With Denis Thatcher (or could it be
John Wells?) and Jenny Agutter at the
Nether Wallop festival, 1984

McGough and McCarthy in Death Valley

With two Petes, Cook and McCarthy,
Melbourne Comedy festival 1987

With Ferlinghetti in San Francisco 1995

At the launch of Robert Graves' *War Poems*
with Spike Milligan, Isla Blair and William Graves

'He's Behind Yer!' Filming *Book Tower*
© ITV Yorkshire

Another hard day at the Palace

Hilary

Matthew and Isabel

With Isabel and Hilary

'The Mersey Sound'. The poets
providing backing vocals for
Willy Russell and Andy
Roberts at my sixtieth

urinal to use? The one at King's Cross Station? The one in the middle of Clapham Common? The one on Hampstead Heath? We didn't think so. The one at the Chelsea Arts would be ideal, so we got in there one Thursday morning when the place was quiet, and I inscribed the verse on to the porcelain and he took the photograph. When we had finished he went to the bar to order coffee while I cleaned the graffito off the urinal. It was summer and I was wearing a white Levi's denim jacket and jeans, and was still crouching, Windowlene and cloth in hand, when a portly gentleman came into the toilet, unzipped and let flow into the stall next to me. 'Jolly good,' he boomed. 'You chaps do a fine job, this place is always spotless.' I looked up embarrassed and opened my mouth to explain who I was and what I was doing, but too late, he had zipped up and swept out, pleased as punch with his good deed for the day.

In 1967 two television scriptwriters based in Manchester, Tom Brennand and Roy Bottomley, who knew me from my days on *Gazette*, invited me to audition for a part in a series they had written for ABC television. *Sat'day While Sunday* was a series that followed the lives of a group of teenagers over a weekend and was transmitted over the two nights. Sarah-Jane Gwillim played Charlotte, a well-to-do student who had two boys in love with her, one the tough working-class son of a docker and the other a mill owner's son. They were to be the first television roles for two young actors straight out of drama school, Tim Dalton and Malcolm McDowell. I'll let you be the casting director and choose which one got to wear the most expensive clothes. Although the series was to be filmed on location in the north-west, the production office was at the studios in Teddington and that is exactly where I turned up for the audition.

The sign on the door said James Goddard so I knocked and, on hearing a growl, went in. Sitting behind a desk in front of a panoramic window, Jim blocked out most of the view. He bulged in a blue denim shirt, had a fierce crew cut and a Zapata moustache, but as far as I can recall he wasn't flicking a bull-whip. Teaching suddenly seemed an attractive occupation. He sat me down, tried to put me at my ease and asked me to read the part of the Narrator. I did my best, but it didn't go well and Jim stopped me: 'It's not you, is it?'

'What do you mean?'

'The Narrator, he doesn't sound real. Look, I'm going for lunch, so why don't you stay here, sit at the desk and rewrite a couple of those speeches in your own voice?' And so I did, and Jim was pleased, and Tom and Roy were happy for me to write my own scenes, and within a month I was rehearsing in Teddington with Tim, Malcolm, and up-and-coming actors such as Michael Pennington, Brian Marshall and David Yelland.

Before the series I would have taken money on the fact that McDowell, because of his Liverpool working-class roots, would be the one I'd pal up with, but it was Tim Dalton and I who pubbed and clubbed together, when we were both billeted at the Brown Bull near the Granada studios in Manchester. It was an infamous drop-in centre for drop-outs, sports journalists, footballers, actors and whoever happened to be passing through town and wasn't in a hurry to go to bed. There's Germaine Greer in the corner being outrageously sexy and loud with Kenny Everett and the team from *Nice Time*, whose young producer John Birt was at St Mary's when I was there. And who's that shy, good-looking feller besieged at the bar? Georgie Best, of course, and don't the journos love him so much that they buy him drink after drink?

'Could be one of the greats,' says one to another, getting them in, 'if he'd only stop drinking.'

Had this not been a true and honest account of my remembered life, I could have exaggerated my part in this ground-breaking drama. Claimed that I had played the leading role in it, that I had blown Tim and Malcolm off the screen, but I won't, because this is a true and honest account. Common sense prevails, of course, but any false claims would be impossible to disprove because TV shows weren't videoed in those days and all the tapes will have been destroyed. I do have a copy, though, of the *TV Times* for October 1967 with a moody picture of me on the front, and a quote from the *Daily Express* critic saying that I was 'The most promising TV newcomer of the year'. And so ended my brief but most promising career in television.

But you want to hear more about those knickers, don't you? I had decided early on to leave drawing, painting and design in the hands of Peter Blake, Patrick Hughes and other experts in the field. My left field would be a short poem, but the idea of knickers didn't really appeal, too flimsy for a start, and the thought of a young lady's mons Veneris cosying up to my words of genius put me into creative freeze-frame. Whenever I get a commission to write something that involves a deadline, I don't usually become motivated until the death threats start coming in. Now this was a commitment rather than a commission, but even so, time was running out and I couldn't crack the knicker problem. The answer, as it always does, lay close at hand.

A tip for the poet, painter, musician asked to create something new: re-create something old. Rummaging through my file of unpublished poems, odds and ends, bibs and bobs, I came across a verse I had written for a British Council touring exhibition in 2000 called 'Inside Out, Underwear and Style in the UK', which had been printed on a card and distributed to all the venues. Seemingly, there or an abundance, nay, a plethora, of hymns of praise in honour of ladies' lingerie, so the curator had specifically requested something about men's underwear, and here was a verse that cried out not for scanties, but for capacious white cotton boxer shorts. After various failed attempts with print and Letraset, I eventually wrote it out in my best joined-up writing using a laundry marker, and they were sold to the highest bidder on St Valentine's night for six hundred knicker.

THE MERSEY SOUND

Although 1967 was to prove, if not an *annus mirabilis*, at least an *annus* reasonably *bonum*, it began quietly, if not glumly. The fact that the Scaffold dirge '2 day's Monday' could be heard regularly on *Housewives' Choice* suggested that the group had lost direction and I had taken a very part-time post as lecturer in Liberal Studies at the Liverpool College of Art. It was Adrian Henri who had recommended me for the job and it was Arthur Ballard who was my boss. Having been canonised by his former student John Lennon, he was already a legend at the college, providing a role model for more than one generation of male students. Arthur looked more like a club bouncer than an artist, with a bald head like polished pumice stone, a thick neck and broad shoulders; he carried himself like the boxer he had been in his youth. Although I've no doubt he could have pursued a successful career as a doorman, his intelligence, sensitivity and skill with either pencil or brush led him to higher things. I rather suspect that he considered Liberal Studies a waste of time for his students, who wanted only to paint, drink and sculpt, but for a poet, he thought that I wasn't too fragrant or foppish, and welcomed me into the staffroom.

There were other good painters on the staff such as Maurice Cockrill, now Keeper at the Royal Academy, and

Sam Walsh who came over to Liverpool from County Wexford for the weekend and stayed for a lifetime that was far too short. Known among the fraternity as 'Spray it again Sam', his speciality was portraiture, and his huge heads of Francis Bacon, W. H. Auden and Paul McCartney (entitled 'Mike's brother') became iconic at the time. Hilary thinks there are far too many photographs and portraits of me around the house and I can see her point, but I'd hang on to the canvas that Sam painted during my Buddy Holly phase.

Even then I especially loved Adrian Henri's paintings and was always surprised at the way his colleagues refused to take his work seriously. It was to do, I believe, with his increasing success as a performing poet and occasional rock'n'roll singer, as much as his ability to charm the birds down from the trees and the media up from the metropolis. Inevitably, Arthur Ballard became increasingly cheesed off with Adrian's extra-curricular activities and gave him the choice: knuckle down and teach fine art, or go off and paint, have exhibitions, publish books, form a poetry-rock band and tour the world. Unsurprisingly, Adrian chose the latter. And just in time, for with the publication in May, of *Penguin Modern Poets 10*, life for three Liverpool poets would never be the same, and for my part, in a couple of months I went from being an occasional Scaffold performer and part-time lecturer to being a full-time poet-of-all-trades.

Because Thelma had found my constant toing and froing hard to take, life in her tiny flat had begun to feel claustro-phobic, so in the previous year I had sought temporary refuge in a room on the ground floor of Adrian's house in 64 Canning Street, with a view to leading the solitary life of an artist. So serious was I about my new vocation that I had a bookcase and small wardrobe brought over from my mother's house in Litherland, which I painted white to match the purity of my ambition. I would live the life of a monk, at least for a few hours during the afternoon, and, free from the fleshy chains that bind, write the great novel. I realised very quickly, however, that if I had to live alone, I could only do it with somebody else, preferably a woman, and within weeks I was talking to the wardrobe: '*Hey, that's a nice coat of paint you're wearing.*'

The best way to stop the wardrobe from answering back, I found, was to pick up pen and paper and start writing, and within weeks I had completed the book that would take the literary world if not by storm, then by a light drizzle. They say that everybody has one novel in them and for most people that's where it should stay, my own included, but I was young and seismic, and nothing beats saying 'I'm writing a novel' when asked 'What are you doing at the moment?' by a young lady, a fellow writer, or even a wardrobe.

On the whole I've been reasonably pleased with the titles of my books, from *Holiday on Death Row* to *Defying Gravity*, from *An Imaginary Menagerie* to *Bad, Bad Cats*, but where on earth did *Frinck, a Life in the Day of* come from? The short list of titles I originally came up with back in 1967 included 'Birdsong', 'One Hundred Years of Being on Your Own', 'The Deaf Watchmaker' and 'The Unbearable Lightness of Being Pissed', and I have often wondered whether the book would have achieved greater success if I'd plumped for one of those. However, Michael Joseph, the rather sedate firm lounging in Bloomsbury who had shown interest in publishing *Summer with Monika* but were not convinced that a sequence of love poems would attract a wide readership, decided to combine the two oeuvres, and on 5 June my first book was published. (Twenty-one shillings net. Hurry, there are a few copies remaining.)

Those of you who have had a book published will recall the pleasure of receiving a package from the publisher and tearing off the paper to reveal a brand-new copy of your own book. Those of you who have not had a book published will not be able to recall this. However, I remember being thrilled, and at the same time disappointed because of the garish cover and the photograph on the back of me looking supercilious. Examining the cover now, I can see that it's witty in a crude, laddish sort of way (a colour photograph of a big-busted girl holding a glass tankard of beer to the lips of a cartoon face painted on her T-shirt), whereas I had hoped for something more lyrical, a soft-focus image, perhaps, that recaptured the maiden lolling immodestly beside a lake in Sweden.

And incidentally, neither Brian, Adrian nor I liked the original Penguin *Mersey Sound* cover, which featured black-and-white photographs of a teenage girl screaming orgasmically and *Yellow Submarine*-type typography that we considered too close to the pop music scene. Given the chance, we would have ditched the reference to the sound of Mersey beat and gone for something more austere and becoming to Byron, Shelley and Wordsworth setting out on that lonely road. But as a young writer you have no say in what the cover looks like, which was just as well in the case of Penguin Marketing.

A few slim volumes later I became exalted enough to be consulted by the publisher regarding the cover, and after one incident began to insist on early and closer involvement.

In 1972 I submitted to Jonathan Cape a manuscript of poems called *Gig*, the title referring to a section of verse written when I was out on the road performing with a recently formed band of poets and musicians known as Grimms. In retrospect, it wasn't a good title because lazy reviewers assumed sniffily that all the poems had been written in the back of a transport van or in a motorway caff. They weren't, they were written, as you would expect, with a nice cup of tea and a Hob-nob, at home in tranquil recollection. One day I received a call from on high telling me that the cover was ready to go to print, and if I was visiting London would I like to call in and give it the once-over. I happened to be down there so I popped along to the office in Bedford Square. Until then I'd been lucky: Ed Victor had guided me through *Watchwords*, followed by Susannah Clapp, who worked closely with me on *After the Merrymaking*, but both had left Cape to find greater glory as agent and theatre critic, and the person brought in to oversee *Gig*, to encourage the Muse, offer suggestions, make cuts, correct spelling, etc. decided instead to quit publishing and ride horses on her farm in Sussex. And so it was with some trepidation that I entered the design office of this august publishing house. In his defence, it has to be said that mine host had probably not read the book, but was pretending that he had for my sake. He picked up the proposed cover from the chief designer's desk and with a flourish held it out before me. 'Good, isn't it?'

What he was holding was a photograph of a tall, elderly man, obviously Irish, wearing a black suit and dancing with a little girl in a white frock. In the background were a marquee, a fiddler and a few glowering onlookers.

'Just right, don't you think?'

'I'm sorry, I don't get it.'

'Jig, they're dancing a jig.'

As the girls in the office turned to the wall and stuffed paperclips into their mouths to stifle their giggles, I explained the difference between a jig and a gig. But our man snatched another photograph from the designer's desk. 'That's our cover,' he declaimed. 'That's our cover.' Paperclips ricocheted off walls as everyone in the design department cheered and applauded. And so the portrait that Sophie Baker had taken of the author on Hampstead Hill for the passport-photo-size inset on the back cover was upgraded. Gig? I'm sorry now I didn't use the first title I thought of, 'Eats, shoots and exits'.

Both *The Mersey Sound* and *Frinck, a Life in the Day of, and Summer with Monika* were pre-empted by the publication in March 1967 of *The Liverpool Scene*, a glossy hardback featuring not only work by Brian, Ade and me, but also by Pete Brown, Spike Hawkins, Henry Graham, Mike Evans and Adrian's girlfriend at the time, Heather Holden. With moody photographs of the poets against stark urban wasteland-scapes, and an introduction by the eminent poet and critic Edward Lucie-Smith, who compared us all favourably with Rimbaud and Baudelaire, it reminded me of a book that had really fired my imagination seven years earlier, *The Beat Scene* edited by Elias Wilentz: 'America's new literary generation in photographs and with an extensive selection of their prose and poetry, including previously unpublished poems by Jack Kerouac, Allen Ginsberg, Frank O'Hara and many others . . .'

Twenty-three years old and teaching in Liverpool? What

was I doing when I could be over there in Greenwich Village reading at the Gas Light Café with Diane Di Prima, helping Ted Joans scrawl '*Le sang des Poètes*' on the wall of his Astor Place studio, sharing a few cold beers with Jack, Allen, Gregory (and a girl called Hazel on page 55)? My poems were as good as theirs, I thought, and my spelling was a whole lot better. Over the years I did get to meet some of the poets who remain youthful and enshrined in Fred McDarrah's black-and-white photographs: Ginsberg, of course, and Ted Joans who read with us at the Traverse Theatre one Edinburgh Festival (no longer throwing wild parties in his Astor Place studio, he had rediscovered his African roots and was living in Timbuctoo), Marvin Cohen, Robert Creeley, Kenneth Koch who became a good friend following a wild week at the Kuala Lumpur World Poetry Reading in 1992, and Lawrence Ferlinghetti.

Remember *American Beauty*? Not the film but the travel series I did with Pete McCarthy for Radio 4? For the second programme we visited San Francisco to include a segment about the Beats which included a trip to the City Lights Bookshop. Although in his eighties, Lawrence Ferlinghetti was still a big, handsome fellow with clear blue eyes and a kitbag full of stories which he enjoyed spinning as he led me round the shop, pausing in front of posters advertising past readings, and the cash till that Gregory Corso had thrown through the window and made off with when he had worked there. (Although angry, he had taken the fallen angel back. 'Whatever Gregory did, we always forgave him.') At ease in front of a microphone, he'd made the tour countless times for countless radio and TV programmes. When we'd finished recording, Sarah-Jane, the producer, asked Lawrence if he'd mind having his photograph taken with me outside the bookshop for BBC publicity. He'd be delighted, but first he'd put on a black baseball cap with the City Lights logo. In between poses I remarked on how the cap suited him.

'Hey, would you like one, Roger?'

'Oh, thanks very much, that would be great.'

'And how about a bookbag? We do a great bookbag too with the City Lights logo.'

'Even better.'

He took me back inside and said to the young man behind the counter: 'Wrap up a cap and a bookbag for our poetry friend here, come all the way from England.' Then he turned back to me: 'That'll be twenty-four dollars.'

The publisher of *The Liverpool Scene*, Donald Carroll, had been born and brought up in the USA and was familiar with the Beats. He was a bespectacled cyclone of energy who launched the book on a French kiss of publicity. As it had been dedicated (by Donald, I assume) 'To the Beatles, without whom . . . etc.' and featured a photograph of Ringo in his underpants on page one, the launch party was held at the Cavern where a local band, the Almost Blues, played, champagne flowed, and cameras whirred as art college beauties jived and twisted the night away with journalists shipped up from London. BUBBLY RUNS OUT AT 'IN' PARTY ran a headline in the *Daily Express* of 4 March 1967, which noted that among the guests were three Liverpool MPs and city council officials, who 'rubbed shoulders with long-haired artists, some wearing wingèd collars and cravats, and mini-skirted girls'.

While Adrian had the time of his life, Brian and I felt

uneasy about the razzmatazz because, although the publicity was exciting, we suspected that once the kissing stopped, some of the reviewers might start chucking their wormy apples. Which many did, in some cases with the branches attached. Thus the Liverpool Poet was born, or as one so wittily put it, 'The three-headed pantomime horse'.

With Brian's first book of poems, *Little Johnny's Confessions*, due to be published by Allen & Unwin around this time, he decided to distance himself by slipping out of the horse costume and leaving the stage. In his own words he 'buggered off to Winchester . . . lived as cheap as I could really. Like a poet.' Although admiring the Keatsian purity of Brian's vision, I decided to stay where the champagne was and on 15 March the corks were popping on the opening night at the Everyman Theatre of my play *The Commission*. Disappointingly, the event proved to be a waste of champagne, but it was great fun to do and anyway, there was no time to wallow in a swill of self-pity, for no sooner had the run started than I was invited down to London by the impresario and film producer Oscar Lowenstein.

McGOUGH, McGEAR AND HENDRIX

I was met at Euston Station by a chauffeur-driven Bentley and whisked off to the film studios in Twickenham to meet Dick Lester, who was in search of a writer to complete a film script that Joe Orton had been working on when he had left Islington for the great cottage in the sky. At this point the Beatles were interested in being involved and I seemed to be the right man for the job, even though I had no experience of scriptwriting. He and Oscar Lowenstein even showed me the small office on the compound where I would put in my eight hours a day. I sensed that Dick Lester would be a tough cookie and I'd find difficulty in arguing my corner, but Oscar was so pleasant I could have taken him home, sprayed him gold and put him on the mantelpiece. Eventually I was given a copy of the script and chauffeured back to Euston. It was a heady experience as I daydreamed the life of a screenwriter, the first rung of a ladder that reached up to the Hollywood of loose cars, fast bucks and big women. Or something like that. Then I read the script of *Up Against It* and couldn't make head or tail of it.

For a long time I pretended to myself that my reasons for turning down the chance of a lifetime were entirely altruistic, in that I didn't want to break up the Scaffold. It was mainly, though, because I was frightened. Frightened of failure, of Dick Lester, of small office with typewriter, of living in London with no wardrobe to talk to. I don't know if it's a failing peculiar to Merseysiders, but I have known so many young people, musicians in particular, who turned down offers to work in London. On the point of signing the contract, they'd opt out and hightail it back to the Liverwomb. As fortune would have it, I probably made the right decision in saying no to the gold bullion because Orton's script was a beast that several writers more experienced than I failed to tame, and eventually the project fizzled out.

'DRUG-CRAZED HIPPIES IN SEX ORGY' headlined an article in the *News of the World* in August of that year, illustrated with a photograph of me wearing one of Thelma's creations, a *Sergeant Peppery* kaftan, standing alongside John Gorman in a military band tunic and a priest's biretta. Nowadays, of course, litigation would have followed, with John and me awarded huge sums for the embarrassment caused by the misrepresentation, but we were tickled pink to see a photograph of ourselves in a national newspaper, even if it had been taken a week earlier at the Alexandra Palace where the Scaffold had compèred a benefit concert for the *International Times* magazine. Presumably Michael had been cut out of the photograph because he didn't look orgiastic enough. Appearing at the Ally Pally with the Crazy World of Arthur Brown and at the UFO club with Pink Floyd, the Scaffold might seem to have been spearheading the psychedelic revolution as the merry pranksters of the English hippie movement, but in truth we were floundering. A change of musical direction was needed and as in a technicolor dream, salvation arrived in the form of Paul McCartney who took a few days off, between recording *Sergeant Pepper's Lonely Hearts Club Band* and setting out on the Magical Mystery Tour, to produce an album with his brother and me. We wanted to do something based around the *Summer with Monika* sequence featuring Andy Roberts's guitar alongside poems, a few songs and a couple of Mike's faux surreal stories, and there was no room for John's subversive clowning. *McGough & McGear* was recorded in two days at the De Lane Lee Studios in Holborn the day after I turned down Joe Orton.

When the Scaffold worked in London we stayed in hotels, the one nearest to Euston Station preferably, to enable a quick getaway back north, but if it was just Mike and me, and Paul was away, then we'd stay at Paul's house in St John's Wood. Comfortable and luxurious though it was, with a Warhol and a Magritte on the walls, you quickly came to realise the price paid. There were never less than twenty people outside the front gate, day and night, fans who would scream whenever music was heard within the house (even though it might have been Radio 1), a light was switched on in an upstairs window, or there were footsteps on the gravel. Photographers patrolled Cavendish Avenue two by two like cops on the beat. For me, it was fun pretending to be a friend of a Beatle, because I knew that in a few days I'd be on the train and back to reality, but for Mike it wasn't so easy, being the younger brother of somebody unimaginably famous. One minute you're fighting over the last slice of Swiss roll and the next he's sending you air tickets to see him in concert in Los Angeles. In the early days it was bad enough . . .

(*Enter photographer from local newspaper*)

PHOTOGRAPHER   Right, Scaffolds, this shouldn't take long. Which of you is the Beatle's brother?

JOHN   Me.

PHOTOGRAPHER   Right, you go in the middle. Which Beatle is it?

JOHN   Ringo.

PHOTOGRAPHER   Thought so. Big smile now.

But as the Scaffold's fame grew, so life became more embarrassing for Mike and in a gallant but vain attempt to escape his brother's shadow he adopted McGear as a stage name.

(*Enter photographer from national newspaper*)

PHOTOGRAPHER   Right, lads, this shouldn't take long. How's your Paul doing, Mike?

MIKE   Fine.

PHOTOGRAPHER   Good, then if you'd just stand in the middle and the other two take a couple paces back. Bit further back . . . bit more, and if you could crouch down a bit . . . lower . . . maybe on one knee looking up at Mike.

MIKE (*with righteous passion*)   Excuse me, we're a group. You take the three of us together or not at all!

PHOTOGRAPHER   Sorry, Mike, sorry.

Earlier this year I was contacted by the perspicacious manager of an Oxfam shop in Henley-on-Thames who, when sifting through a bunch of albums that had been dropped off in a black bin liner, came across one with a photograph of two little garden gnomes on the front cover and a lot of handwriting on the back. Was some of the handwriting mine? It was. Was the rest of the handwriting Michael's? It was. Was the Jimi we were thanking for playing on the album Jimi Hendrix? It was. *McGough & McGear* was subsequently taken off the shelf, put up for auction at the Marquee Club and raised a thousand pounds for Oxfam. Thirty-seven years earlier, as producer of this gift to charity, Paul had been able to call on some of the best musicians around who were more than happy to sit about, share a few spliffs and strum/hum/drum/blow as required: Dave Mason of Traffic, Graham Nash, prior to leaving the Hollies and seeking his fortune with Crosby & Stills, John Mayall as well as Hendrix, who brought along his drummer Mitch Mitchell and bassist Noel Reading for the experience. Even Paul's girlfriend at the time, Jane Asher, invited her mother to one of the sessions where she sang and swung with the best of them. There was something quite magical about turning up at the studio at lunchtime with a little poem called 'Ex-Art Student' and at three the following morning listening to a song transformed by a shy guitarist known as 'The Wild Man of Pop'.

For contractual reasons, none of the musicians could be named, but when the record was launched in May 1968 at EMI, the former Beatles Press Officer, Derek Taylor, handed out a press release naming those who took part. As well as those listed above, other musicians included Spencer Davis, Paul Samwell-Smith (Yardbirds), Zoot Money, Barry Fantoni, Mike Hart, Gary Leeds (Walker Brothers) and Viv Prince (Pretty Things). Fun though it was, making the album reinforced my feelings of being a stranger at my own party, for once these guys picked up an instrument and conversed through music I became the dumbstruck outsider, the table-tennis player adrift on a beach volleyball court. Despite being well reviewed by the music press – indeed, it was *Melody Maker*'s Album of the Month – *McGough & McGear* never made it to platinum. Or gold, or silver, or tin, although, of course, it did make it to black plastic, as in bin liner. How it got there remains a mystery, although Jimi did have a girlfriend who lived in the Henley-on-Thames area who might have cleaned out the garage and missed the collector's item. If only that album could talk, what a story it might tell!

After being pressed, I left the factory and was dispatched, along with five of my brothers, to Mr Michael McCartney's house on the Wirral, where I was inscribed by him and another gentleman before being posted to an address in London. I had rather hoped that my new owner, Mr Hendrix, would put me on the record player and listen to me, but instead he stood me on a shelf with hundreds of my fellows, all of whom I found to be loud and arrogant. I was to remain there, unopened and unplayed, for several years until one morning I was taken down by my owner and presented to a young lady. You can imagine my excitement when she took me to her flat in Henley-on-Thames where she undressed me and laid me on the turntable. I was soon in a spin, what a spin I was in. Round and round I went, the needle working that old black magic, when suddenly . . . You can imagine my disappointment when only halfway through the first track I was taken off, put back in my sleeve and pushed into the musty darkness of a cupboard containing shoes, magazines and old toys, where I was to remain for three score and seven years. Now, of course, I am famous thanks to the lady in the shop who rescued this poor foundling from death by recycling. My new owner wears purple loons and an anorak, and at least once a week, usually at weekends, he takes me down, wipes my sleeve and kisses me before putting me back on the shelf. Am I happy? At least I'm content, although I still wrestle with that one big philosophical question: What do I sound like?

In the summer of 1967 as China exploded its first H bomb, summit talks began between US President Lyndon Johnson and Soviet Premier Kosygin, homosexuality was legalised in Britain and *Fiddler on the Roof* played in the West End, I rehearsed and filmed the series *Sat'day While Sunday* with Tim Dalton, Malcolm McDowell and company. (I hope you haven't forgotten about that 'Most promising TV newcomer' quote in the *Daily Express*, it means a lot to me.) The drift away from the Scaffold seemed increasingly on the cards, particularly as I was spending more and more time in London working on scripts for *At the Eleventh Hour*, a late-night politico-satirical show for the BBC scheduled for the new year, as well as popping along to the TVC studio in Soho to start work on the script for *The Yellow Submarine*. Then, on 4 November, 'Thank U Very Much' was released.

THANK U VERY MUCH

Thank U Very Much was the title Mike McCartney chose for his autobiography, and as titles and catchphrases go it's hard to beat. According to its author, he came up with the idea for the song when he was on the phone to Paul thanking him for the birthday gift of a Nikon camera, but by the time he sang the first version to John and me, the camera had given way to an Aintree Iron, Gertie the girl with the Garston gong, and something about a Fazakerly fishcake. We played around with the lyrics to extract all references to Liverpool suburbia (save one), for obviously it was a song with the potential of appealing to an audience worldwide. So in came the *Sunday Times,* 'Our gracious team' and the 'napalm bomb', as well as the 'family circle', meaning Mum, Dad and the kids, which prompted Huntley and Palmer to send us each a tin of their 'Family Circle' biscuits as a little thank you for promoting their brand. (With a little fore-thought we might have been better off giving thanks for Jaguar cars, Philips TV sets and Glenmorangie whisky, but we weren't to know.) And even though John and I threw in our tuppence worth, it was very much Mike's creation and all credit, then, must go to him. As well as PRS, of course, publishing and mechanical royalties, together with all ensuing advertising and commercial revenue. George

Martin was our producer at the Abbey Road Studios and within a month of its release in November 1967 it reached number four in the charts and we were on *Top of the Pops*.

The single reference to a Liverpool placename we kept in the song was the 'Aintree Iron' and if there's one question I'm always being asked (apart from 'Why poetry?' 'Where do you get your ideas from?' and 'How did you manage to keep your affair with Michelle Pfeiffer a secret for so long?') it is 'What is the Aintree Iron?' Usually there's somebody on hand who will wink conspiratorially and announce, 'It's Brian Epstein, isn't it? Rhyming slang, iron hoof – poof?' Or, 'It's Tommy Smith, isn't it? Used to play centre-half for Liverpool?' Or, 'It's Aintree Racecourse, isn't it?' Whatever answer is on offer I'm only too happy to concur. But if you're of a certain age, interested in pop music ephemera and would genuinely like to know the answer to a problem that has puzzled generations for nearly forty years, you will certainly be looking forward to finding it in the second volume of this autobiography whose working title is 'The Aintree Iron, Myth or Mythology?'.

The prime minister of the day, Harold Wilson, was not amused by a lyric I had written for a pugnacious BBC television documentary called *Yesterday's Men*, which was turned into the theme song and sung by the Scaffold. It began:

> *Like Humpty-Dumpty, he sat on a wall*
> *Giving the orders and then*
> *In the midst of it all, he had a great fall*
> *Now he's one of yesterday's men.*

The MP for Huyton let it be known that he found the song personally offensive, so plans for 'Yesterday's Men' to be the catchy follow-up to our surprise hit were ditched. The irony is that he had previously named 'Thank U Very Much' as his favourite record, so I have the dubious achievement of being associated with a prime minister's most-liked and most-hated song.

What was wonderful about the sixties was the way class barriers came tumbling down. Isn't that right? A whiff of patchouli plaited with marijuana, communal changing rooms at Biba, working-class photographers and rock stars cavorting with toffs, it was time to garage the tumbrils and dismantle the scaffold. Not the 'fresh, highly original, self-sufficient comedy unit', of course, for I like to think that in our own small way we helped bridge the class divide as the following vignette illustrates.

We were invited one evening to perform at the Savoy Hotel. It was all quite hush-hush and we were given few details of the event until the day before. All we knew was that we were to sing 'Thank U Very Much' at a private dinner party in honour of Sir Tommy Sopwith, the pioneer aviator and designer of the Sopwith Camel, the First World War fighter plane.

'Shall we do a few other songs as well?' we asked.

'No, just the one song, it's his favourite apparently.'

'How about a couple of funny sketches, perhaps with a Great War theme?'

'No.'

'I could write a poem in his honour?'

'Just the song.'

So we duly turned up with five session musicians and

asked to see the stage where we could set up and sound check.

'Stage? Oh, dear me, no,' said Jocelyn Stevens, then editor of *Queen* magazine and our contact for the evening. 'You'll be doing your thing here,' ('here' being a chintzy sitting room) 'and when supper is over the guests will wander through and, once they're settled, Lady Sopwith will wheel Tommy in. It's his eightieth birthday today and he's no idea that you're here and so it will be a wonderful surprise.'

Left to our own devices for a couple of hours, we mimed a rehearsal, made short work of the sandwiches and watched television with the sound turned off, until near enough to midnight the audience drifted in. I use the word 'audience' in its narrowest sense in that the performers outnumbered it. Jocelyn Stevens brought Sir Max Aitken over to say hello but there was no time for further introductions as the door opened and a wheelchair taxied down the runway.

> *One, two, three and . . .*
> *Thank you very much for the Sopwith Camel*
> *Thank you very much*
> *Thank you very, very, very much.*

At first it was all too much for the great man, who was nonplussed, thinking perhaps that a gang of burglars, caught on the job, had burst into song. But once his wife had reassured him he joined in the chorus and insisted we sang it again;

> *Thank you very much for the Sopwith Pup . . .*
> *Sopwith Tabloid . . .*

Sopwith Snipe . . .
Sopwith Dolphin . . .
Sopwith Salamander . . .

(We'd certainly done our homework.)

Thank you very, very, very much.

Flushed with triumph we were introduced to the Sopwiths, Princess Alexandra and Angus Ogilvie while the champagne circulated and the conversation sparkled. Which brings me back to my point about hurdling over those class barriers. I mean, their lord- and ladyships could have said, 'Right, you lot, here's your money, now piss off back up north where you belong.' But they didn't. No, they were more than happy to let us stay in their company for twenty minutes or so. Well, fifteen, but it was getting late. Thank you very much.

THE YELLOW SUBMARINE

I am holding a 'Client remittance advice' from Hope Leresche dated 19 September 1968 which reads:

Fee in payment for story boards and dialogue of *THE YELLOW SUBMARINE* $1000 = £417 10 9
Less Commission   41 15 1
Less Bank charges   15 6
Total   £375 0 2

The making of the Beatles' animated classic would make an intriguing film in itself and has indeed spawned a number of books, the best of which is *Inside the Yellow Submarine* by the heroically named Dr Robert R. Hieronimus. The Beatles' contract with United Artists required them to make three films, two of which, *A Hard Day's Night* and *Help!*, came out in 1964 and 1965, but in the following year, as their music transported them into the stratosphere, they were disinclined to take time off and rejected all the scripts that came their way. Enter Al Brodax, a New Yorker wearing an Hawaiian shirt and smoking a fat cigar. As head of King Features he had produced a highly successful cartoon series, *The Beatles,* that was broadcast only in America, and he persuaded Brian Epstein to let him make a full-length animated cartoon, which would free the lads to sit at the feet of the maharishi in India while at the same time fulfilling their contract with United Artists.

Suspicious of anything that wasn't their own idea and having disliked the US cartoon series for reasons that Brodax openly admits to – 'The Beatles didn't like the caricatures and they also objected to the fact that I had American voice-overs. Because it was difficult for Americans, in my experience, to understand Englishmen. They tend to have a mouth full of marbles . . .' – the Beatles assumed a King Features full-length animation would be another candyfloss rip-off and decided to have as little to do with it as possible. The fact that they were won over eventually, and indeed regretted not having involved themselves more closely, has almost everything to do with a small band of artists at TV Cartoons in London.

TVC producers John Coates and George Dunning had not enjoyed the experience of churning out the weekly half-hour *Beatles* cartoons, so when Brodax offered them the opportunity to make a full-length feature they put the newly released *Sergeant Pepper* on the turntable and determined to look for an illustrator who could visualise the music in terms of graphic art. The man they found was a Czechoslovakian-born illustrator, Heinz Edelmann, whose designs helped shape the plot and direction, and who inspired all those who worked around him, myself included.

I was brought in to the project early one morning very late in the day, if that's chronogrammatically feasible, because all the Brits at TVC felt that the script was far too American. There is an adage that 'movies are not written – but *rewritten*', and by the time I arrived on the scene there had already been numerous writers, rewriters and script consultants hired, fired, dismembered and buried in wet concrete. There was also a sense of panic orchestrated by King Features, who wanted to speed up production for fear that by the time the film was released the Beatles' glory days would be well and truly over. The late Erich Segal, a former Professor of Classics at Harvard and author of *Love Story*, had finished what he considered to be the final treatment, and his script was passed on to me with instructions to rewrite the Beatles' dialogue and inject some Liverpudlian humour. As my job description seemed to imply little more than a few days' script doctoring, my agent was happy to agree to the $1,000 fee and no screen credit, whereas $1 and a credit would have been the better deal, because the writers' residuals would have bought me that massive ranch in Montana, the one I've always dreamed of.

At first I worked directly from Segal's script, having no idea of how the characters were evolving in the animation studios. I took the dialogue line by line and whenever the Beatles sounded like the Bowery boys or the Goodfellas I would take them by the scruff of the vowels and drag them back to the Pier Head. George Dunning, a quiet, dignified Canadian, was the film's director and it was his genius that elevated a simple cartoon film to a production that the Beatles eventually embraced. After reading my revisions and laughing at the jokes, he invited me to the studios in Soho Square to work directly with the animators, particularly Bob Balser and Jack Stokes who were devising scenes like 'The Sea of Monsters' that weren't in any of the original scripts. Occasionally J, P, G and Ringo would whizz into the Dean Street office for a swift viewing on the moviola, say a few whizzy things and whizz out. Although John was to claim later that the vacuum cleaner monster had been his idea, the 200 people who worked on the film denied it.

When it comes to making a cartoon, the recorded voice track is the horse that comes before the cart carrying the animators, and as the Beatles didn't fancy climbing into any saddles, George Dunning was keen to find actors who could impersonate them. Paul Angelis provided the lugubrious voice of Ringo, Geoff Hughes, another friend from Liverpool who wouldn't be mistaken for McCartney in a police line-up, played Paul, John Clive got to be John Lennon and Peter Batten came in at number four. Rumour has it that the producers were having a few drinks in the crew's local, the Dog and Duck, after a hard day auditioning unsuccessfully for somebody to voice George Harrison, when they heard the man himself talking loudly on the other side of the bar. And you're right, it wasn't George, it was Peter. To this day, who is to say that Batten's girlfriend at the time, a woman who was working for TVC on the film, didn't whisper: *'Hey Pete, look who's just come in after a hard day auditioning unsuccessfully for somebody to voice George Harrison. Go on, do your impersonation . . . Louder! . . . Oh, good, I think they're coming over.'*

The great twist to the story is that not only was Peter Batten not an actor, but he was a deserter from a British Army barracks in Germany. As he told the *Sunday Telegraph* in 1999:

It was all very strange. One minute I'm a soldier on the run, the next I'm meeting the Beatles and bumping into actors like Peter O'Toole. All that and

I was being paid fifty quid an hour thirty years ago. It was brilliant. There was some whingeing from some people because I wasn't a member of Equity, the actors' union, but overall I felt very lucky.

Lucky indeed, although the company weren't so lucky when he was hauled off by military police in the middle of recording the dialogue track, and Paul Angelis had to step in and complete the remaining lines of George's character. With an aversion to 'mouth-marbles' verging on the paranoid, Brodax worried throughout the recordings about the actors' voices being indecipherable in upstate Buffalo, but Dunning was insistent on keeping the Mersey sound, although, as Paul Angelis recalls, 'We spoke very, very slow.'

Needless to say, spending time in the studios, I was to become aware of the various tensions between the 'Yanks' and the 'Brits', or the producers and the creators, but considering the deadline to which everyone was working, friction was inevitable and I feel honoured to have been involved in the making of a classic, even if my part in the creative process has been kept a closely guarded secret. Until this year, in fact, when Walker Books published *Yellow Submarine* and on the title page it says:

Story adapted by Charlie Gardner from the screenplay by Lee Minoff, Al Brodax, Jack Mendelsohn and Erich Segal.
With thanks to Roger McGough.

So in the end it all worked out happily. I mean, what would I do on a massive ranch in Montana?

AT THE ELEVENTH HOUR

Discretion is the better part of Valerie
though all of her is nice
lips as warm as strawberries
eyes as cold as ice
the very best of everything
only will suffice
not for her potatoes
and puddings made of rice.

I remember half waking one morning in the sun-filled bedroom of a house in north London and listening to the first four lines of the poem 'Discretion' repeating in my head as clearly as if they were being broadcast on the radio. Having satisfied myself that there was no radio in the room and that I hadn't overheard anybody else saying them, I got up, made coffee and wrote the first draft of the poem in one sitting. It's a rare occurrence when a poem gifts itself to the brain in that way. Had it simply offered up reworking of 'Discretion is the better part of valour' that might have been the end of it, an amusing turn of cliché, but in this case Valerie appeared not only fully formed as a character, but humming a tune and carrying a rhyming scheme . . . 'nice, ice, suffice, ice, vice, trice' . . . all those 's's, the serpent in the Garden of Eden. All I had to do was pick up a pen and follow instructions.

> *Valerie is corruptible*
> *but known to be discreet*
> *Valerie rides a silver cloud*
> *Where once she walked the street.*

runs the last verse, which I thought rounded off the portrait of a high-class hooker, until I had a letter from a writers' group in Hampshire wondering if I could settle a little argument for them. Could I explain what the poet was getting at in the last verse, because half of the group believed that 'Valerie rides a silver cloud' suggested that she was in heaven and that 'Discretion' was, in fact, a love poem about necrophilia.

The house in Kilburn belonged to Anthony Smith, later President of Magdalen College, and head of the British Film Institute, but then the young producer of *At the Eleventh Hour*, the BBC's satirical programme that went out live on Saturday nights beginning in January 1968. The cast included Richard Neville, one of the founders of *Oz* magazine, Miriam Margolyes, having stepped straight out of the Cambridge Footlights and still blinking, as well as a journalist who, despite his orientation, played the straight man. Ray Davies, loosening the ties that bound him to the Kinks, provided a topical song and I wrote a sketch each week for the Scaffold, becoming quickly aware of the limitations of having to include three male characters every time. (Unlike the Pythons, we wouldn't be seen dead wearing women's clothes.) I was also commissioned to write and perform a poem relating to the week's events. By Tuesday I would have written a poem about the subject that Tony had chosen and sent it down from Liverpool. He was always enthusiastic about it, but when I arrived at the BBC's Lime Grove Studios on Thursday he would have cooled: 'Really fine piece of work, Roger, but . . . well, perhaps too personal . . . Too poetic. Besides, we're not doing the devaluation of the pound this week; instead, we'll be looking at student unrest in Poland.'

Tony had kindly invited me to stay over at his house while in London writing and rehearsing, but inevitably, whenever Saturday loomed large and threatening, I would not have written the dreaded poem and so would lock myself into a dressing room with my Muse (the one called 'Panikos') and would not emerge until I had the requisite number of verses. Tony's assistant and the PA on the programme was a bright slip of a girl called Esther Rantzen who, despite being just down from Oxford (or because of it), had the Scaffold sitting up straight and minding their 'p's and 'q's in a way that grown men, looming large and threatening, had never managed to do. It was she who would come to my dressing room with a sandwich and a cup of tea at midday with instructions from the control box that after a timing of the first run-through, the programme was short by four minutes ten seconds, so that was how long the poem should be, only to return later in the afternoon with the news that Ray Davies would be repeating a chorus and so the poem should be cut to two minutes twenty.

I was never fazed by the discipline of writing to order under that sort of pressure and always managed to turn out verse that worked when performed live on camera, although I have to confess that the weaker the poem, the more time I'd spend in wardrobe picking out a natty outfit and the longer I'd spend in make-up. While some of my efforts written at the eleventh hour were never to see the printed page, others were to form the core of my first book to be published by Cape in 1969, *Watchwords*, which at my request they stopped reprinting in 1983 because the only poems that were still breathing were ones that had never seen the inside of a television studio.

Luckily the Scaffold were able to escape the confines of the studios for a few hours each week when the sketches were filmed on location, somewhere exotic like on the pavement in Lime Grove, or outside a pub in Shepherd's Bush. Our director was a young man who always looked as if he'd been partying into the early hours and rushed to the set straight from the arms of a pouting Turkish belly dancer. No doubt totally unkind and untrue, and for all Stephen Frears's rumpled wistfulness, we got along so well that he was later to be immortalised in the Scaffold's most famous song:

> *Stephen Frears had sticky-out ears*
> *And they made him awful shy.*
> *So they gave him medicinal compound*
> *Now he's learning how to fly.*

For the record (not the vinyl), Stephen's ears were perfectly formed and much admired by those who worked with him on both sides of the camera. And while we're being honest, I think that Mike, John and I couldn't help but be disappointed in the years that followed that, having learned his trade with us on the streets of Shepherd's Bush, he never offered us roles, even small cameo parts in any of the films he directed. *High Fidelity* might have been written for us and *My Beautiful Laundrette* would have provided just the challenge we enjoyed.

Ridley Scott is another famous film director who worked with us, and surprisingly failed to spot the Hollywood potential. We spent a couple of days together on the Thames near Maidenhead, filming a TV commercial for Watney's Beer. It was in early March and the sun was as watery and pale as the ale whose virtues we extolled to the tune of 'Lily the Pink'. We spent most of the time in our white suits, punting up and down the river through a fog of green smoke pumped out from the banks, lit from above by a lighting rig on loan from Wembley Stadium, and it felt most of the time as if we were crossing the Mekong Delta. Even though Watney's Pale was perhaps the only beer we found undrinkable, we acted our little thermal socks off and the clients were duly pleased with the commercial. Moreover we three men in a boat, having got along famously with the young director, looked forward to working with him again. For some reason it was not to be. And although a great film, am I the only one who believes that *Alien* would have been even more successful had it included a couple of scenes in which three Scousers say funny things and perhaps sing a song or two?

LILY THE PINK

If you ever get the chance, write a song that gets to number one in the charts and then appear on *Top of the Pops*. It's great fun. Writing novelty songs was still something of a novelty for me in those days, but following the success of 'Thank U Very Much', the pressure was on for the group to provide a follow-up. At first we toyed with titles like 'Thanks a Million' and 'Ta Ever So', before deciding on 'Do you Remember', a summer-of-love kind of toe-tapper that began:

> *Do do do do do you remember*
> *Do do do do do you recall*
> *The day we went out into the country*
> *Just to get away from it all*

Although they were very much like myself, naïve and sentimental, I still retain a fondness for the lyrics, which prescribed the tempo and almost wrote the music. Mike crooned the verses save one, which I voiced in the manner of a lovelorn poet, and into the middle eight we introduced a soft-shoe shuffle for John to perform on stage, for whenever we made a record it was always with theatre performance in mind, not a sound policy, as it turned out, because although Mike looked like a singer, I could pass for a poet and John was hilarious hoofing about on stage, we weren't visible on record and 'Do You Remember' became only a minor hit. The pressure was on, if we didn't come up quickly with big seller it would be back to the ladies' hairdressers for Mike, the circus for John and the classroom for me. Luckily for us all, Lydia E. Pinkham, the inventor of a vegetable compound 'For relieving hot flashes and certain other symptoms associated with "Change of Life" (Menopause) and cramps and other distress of monthly periods (Menstruation) not due to organic disease. Acts as a uterine sedative' was to provide the unlikely inspiration. I remember joining in the drunken chorus of 'Lily the Pink' on the coach after university cricket matches and in the student bar, but I could never bring myself to sing any of the outrageously rude verses. It was also one of the songs that would lift Scaffold spirits on the way home from a gig in the Black Country, with Hewo at the wheel beeping time on the car horn, while achieving a syncopatic effect using the windscreen wipers.

If I had kept a journal rather than an appointments diary, Friday 21 June 1968 might have read:

Two o'clock this afternoon we're off to Aintree Motors, to open the new forecourt (providing space for an extra 200 second-hand cars in excellent condition) by singing 'Thank U Very Much for Aintree Motors'. Pick up cheque and make a run for it. Saturday and Sunday we're playing Bradford University. We'll do our two-hour show of sketches and sing maybe three songs (including the new one, 'Do You Remember?'). Train down to London on Tuesday for production meeting with Norrie Paramor at EMI about our next single, and a fifteen-minute spot in the anti-apartheid concert at the Albert Hall next evening. (Looking forward to meeting Sammy Davis Jr.) Back up to Liverpool for gig in St Helens, then grab poetry hat and head back down to London on Sunday for Late Night Line-Up *with Joan Bakewell on BBC 2. Back oop north for cabaret in Southport on Tuesday, followed by* The Basil Brush Show *at TV Centre in London the following day.*

Had I kept a journal in those days, the title 'Up and Down Like a Blue-arsed Fly' might have been appropriate, but now I can understand why I never did: I wouldn't have had the time to fill it in. Sadly, I can't remember my meeting with Sammy Davis Jr, nor my brush with Basil, but the recollection of my appearance on *Late Night Line-Up* still brings an apricot tinge to my finely chiselled cheekbones. This rather highbrow, but popular, programme went out live every Sunday evening and consisted of a number of guests discussing the arts and various topics of the day with Joan Bakewell. I was very flattered to be invited, to be admitted to the inner sanctum of cosmopolitan trendsetters. I did worry, though, as I nibbled my BR cheese sandwich on the journey down, if I would be able to hold my own among the intellectuals whose wit and erudition refracted like a diamanté rainbow into our living rooms each week. In a word, would my *mots* be *bons* enough? Maybe they'd invited me by mistake, or I imagined an even worse scenario: one of the producers is a poet whose verse has been rejected by Penguin and, seething with hatred, he is having me on the programme so that I can be exposed, live in front of millions, as the talentless, pushy Scouser he wishes me to be. It takes three cans of lager to take away the taste of the sandwich.

I'm sure that Joan Bakewell became irritated hearing herself referred to all the time as 'The thinking man's crumpet' but when *Time Out* once referred to me as 'The thinking woman's David Cassidy' I was terribly disappointed that the phrase didn't pass into common parlance. Could it be that she was a beauty with brains, whereas I was no David Cassidy? Possibly. But here she is in the Green Room at TV Centre failing to put me at my ease as she introduces me to Sir Edward Boyle and Yehudi Menuhin, for with a sinking feeling I realise that I have more in common with the half-coated chocolate digestives on the table than with my fellow guests.

'Wine? No thanks, I'll have another lager.'

This will be the last one, definitely. Need to go to the toilet, but try and hang on until the last minute, because if you go now, you might want to go again during the programme, and it's live remember. Five minutes before we're due on air, I slip away from the throng and head for the gents. I'm just installed, unzipped and, as they say in ceramic circles, pointing percy at the porcelain, when Yehudi rushes in and stands next to me. Suddenly I get writer's block, as he chats away and micturates melodiously. He is still talking as he puts the finely tuned instrument back into its case and goes to the washbasin. I can't admit to not having started, so I do what men always do, let out a pretend sigh of relief, shake it all about, and say 'Oh, that's better'. Then I follow him first to the washbasin and then into the studio.

At the time I hadn't seen Tom Stoppard's *The Real Inspector Hound*, nor Alan Bennett's *Forty Years On*, nor had I read Norman Mailer's *Armies of the Night* or *Cancer Ward* by Solzhenitsyn, and so had nothing to add to the lively discussion that took place during the hour that followed. I have always been a good listener as opposed to a fulsome talker which, although an asset in the confessional box and at a hospital bedside, is a quality that is less appreciated on chat shows. I listened and nodded wisely, I smiled and tutted as conversation, sometimes *prestissimo*, sometimes *rallentando*, ranged from Vivaldi to Vietnam from t'ai chi to Tchaikovsky. Seated between Menuhin and Boyle, I was like a spectator at Wimbledon as the two of them lobbed, volleyed and served verbal aces. Not only did my neck ache but I was finding it increasingly difficult to concentrate on anything save the half-gallon of lager fermenting in my bladder. When the recent assassination of Robert Kennedy was referred to, the anguish that seemed to take hold of my body, hands clenched and thrust between my thighs as I rocked to and fro, the pained look on my face, said it all ('I'm dying for a pee!'). When would they start talking about Everton, I wondered, or Sammy Davis Jr? I could tell some fascinating stories about my meeting up with him backstage at the Albert Hall. Suddenly it was my turn to walk out on to the centre court. On the previous day there had been student riots in Berkeley, California, had I been moved to write a poem? asked Joan.

'Er, no, but I do have one with me about the assassination of Martin Luther King.'

But time was against us, she was afraid, thanked us all for taking part and bade the viewers goodnight.

Before the credits had finished rolling I was out of the studio, down the corridor and into the gents. And guess who was up there on the rostrum before me, baton in hand, conducting Handel's *Water Music*? Yes.

A couple of days later I was on the train down to the recording studios in Abbey Road writing lyrics in a BabyChic appointments diary, a rag-trade giveaway, given away to me by Thelma on New Year's Day. George Martin was now too tied up with the Beatles to work with us after 'Thank U Very Much', so EMI had brought in Norrie Paramor as producer. Norrie Paramor (was that his real name we wondered?) had been a bandleader in the forties and fifties, and as producer, composer and arranger had launched the careers of many singers, including Cliff Richard, Helen Shapiro, Frank Ifield and Ruby Murray. But by the time we landed on his doorstep I had the feeling that he was looking forward to retirement. Always the gentleman, he was easygoing and a pleasure to work with, but, in retrospect, I think that if he'd been more critical of our recording material post 'Lily the Pink', he could have saved EMI and ourselves a lot of money.

If Norrie was laid-back, his young assistant, an amazing dreamboat by the name of Tim Rice, was a maelstrom of exuberance. Tim had joined the Paramor organisation having been a management trainee at EMI, and his enthusiasm for pop music would have been infectious had I not been immunised against it by Tommy Steele singles when young and impressionable. At those early meetings in Norrie's grand apartment in Regent's Park, Tim would make tea, stick labels on reel-to-reel tapes and refer to obscure songs by American bands we'd never heard of, but as the shyness wore off (ours, not his, he'd been to Lancing College) he became more involved in our various projects, and when we recorded 'Do You Remember' in February 1968 Tim was very much part of the team, even joining in the chorus.

It must have seemed to me like a good story, a rock'n'roll myth that I continued to perpetrate down the years, the one of me writing the lyrics to 'Lily the Pink' on the train to London, tidying them up in the back of a cab bound for Abbey Road and copying them out in my best handwriting so that we could sing them in the studio. But looking now more closely at the lyrics scribbled on three pages for July in that appointments diary, it's clear that they had been written at more than one sitting. Some verses are in pencil, while others reveal the use of both ballpoint and fountain pen, so I had obviously worked on them over a period of days, even weeks, before the final revision en route to the studio. Some of the characters who swallowed the medicinal compound and never made it to vinyl included Uncle Leo who had terrible BO, Cousin Eva who suffered hay fever, Jimmy Cagney who had awful acne and Aunty Mary who was very hairy. Sorry, guys.

John, though, who was by no means a Tump, would have typed out his verses about his bony brother Tony and his 'Aunty Milly who ran willy-nilly'. At the time the Hollies had scored a hit with a song called 'Jennifer Eccles', which had inspired one of my verses about a certain Jennifer Eccles who had terrible freckles, and in a stroke of postmodern ironic genius we invited Graham Nash along to sing the verse, which he did so well that I joked that he should quit the Hollies and join the Scaffold. Tempted though he must have been, he decided to stay with music and joined Crosby, Stills and Young in America instead. Jack Bruce played bass on the record and, although he was an intelligent and talented musician, I reckoned he'd be better off staying with Cream and playing to vast audiences all over the world than doing the north of England cabaret circuit, so I didn't invite him to join us.

'Lily the Pink' was released on the Parlophone label on 18 October 1968 but not as the A-side. Following the success of 'Thank U Very Much' we had spent more time doing cabaret dates and kiddy TV than we had playing to our student and theatre audiences, and we shared a collective sense of guilt: Are we selling out? Can we be taken seriously as artists if we continue to record silly songs? Do we have to wear white suits all the time? Whatever happened to the poetry? It was Mike rather than me who worried about our public image – I suppose because I had an artistic life outside the group I was less concerned, at least at that time. We had recorded a track called 'Buttons of Your Mind' (which I think preceded 'Windmills of Your Mind' and 'Handcarts of Your Mind', but I can't be sure), a love song that featured Mike singing and me reciting verse about 'Not being drawn into the bedroom of your eyes' and about 'The buttons of your mind being difficult to find, and my fingers far too clumsy', lyrics that Rod McKuen would have put down his big white sheep-dog to have written. Although a pleasant enough tune, it was never chart material; however, at Mike's insistence and with the group's best interests at heart, the record was released as a double A-side, in the hope that 'Buttons' would get an airing on Radio 1 and people would say, 'Gosh, there's more than one string to the Scaffold's bow.' Within weeks 'Lily' was racing up the charts and 'Buttons' remained fastened, with the result that people could be heard muttering, 'Gosh, there's only one string to the Scaffold's bow . . . Whatever that means.'

Having favoured black as our stage outfits in the early days, we wanted to suggest summer and light for 'Do you Remember', so we nipped down to Carnaby Street and chose the white suits that were to become our trademark for a few years and which we wore on *Top of the Pops* while 'Lily' was number one in the charts over the Christmas period and into 1969. Twelve months later, however, when we featured on the first *TOTP* of 1970, we were no longer top of the pile, so we came up with the concept of looking as if we hadn't worked for a year. We dirtied up some old white suits, frayed the cuffs and pulled off buttons, and John unstitched a sleeve that was to come off during the final chorus. I doubt if many of the audience either at home or in the studio sensed the Dadaesque significance of our performance, but assumed we were acting soft, as usual. BBC top brass, however, were not amused and the show's producer nailed us in the bar afterwards and accused us of sending up the programme, the jewel in the Corporation's popular music crown. Not the programme, we countered, but ourselves. But he'd have none of it and our copybook had been well and truly blotted. That Mr Dada has a lot to answer for.

And talking of jewels in crowns, 'Lily the Pink' must have been bobbing about in my subconscious, the result of writing this, when I went to see the Queen yesterday at Buckingham Palace. As one does. The date was Tuesday 12 October 2004 and the occasion was to receive my CBE, news of which had prompted a fusillade of apoplectic e-mails through my spam and porn filter: 'How dare you accept a gong from warmonger Blair?' . . . 'My children used to love your poems, but not any more, since I have burned your books' . . . 'We thought you were one of us, but all the time you were one of them' . . . 'Horny ladies in spam orgy'. I was hardened this time round to these bunches of sour grapes, having had them thrown at me when I was awarded the OBE in 1996, together with letters to the newpapers that tut-tutted about 'working-class heroes' selling out and leaping over the barricades to join the ruling classes. I must confess that I hadn't seen accepting an honour in quite those terms. Even though I can understand those who wish to have nothing to do with an award that has 'Empire' in the title, and I admire friends who, without fuss, have turned it down for their own very good reasons, I was surprised and delighted to be nominated, and the hundreds of letters and calls I had from relatives, old school pals, even ex-lovers and poets, confirmed that in my case to have said no thank you would have been arrogance. What happens is that the Secretary for Appointments at 10 Downing Street writes 'In Confidence' that the Prime Minister has it in mind to submit your name to the Queen with a view to your receiving the award, and you must complete the enclosed form and send it back by return of post. Unfortunately, when the first letter arrived I was in Bulgaria at the invitation of the British Council, and I wrote this at the time in my journal:

There are very few things in life more grown-up than going into a restaurant on your own, particularly in a country where the only word you know is the unit of currency (in this case, the Leva), but I just love the excitement of pointing to the menu and hoping that you will recognise something on the plate the grim waiter bangs down on the table before you. On the fifth floor of the hotel I find the Panorama and slink in with all the confidence I can muster. After two glasses of red wine and a plate of food (pork stuffed with fish? Vice-versa?), I go up to my room.

The double bed is low and sags alarmingly in the middle, and the pillowcases only half cover the pillows, which are yellow, tired and obviously desperate to escape. It is eleven thirty here and nine thirty in the UK, so I ring home. Isabel is asleep, but Matt is his usual chatty self. Hil comes on and after some lively banter about washing machines and kiddy stuff, teasingly mentions an important-looking letter that had arrived for me this morning, marked 'Private', 'Confidential', 'Not to be opened by anyone other than' etc.

'So what did it say?' I asked.

'Oh, John Major wants to give you an OBE but you've got to reply by return of post.'

'But I won't be home for a week, Can't you fill it in for me?'

'No, it needs your signature. Do it as soon as you get back.'

A week later I did just that, rushed into the house, grabbed the form, put a tick in the box, added my signature and sent it off. Then panicked on my way back from the pillar box, convinced that I'd ticked the box refusing the award, and as there was no way of checking, started to make excuses: '*I was offered the OBE but I turned it down. Imagine me, a working-class hero, leaping over the barricades to join the ruling classes*' . . . '*Accept a medal from the monarchy? I don't think so.*'

But, of course, I had ticked the right box as I did flawlessly when invited seven years later to accept an upgrade to Commander class, necessitating a further visit to Buck House. On the first occasion my expectations of the conversation I would have with the Queen had been ridiculously high. While pinning the medal to my noble breast, would she tell me how important *Summer with Monika* had been in fanning the flames of royal desire during the love life of herself and Philip, and how much she regretted that my children's books hadn't been available when Charles and Anne were toddlers and in need of exciting, yet essentially moral, bedtime stories? How different their lives might have turned out, she would muse sadly. In fact, when I moved the four steps towards her on hearing my cue from the Lord Chamberlain, 'For services to poetry', her first words were 'Congratulations. What do you do?'

Slightly miffed, but with as much grace as I could muster, I made what sounded like an excuse about writing poetry, then mumbled about being published by Penguin and Puffin in the vain hope that her well-known fondness for little creatures would see me through.

Yesterday my expectations were more realistic. As long as her first words weren't 'Congratulations. What was it you said you did?' I would consider myself one of the family. In fact, she referred to the sterling work being done by her

Laureate, but not wanting to waste my allotted two minutes chewing the fat about Mr Motion, I panicked and blurted out 'Lily the Pink'.

She paused. 'Pardon?'

'"Lily the Pink". I wrote the words to "Lily the Pink".'

As her jaw dropped and her brow furrowed, I just about managed to stop myself from trying to jog her memory by bursting into the chorus. Luckily for me, Her Majesty and the assembled crowd in the Palace Ballroom, the penny dropped and she smiled in recognition. 'Oh, yes, "Lily the Pink".' And as she took my hand, the signal that the audience was at an end, was it only imagination, or did I really sense that there was a special warmth in that handshake? For those royal blue eyes seemed to say thank you, thank you for all the pleasure your song has given us during our reign. And finally, the investiture over, as she walked down the aisle flanked by her Gurkha guards, past row upon row of her loyal subjects, was she singing softly to herself:

Old Ebeneezer thought he was Julius Caesar
So they put him in a ho-o-ome . . .

OPEN SPACE

If you are lucky enough to have a number one in the charts for twelve weeks you have the opportunity of making a lot of money by getting out there and playing to the adoring fans. So why not go on tour? Play all the major venues in the country taking with you a few quality support acts so that you won't have to perform more than thirty minutes a night? Alternatively, why not write a revue without any music whatsoever, give it a weird title that will be off-putting to your average fan-in-the-street and run it for three weeks at a tiny experimental theatre on Tottenham Court Road?

OK, we'll do that.

The Open Space Theatre, formerly a disused old people's home, founded in 1968 by febrile New Yorker Charles Marowitz and Thelma Holt, was already gaining a reputation for the quality of work produced and we felt very proud to be invited to perform there. In the words of Patricia Burke at the literary agency, 'It's small, darlings, but it echoes far.' Except for John Gorman's wildly irreverent church sermon and 'Boxes', a sketch we'd co-written about a TV quiz game hosted by Michael Miles, *The Puny Little Life Show* consisted of poems and sketches I had previously written, dressed up in a loose-fitting dramatic outfit and directed by my old pal Jim Goddard. 'Culturally, they are the perfect example of "Pop Theatre",' wrote film-maker and critic Tony Palmer, 'and although they might have long hair and funny accents, their material would be acceptable in the most genteel surroundings if only as an example of the avant-garde. Thus, they can be patronised, even if not actively promoted.'

The show opened on 9 January 1969 and although we only did fifteen performances and had no intention of taking it elsewhere, *The Puny Little Life Show* continues to be performed, usually in the drama departments of Australian colleges, and for some reason at girls' public schools over here, because the script appears in *Open Space Plays Selected by Charles Marowitz*, a book published by Penguin in 1974, mouse-eared copies of which must still be kicking around. Although what the sixth formers at Knaresborough Ladies College make of this cut-and-paste of television commercials and political slogans of the early sixties I'm not sure.

And so you've turned down the chance of a national tour or a season in panto in order to pursue your dreams in a tiny basement theatre. If you insist on suffering for your art, is there anything else you can do to make the experience even more penitential? Like doubling up, for instance?

What do you mean?

Well, why not do another show the same evening at a different venue?

Like which venue?

Ronnie Scott's, the jazz club in Soho, only a short walk away from the Open Space.

Would we do the same show, more or less?

No, completely different material suitable for a late-night

audience who will have paid to listen to Stan Getz.

Mmm . . . sounds like a challenge. OK, we'll do it.

Oh, and by the by, in case you'd like time to rehearse both shows prior to the London opening, might we suggest instead that you spend the week at the Fiesta Club in Stockton-on-Tees? White suits, Aintree Iron, bolshie band, soup-in-a-basket, usual sort of thing?

Excellent, how soon can we start?

Our season at Ronnie Scott's was great fun, despite having to listen to Ronnie's repertoire of hairy chestnuts and practised ad libs every night, and we were made to feel very welcome. There was something very civilised about sitting at our regular table at the back of the club, with a bottle of red wine, matzos and plate of chicken livers, letting the music wash over us. I used to imagine we were a jazz trio relaxing between sets. I notice the stunning Brazilian girl sitting with a group at a table in front of the stage and decide to play for her. No doubt she's come to listen to Stan, but when she hears me playing the blues, like she's never heard them before . . . Half an hour later I'm up on stage making jokes she doesn't get and reading poems in a language she doesn't understand, wishing I could play a melancholic, mutilingual tenor sax. Non-English speakers apart, we managed to win over jazz aficionados who would not normally have crossed the street to watch the Scaffold, including club regulars like Spike Milligan and Marty Feldman who sent a note backstage which I still treasure. Scribbled on the torn-off flap of a cigarette packet, the heartfelt and warming tribute: 'Brilliant you cu★ts'.

I'm not sure if Stan Getz, the legend who had played alongside Benny Goodman, Oscar Peterson and Gerry

Mulligan, ever caught the act. Then in his forties and still fighting the battle with narcotics ('What Stan wantz, Stan Getz'), he could be forgiven, but he never scribbled any billets-doux, nor invited us to accompany him on a tour of the States; in fact, I don't remember him saying hello the whole time we were there. Mind you, he couldn't half play the trombone.

NEW YORK, NEW YORK

New York today is as safe as, if not safer than, most cities to visit but in 1969 it had a reputation for muggings and violence that was second to none. It would be asking for trouble, our agent warned, to run around Central Park in our underpants after midnight, waving fistfuls of $100 bills. Luckily, when the Scaffold arrived at La Guardia airport at 3 p.m. on 4 November it was a bitterly cold day and we sensed, to a man, that we'd have no difficulty keeping our clothes on and avoiding Central Park after dark. We had been booked to play for two weeks at the Bitter End, a folksy venue on Bleecker Street in Greenwich Village and, checking into the Chelsea Hotel on West 23rd Street, I felt like the young gun new in town, and the world was my holster. The macho sensation lasted all of twenty minutes, then I took a shower in room 1208, and roaches the size of castanets appeared out of nowhere and had me hopping about on the tiles like a nude flamenco dancer.

Each night after the gig I would lie in bed listening to the gurgle of the pipes and the ghostly tip-tapping of an old typewriter from somewhere down the corridor. Was it Dylan Thomas dying for a whiskey, starting a new poem he would never complete? Jack Kerouac up to his waist in a stream of consciousness? Tennessee Williams? Arthur

Miller? They had all stayed here at some time, perhaps in this very room. Come to think of it, it was probably Archy, the cockroach with the soul of a poet, lower-casing eternal love letters to Mehitabel, his beloved alley cat.

Tom Rush was the headlining act with his nifty guitar playing and warm expressive voice, and although he didn't invite us to accompany him on a tour of the States, he was a pleasant guy to get along with. If most of the audience came to see him, quite a number turned out to see us as well. Mainly to gawk at Paul McCartney's brother in the flesh and try to make sense of what we were saying. If there was ever a case of culture divided by language this was it. Naïvely we had assumed that as long as we avoided the usual gaffes: pavement/sidewalk, suspenders/braces, rubber/eraser, the rhythms and images we conjured up on stage would be as accessible as they had been to the hen parties at the Stockton Fiesta and the sophisticates at Ronnie Scott's. Wrong. The young crowd sipping sodas wished us well but were immune to puns and irony. Jokes came apart at the seams, punchlines dropped to their knees, poems curled up in embarrassment. But not every night, for we had our fans, and there is no one in the world who is quite as fanatical as an American fan. One lad from Hawaii who visited backstage could recite all the words of a Scaffold LP, *Live at the Queen Elizabeth Hall*, which meant not only knowing the poems off by heart but the sketches as well, which he reeled off parrot-fashion impersonating our voices. Clever, uncanny and decidedly spooky though this talent was, I did make a note of his telephone number in case we became too famous to appear in public, when he could be hired to tour as a one-man Scaffold.

After the show on the second night, three stunning girls

came into the dressing room while we were ironing our puns and thought us so cute that: 'Hey guys, why not let us show you around our beautiful city?'

We couldn't believe our luck: 'That would be great, thank you. We take it you enjoyed the show, then?'

'We ain't seen it yet, but when we heard that one of the Beatles' brother's group was in town, we just had to come and say hello.'

As good as their word, they collected us from the Chelsea next morning to offer our first bite at the Big Apple. The Empire State? The Lincoln Center? The Staten Island Ferry? Which would it be first? Our first stop was a dinky dress shop two doors down from the hotel, which John, Mike and I agreed was lovely. After lunch at the Love and Quiches, we were strolling through Washington Square on our way to a really trendy clothes store the girls insisted we'd go crazy for, when we paused to admire an exhibition of what we took to be pavement art. Life-size silhouettes of figures in various poses outlined in white paint. Six in all, arranged round the fountain as if they had fallen to earth from outer space. The girls must have thought that we'd fallen from outer space too when they explained that there was no artist involved, just a scene-of-crime officer doing his job after a brutal shooting the previous night. It was some relief to be hurried along to a clothes store two blocks away, where we admired the tops and skirts that the girls tried on.

'Do you guys like fur coats? Wait until we see the stuff they're selling right across the street from here.'

This was fun certainly, but any chance possibly of a landmark? A photo, perhaps, of the Scaffs standing in front of something recognisably Manhattanish?

'Photographs? Of course, there's a swell boutique on 42nd Street. Let's take a cab.'

While John and I discussed the pros and cons of marrying leggy black chicks and settling down in the Village, and Mike took photographs of them modelling for us, their conversation took a decidedly pointed turn: 'The Small Faces bought you a terrific dress here, didn't they, honey?'

'They sure did. And remember the fabulous coat Mick Jagger bought Dinah?'

'Those English groups, my, they're so so generous.'

Now that the penny had finally dropped, we had to come clean: 'Sorry girls, we're not really a group and we're not really English, we're Scousers.'

In the face of such heart-warming honesty, the girls laughed gaily and confessed that it was our company they sought, not our money, so we all went back to the Chelsea and had a six-up in room 1208.

Except, of course, that we didn't.

In the face of such heart-warming honesty, the girls told us to piss off and long-legged it up 42nd Street.

It was in the Coffè Café on 42nd Street a few days later that I scribbled the following on the back of the bill. It's a cut-up of items on the menu with a little local colour thrown in:

> orange-juice scrambled
> over easy followed by
> New Jersey bred
> duck-flavoured bacon
> with a choice of either
> coffee or unlimited abuse
> $1.85

Mike, always indecisive and unhurried when faced with a menu, would bring out the beast in waiters, and in particular those who served behind counters in busy cafeterias. 'Excuse me, what's mayo?'

'Whadderya mean, what's mayo?'

'I mean, what is it?'

'It's fuckin mayo, dat's what it is.'

'Oh, then what's the difference between pastrami and corned beef?'

'Look, you wanna order, or you don' wanna order. If you don' wanna order, fuck off.'

'There's no need to get stroppy, young lady.'

Frinck and Summer with Monika had been published in the USA by Ballantine two years earlier, but I was so embarrassed by the cover and the blurb ('McGough is cool, tender, angry, funny – the most exciting writer/performer since John Lennon') that I kept quiet about it, but I had hoped that when we performed our material on nationwide television the country might take us to its heart. This was not to be, however, for although we guested with Diana Rigg and did a sketch or two on *The David Frost Show* while in New York, when we flew out to Cincinnati and Philadelphia to appear on networked afternoon chat shows, producers were interested only in Mike's opinion of the 'Paul is Dead' rumour circulating at the time.

'But you must admit, Mike, that Paul not wearing shoes on the cover of Abbey Road could mean that he's dead?'

'Rubbish, I spoke to him on the phone only this morning.'

'Are you sure it was him, not the spirit of your dead brother?'

'Bollocks!'

'There's no need to get stroppy, young man.'

We had an early-morning flight back to Manchester, and John and I were in the lounge of the Chelsea waiting for Mike as usual. If the train departed at 11.05, he would plan to arrive at the station at 11.04, and the same with planes. We had given up explaining about traffic hold-ups and queues at check-in; he always assumed they would hold up the plane/train for him (and dammit, if they didn't on occasion). Eventually John and I went outside and hailed a yellow cab, put all the cases into the trunk and climbed in to await his nibs. We didn't hear or see anything because the lid was up, but the driver must have felt a shift of weight at the back and with a yell jumped out of the cab. We did likewise in time to see a guy running up a deserted West 23rd Street with a case in each hand. We all gave chase until the trunk raider, torn for an instant between greed and common sense, dropped the swag and disappeared into the morning mist. As we retrieved the cases, both Mike's as it turned out, he emerged from the hotel, not a hair out of place, python-skin coat draped over his shoulders, looking every inch the cultural ambassador for the Wirral he was destined to become: 'Hurry up, lads, and get those cases in, we've got a plane to catch.'

THE BATHROOM TOUR

The Japanese lady seated in front of me on the 9.45 out of Lime Street has blonde wavy hair. Unusual, that, in a Japanese lady. As she turns to look out of the window I notice, too, that she has blue eyes. Large, quite rounded. When the inspector arrives to examine her ticket, she asks what time the train will arrive at Newcastle. Her accent is unmistakably Geordie. Perhaps she is not Japanese after all? That's the mysterious north-east for you, things are never quite what they seem.

On 27 November 1972 I took the train from Liverpool up to Sunderland, changing at Darlington, to read in a jolly venue above a pub. The Londonderry Hotel was heaving with students from the local art college and afterwards half of them came back to the house where I was staying and partied until the sun rose above the Wear. The next morning I stepped over the bodies huddled on the floor and made my way to the station.

(*I want you to give the following paragraph your fullest attention, because although the detail may seem wearisome and irrelevant, there may be questions later.*)

At the ticket office, as well as my single to Newcastle, I was given two travel vouchers worth 5p each to travel on Tynerail, as well as a programme of events for Tynerail's forthcoming 'Festival of Music 1972'. On arrival at Newcastle I was handed an orange-and-white plastic bag with a metro map printed on each side and the slogan 'Come shopping on a Tynerider train'. Having time to spare before my connection to London, where I had a meeting later in the afternoon with my publisher in Bedford Square, I wandered around the concourse and bought the *Daily Express* (price threepence) and a packet of Wrigley's spearmint chewing gum. At 10.12 I boarded the train for King's Cross.

Whenever I'm performing out of London I will stay in a decent hotel and I look forward to it, the chance to relax as best I can before going along to the theatre for the sound and lighting check. Perhaps I will have a swim. After the show I'll go back and unwind with a light supper and a glass of wine in my lonely but luxurious room. It's partly because I don't drive that I usually stay over after a gig rather than rushing back home, but it's mainly because I find it more relaxing.

Not all poets do, and most musicians will have the gear loaded in the transit van and be on the motorway before the audience have reached the foyer. But of course, I'm older now and can afford to take some of the pain out of being on the road. But 'twas not ever thus.

People who organise readings in small venues will often invite the visiting poet to stay overnight with them, not only as a way of keeping costs down, but for the chance to spend a little time getting to know someone whose work they probably admire. For the poet though, it can be a minefield. One series of readings I made in the seventies I still refer to as the 'Bathroom Tour' because when the lady who was showing me around her neat, suburban house came to the bathroom she said:

> 'We've had them all staying here, you know. All the poets. Good ones like that G***** ******. Do you know, he left this bathroom spotless, you wouldn't know he'd been here. A really good poet he is. Mind you, we had that er, whatsisname? T** ****** staying. He's a very bad poet. Do you know, he left the bathroom in a terrible state. Sick everywhere and left it for me to clean up. No I'm sorry, but I don't call that poetry!'

Consequently, I spent most of the next morning polishing the bathroom tiles and cleaning out the showerhead. 'Ooh, we had that Walter McGough here last month. Clean as a whistle he was. Good poet.'

The other problem is the sheaf of poems that will appear just as the poet is about to retire. 'I bet you get fed up with people giving you their poems to look at, especially as you must be tired after the reading, but I thought as you're here, you might . . .'

Food is another. The organiser will usually prefer you to fit in with the normal family routine (your first mistake, of course, was to say, 'Don't go to any trouble') and you'll eat with Mum, Dad, Grandma and the twins at half past six. Now a pair of Barnsley chops with carrots, peas and mash, followed by spotted dick and custard, washed down with a couple of bottles of Theakston's Old Peculier may set you up for a night sprawled in front of the telly, but does little for the digestion half an hour later when the buttocks are clenched and you're standing in front of an audience trying to control the leg wobble.

Worse, perhaps, is the assumption that poets don't eat. After the reading in a local village hall, the organiser apologised for having to stay behind and help clear up, so he rang his wife who drove over and gave me a lift back to the house. We sat facing each other in the living room. The clock drummed its fingers on the mantelpiece. Eventually she said, 'Would you like a drink?'

'A drink? Mmm, not half.'

'Tea or Coffee?'

'Oh . . .' The clock missed a beat.

'Or would you like something stronger?'

'Yes, please.'

'Whisky all right?'

'Whisky would be fine.' A large whisky in hand, the conversation went as follows:

'By the way, are you peckish? I never thought of asking.'

'Well, yes, actually.'

'I could make you a sandwich?'

'Thank you.' She disappears into the kitchen.

'There's cheese, or tuna if you prefer?'

'Tuna would be fine, thank you.'

'Actually, there's a nice piece of steak here, would you rather have that in a sandwich?'

'If it's not too much trouble?'

'No trouble at all, in fact, shall I fry some chips with it?'

And so it went on, until by the time the organiser arrived back home, I was sitting at the kitchen table, tucking into a sirloin steak, with fried onions, chips and petits pois, and sharing a decent bottle of Châteauneuf du Pape with Laura.

On 27 November 1973 a parcel arrived for me at my house in Liverpool. I opened it to find an orange-and-white plastic bag with a metro map printed on each side and the slogan 'Come shopping on a Tynerider train'. Inside the bag was a single train ticket from Sunderland to Newcastle, two 5p travel vouchers, a 'Festival of Music' programme, a packet of Wrigley's spearmint chewing gum and the *Daily Express* dated 27 November 1972. Nothing else. No letter, no address.

Even though I prefer hotels for the privacy and anonymity they afford, I've always been well looked after in people's homes. (Sunderland scored nine out of ten in the bedroom department, incidentally, but the curtains remain firmly drawn on that one.) Just occasionally, however, I have been made to feel like the ghost at the banquet. Like the time I was invited to give a reading at a university in Yorkshire in aid of Amnesty International. I was met at the station by the organiser, who was a consultant at the local hospital, and on the drive to the venue he twittered on about how grateful the committee were to me for travelling such a long way and giving my services free in aid of this good cause. I concurred modestly. On arrival he showed me to the dressing room and told me that he'd arranged for me to stay overnight with a couple of students, would that be all right? He then left me alone with my running order, a packet of crisps and a pint of lager.

The hall was packed and I was pleased to reckon that Amnesty would be a grand or two better off by the end of the evening. During the interval the students who had kindly offered to put me up for the night popped in to say hello. 'Have you brought a sleeping bag?' asked the hippie with the beard.

'Er, no,' was my straight and honest answer.

'Oh, dear,' said the hippie with the breasts, 'it can be freezing in the attic. But never mind, we've got a stash of good dope and the dog's got a spare blanket.'

My performance in the second half was fired by a sense of injustice and the prospect of a night spent hallucinating on wooden boards beneath a dog blanket, so when it was over I went in search of the organiser. I spotted him in the foyer about to leave with a group of well-heeled friends. 'Oh, Roger, I'm glad you caught me before I left, and may I just say on behalf of . . .'

I cut him off mid-twitter and explained that I wasn't happy about the sleeping arrangements.

He looked slightly miffed and went into a huddle with his friends. There were mumblings of 'poets in garrets' and 'enough canapés to go round' before he came back to me. 'I've got an idea, why don't you come back with us to my house? Caroline's up at Oxford and I'm sure she wouldn't mind you using her room for the night. I'll ring Fiona, that's my wife, and tell her to expect one more guest. Jolly good, why didn't I think of it before?'

The reason he didn't think of it before may have been that I wasn't seen as an equal, but as a poet from Liverpool who'd feel more at home with a party can of Watney's ale and a bag of fish and chips. His grand house was already full when we arrived, all the hard-working committee members and their partners tucking into poached salmon, coronation chicken and the rest. To be fair, I was warmly received and, basking in the warmth of their embarrassment, made short work of the salmon and a bottle of Sancerre before retiring to Caroline's room. There was a sexy photograph of her on the bedside table and I must say she was a beautiful girl and

I often wonder, when she came home at the end of term, if she noticed anything different about the teddy bear.

On the morning of 27 November 1974 a parcel arrived for me at my home in Liverpool and inside it was . . . yes, you've guessed, an orange-and-white plastic bag advertising the Tynerider metro system, containing chewing gum, a rail ticket and a newspaper, two years out of date, etc. It was a dislocating experience on the edge of being scary. But this time there was an envelope containing a written note that said, 'Are you sure you are really Roger McGough?' My identity was to be questioned again a year later when another parcel arrived, and inside the spookily familiar plastic bag was another newspaper, rail ticket, music festival leaflet, chewing gum and an envelope. Written on the note was, 'Are you still sure you are really Roger McGough?' But this time, pinned to the bag was a card which said, 'Reproduction of "An Incident Regarding Identity" accompanied by relevant articles.' As I had suspected all along, I was a work of art.

Although I had always suspected that art students from Sunderland were involved, I never followed it up, but many years later, after a lunchtime reading at the Edinburgh Festival I met a teacher who confessed all. There was this female lecturer, she explained, who devised the plan to have me stalked by a small group of students with instructions to copy where I went, what I did and what I bought on a particular day, with a view to creating an ongoing and unsettling work of art. What became of her? I asked, but she had no idea. When I came out of the theatre I walked along George Street and considered buying a sandwich and a copy of the *Scotsman*, but with a nervous look over my shoulder thought better of it.

A STING IN THE TAIL

'Life on the road with one of today's supergroups. What it's like from the inside. A no-holds-barred story of love-hungry young men and the girls they meet. The lesbians, the plastercasters, the groupies out for thrills. The weirdos, the junkies and the perverts. Gangbangs, orgies in the van. Excitement . . . Ecstasy . . . Sexual delinquency . . . There's no business like . . .' runs the preface of *Gig* published in 1973, my fourth single collection in six years. Unfortunately, the title was a misnomer as relatively few of the poems were about life in a band, but I was perceived in some quarters as a pop star with pretensions, and several literary critics chose to skip the poems and reviewed only the preface. Transit vans were not allowed to park at the foot of Mount Parnassus, and rock'n'roll was not considered the stuff of poetry. I make no claims for the quality of the verse written on tour, some of which appears more like notes awaiting considered reflection, but there is nothing macho or glitzy here, as the last few lines of the opening poem show, written after a bleak midwinter performance at Huddersfield Polytechnic:

> *in bed I wear socks and my grey woolly hat,*
> *shiver, and regret not having filled the 'Kozeeglow'*

hot waterbottle
with vindaloo.

At home, lonely and dislocated, I had felt driven to escape, but what did escape offer? A world of cheap hotels where terrifying landladies goose-step down corridors. Where ashtrays are nailed to the mantelpiece and spiders hold their winter sports in icy bathrooms. Humour is never far away from the mildly tragic, but it deflects rather than hides the horrors, when everyday habits, usually so reassuring, are transformed into nightmares. After all, you can't beat the full monty, the good old English breakfast:

I pick up cold steel talons and tear into the heart of Egg
which bleeds over strips of dead pig marinated in brine.
Grey, shabby Mushrooms squeal as they are hacked to death
slithering in their own sweat.
Like policemen to a motor accident, Toast arrives,
the debris is mopped up. Nothing remains of the slaughter.

On receiving reams of wild paranoia like this, I wonder why my editor at Jonathan Cape didn't call Social Services, or at least recommend a decent psychiatrist. Here was a guy with a problem. Because she had left the company halfway through publication, I had always felt resentful, but now I can see that revising a manuscript in a tiny office with a deranged psycho was not part of her job description.

Those of you who are keen on astrology will be interested to know that I am a Scorpio, and exhibit all the positive qualities associated with my birth sign: loyalty, generosity, wisdom and raw animal sexuality among them, with none of the vices, particularly the one about harbouring vindictive feelings. Revenge, unlike Lancashire Hotpot, is a dish best served cold, but I have never been troubled by it. This Scorpio does not have a sting in his tail. Although I must confess an inclination towards John Betjeman's view when he said: 'Our poems are part of ourselves. They are our children and we do not like them to be made public fools of by strangers.'

In my study I have a paperweight that somebody brought me back from New Mexico. It is a dome of solid glass containing a scorpion, about two inches long with lobsteresque claws and a tail like a curled rattlesnake. I am extremely careful when handling it for fear of dropping it, the glass shattering and the scorpion, free at last after thirty years, panicking and running up my trouser leg. I will never bad-mouth those poets and literary journalists, the critics whom I feel have stuck the knife in, but I have written down their names on a circular piece of gummed paper: seventeen in all, some still hacking a living as nightwatchmen in cemeteries, others now forgotten and unknown. Only one is a woman, a poet whose photograph never appears on the back of her books, and on meeting her recently for the first time I could understand why and it cheered me up no end. But I would get no satisfaction from naming them, for some have passed on and others perhaps may regret their youthful bile. But this is just to let them know that their names can be found beneath the scorpion, weighed down by glass.

Gig is divided into two sections, 'On the road' and 'At the roadside', and in the second is a poem that took me several months to write called 'The Identification'. The television news on the evening of 4 March 1972 reported yet another bombing in Belfast, at the Abercorn Restaurant filled at the time with women shoppers and children. And after all the horrific scenes of carnage, there followed an interview with the father of one of the young victims. He was a Presbyterian minister and the dignity of the man almost transcended his grief, as he described the harrowing process of having to identify the body of Stephen, his son. The American poet Robert Lowell seems also to have been moved by the interview because the same incident is described in a collection of his called *Notebooks*, although in his poem the father recognises the body by a book of 'toy matches' in the child's pocket. In my version there are no matches, but the father is puzzled by a packet of cigarettes:

> *Cigarettes? Oh this can't be Stephen,*
> *I don't allow him to smoke, you see.*
> *He wouldn't disobey me, not his father.*
> *But that's his penknife. That's his alright.*
> *And that's his key on the keyring*
> *Gran gave him just the other night.*
> *So this must be him.*
>
> *I think I know what happened . . . about the cigarettes,*
> *No doubt he was minding them for one of the older boys.*
> *Yes, that's it.*
> *That's him.*
> *That's our Stephen.*

I think it's a poem that works and I rather suspect that the critics at the bottom of my paperweight thought so too, because none of them referred to it in their petulant reviews.

I was delighted, then, when last week Izzy, my fourteen-year-old, broke off from her saxophone practice and said,

'Oh, by the way, Dad, we did one of your poems in class today.'

'Which one?'

'It's about a father identifying his son.'

'"The Identification"?'

'Yes, that's it.'

'Ah, well, do you know what happened?'

I explained the political background to the poem, about the interview on television, as well as information I'd gleaned over the years about the father who had since emigrated to Canada. And of how the tragedy had been brought home to me again recently after a reading at the Waterfront Hall in Belfast, when I met people who had been at school with Stephen and who spoke warmly of their friend.

Izzy listened with that intent but glazed expression that girls have when grown-ups are banging on: 'Teacher said it was about a boy who had been in a fire.'

'Well, there was a fire, but it was a bomb that caused it.'

'That's what teacher said.'

'Never you mind what teacher said, I wrote it.'

'Whatever,' said Izzy, going back with some relief to her sax.

It's hardly surprising that the poem took a long time to write, having less to do with gestation and quiet recollection than being in one place long enough to put pen to paper. John Gorman's passion for providing Liverpool with an arts centre led to the Scaffold's funding of the expensive renovation of a building on Renshaw Street. The venture, which would provide performance space, a recording studio and 'Scaffoscope', an agency to discover and promote local talent, proved a disaster and in April the Scaffold had been declared bankrupt and the police had issued a warrant for our arrest concerning non-payment of debts. Thelma had found another lover and I was living out of a suitcase. (I had thought of writing 'battered suitcase' there, but feared it might conjure up an image of something deep-fried.)

Brian Patten, on the other hand, had struck gold in London. To his small flat near Notting Hill Gate came a procession of young women, the beautiful, the gifted and the wealthy, eager to tame this wild young poet, a burning genius with the looks of a mischievous faun. (He remains to this day untameable, although I entertain high hopes for Lynda Cookson, his partner for the last twelve years.) For most of them it was in one door and out the other, but his relationship with Mary Moore, with whom he lived for four years, was an intense and mutually profitable one and she it was who, taking pity on me dossing in Brian's spare room, offered me the use of her father's former studio in NW3.

The Mall Studios had been purpose built for use by artists and I could easily imagine her father Henry Moore chipping away in the bright airy space, or Ben Nicholson before him, painting his geometric abstracts. As well as a kitchen and bathroom on the ground floor, there was an open-plan bedroom built on to a balcony some twenty metres above ground. The whole effect was like inhabiting a white clapboard cathedral and at first I couldn't believe my luck to be living there. The trouble was that I hardly ever did. I was either on tour or skulking around Liverpool. When I did spend time there the space closed in, mummifying me in its faded whiteness. That's either the appeal or the worry of poetry, the silence of its creation. Late at night, sitting on one of the long leather sofas, pen and paper to hand, trying to write, I would worry that the room might be suffering from tinnitus and in need of aural distraction. A Mozart piano concerto, the scraping of brush on canvas, the ringing of hammer on metal. Three months later I cast off the winding-sheet, had a farewell drink in the Sir Richard Steele on Haverstock Hill, and caught the train back to Liverpool.

> *His life like this poem,*
> *out of sequence,*
> *a series of impressions,*
> *unfinished, imperfect.*

DOCKER'S SON DESERTS WIFE AND
FAMILY TO LIVE WITH HEIRESS

A month ago, at the funeral service of a friend, not a bosom pal but a local poet and artist whose reputation didn't extend beyond the pub, I read a poem I'd written. Next Thursday I'll be standing in another pulpit in another church to read another poem for another friend. A closer friend, this time, and I have yet to write the poem his widow and family have requested. It's always difficult to write verse for such an occasion, not resorting to easy clichés that will have the congregation, already brimming with emotion, turning on the taps. I should talk *to* him rather than *about* him. Perhaps write him a letter or chat as if we were in the pub, find a tone of voice that won't buckle under the weight of metaphor, that doesn't sound like a chopped-up sermon. There are now more funeral than marriage services, the wreaths outnumber the bouquets, the eulogies the epithalamia. It comes with the uncharted territory, of course, all the vacated perches swinging gently in the late evening breeze, and although not a hypochondriac as many of my fellow poets confess to be, I do worry about becoming one, and this chronic state of anxiety brought on by the fear of developing hypochondria can affect my work. Quite a few poems deal with suffering, ageing and dying, and although some are the result of real experience, others have been written almost as spells, to charm and counter evil spirits, to take the sting out of their tails.

I have recently been reading favourable reviews for Simon Gray's memoirs, addictively entitled, *The Smoking Diaries*, and most reviewers refer to this 'curmudgeonly old man' who writes wittily and movingly about mortality on a path strewn with fag-ends and empty champagne bottles. A literary warrior of bygone days, still able to throw punches and settle a few old scores. When I reach his age, I thought, I hope I still have a sense of humour and, more important, the energy to sit down and write my non-smoking diaries. Then I notice that he is practically the same age as me and feel suddenly curmudgeonly. I mean, I realise that it wasn't a computer virus that caused various government departments to send me senior travel passes, winter fuel vouchers and weekly pensions, and that the occasional young man (usually Italian) who offers me his seat on the Tube, isn't taking the piss, but even so . . . Ageing? Possibly. Old? Not in a million years. (No, that can't be right, can it? In a million years I'll be 1,000,066 which *is* getting on a bit.)

But despite the book's good notices, I probably won't be reading Gray's memoirs because he married a favourite ex-girlfriend of mine in 1997 and, being a Scorpio, I would find it hard to sit back and enjoy heart-warming recollections of the good times they have shared.

John Brown, who became a hugely successful publisher, was a young dynamo in the publicity department at Jonathan Cape when they were publishing my books in the seventies, and he liked nothing better than being out of the office on Bedford Square and on the road with the poet, armed with a case full of slim volumes to flog after the reading. We became chums, so when he mentioned how he had always wanted to watch the Grand National at Aintree, I invited him up to Liverpool to stay the weekend at Windermere House. Had John been a racehorse, he would have been a thoroughbred, raised in swanky stables and fed on a diet of top-class hay, and when he joined me for breakfast on that first morning wearing his silk dressing gown with a white linen handkerchief tucked into the top pocket, I could not escape the feeling that Windermere House was really his and I was merely the valet.

Deep down, of course, I knew that I owned the house because I had bought the white stuccoed Palladian pile in Princes Park in 1970 in an attempt to cheer myself up after breaking off with Thelma. Rumour has it, according to the nuns from Bellereve Convent next door, that I turned up one morning with a brown canvas bag containing bundles of used fivers, profits from the weekly sales of 'Lily the Pink', and made the owner an offer he couldn't refuse. My own recollection, however, is more mundane, involving a Halifax mortgage and a brown canvas bag filled only with poems and dirty laundry.

I think I may have been under pressure from my accountant to invest in property, and certainly John and Mike had bought houses, but I can only put down the purchase of a six-bedroomed mansion built for Sir Joseph Paxton, with a garden the size of a small jungle, as a symptom of mental instability. Within months of my moving in Thelma, now pregnant, joined me and we lived happily for a couple of years until, a wedding and two sons later, the rot set in:

It began in a corner of the bedroom
following the birth of the second child.
It spread into the linen cupboard
and across the fabric of our lives.
Experts came to treat it.
Could not.
The Rot could not be stopped.

Dying now, we live with it.
The fungus grows.
It spreads across our faces.
We watch the smiles rot,
Gestures crumble.
Diseased, we become the disease.
Part of the fungus.
The part that dreams, that feels pain . . .

In November 1976 Thelma moved into the side of the building we had converted for letting to tenants, taking the boys with her, while I was confined to solitary in the main house. Like most half-brained, stupid-assed ideas, this seemed like a good one at the time. There would be easy proximity, the children wouldn't feel the full pain of separation and it left open the possibility of an eventual reunion. In reality, of course, it merely enlarged the boxing ring.

Instead of thrilling to the sound of horses' hooves thundering towards Beecher's Brook, and marvelling at the sight of scarlet, sky-blue and gold, John bore open-mouthed witness to a no-holds-barred slanging match that lasted all weekend and wilted his linen handkerchief. Although there was no actual violence, Thelma drawing the line at physical abuse, it must have been a frightening experience for gentle

John, rather like being hurled through time into the future, to be saddled with a non-speaking part in a particularly tacky episode of *Brookside*.

Whenever I look at my diaries for the years 1974–7 I am overcome with a sense of fatigue and have to go for a lie-down. I hardly seemed to be in one place for more than a day at a time. There were long, gruelling tours with Grimms – the poetry/comedy/rock outfit; recording sessions in out-of-the-way places with strange-sounding names; the demise of the Scaffold involving tax inspectors toting small firearms; poetry festivals at home and abroad; creative writing courses at the Arvon Foundation; presenting *Focus*, a long-running series for BBC children's television; as well as popping over to Loughborough University on my days off to carry out my duties as Poetry Fellow. Thelma might claim with some justification that one of the reasons for the breakdown of our marriage was my constant travelling. She needed stability and there were those nearer to hand who could provide it, so we called in the lawyers.

I needed to move away from Liverpool and began to spend more and more time in London, either with Brian in his dark but flower-filled basement in Holland Park, or with Jim Goddard in his luminous top-floor flat round the corner. On the other side of Holland Park, in the house that would loom large in *The Smoking Diaries*, lived Victoria Rothschild who was a friend of John Brown's, and one evening, after a reading in Guildford, we dropped in to catch the tail end of a small party. As well as being super-intelligent and darkly beautiful, Victoria was bruised fruit, still recovering from the break-up of an intense affair, and I made her laugh. I think it was probably as simple as that. We started seeing each other and before long, and far too soon, I moved in with her.

If I'd hurried through the divorce as soon as it became obvious that the marriage was over, sold White Elephant House, agreed on a settlement and moved to London, who knows? I might have been the next Lord Rothschild. At least we could have done a bit of old-fashioned courting, phone calls, flowers, evenings at the cinema, instead of a few jokes and a long kiss followed by a brown canvas bag in the hall.

Although not divorced from Thelma, I was divorced from reality and living in a dream world in which I was single and free from all responsibilities. The truth hit me like a kick to the shin, twelve days after I had moved into Victoria's house in Addison Avenue, when Thelma arrived with the responsibilities, aged three and five, and keen on them spending time with me, dropped them off at the front door with suitcases full of their toys and clothing, and drove straight back to Liverpool. I sensed the going might be uphill after that and I was right. To add injury to insult, Tom was a toddling time-bomb, and within days Victoria had contracted chicken-pox and was unable to continue in her new post as a lecturer at Queen Mary College.

The following Monday afternoon, while Finn was sledging down the stairs on a tea tray, the invalids were in darkened bedrooms, whimpering softly and I was making an origami revolver out of a Nigel Dempster column in the *Mail* headed 'DOCKER'S SON DESERTS WIFE AND FAMILY TO LIVE WITH HEIRESS', when the front doorbell rang. It was Lady Rothschild with a flower stall wrapped in cellophane for her daughter, and, although she must have been mightily unimpressed with the latest boyfriend, and rightly so, she was too gracious to let it show. If I'd been her ladyship I would have kicked me out on my Scouse arse; instead, she sympathised with my predicament before going upstairs to comfort Victoria and cheer up Tom.

I was later to meet Lord Rothschild too, a meeting that was far scarier because his children were very much in awe of him, but he didn't attack me physically, as I feared he might. Instead, he made it clear that his daughter had been through an emotional wringer and needed a carefree settled life to enable her to enjoy her new academic post. He hoped that Victoria and I could sort out the arrangements with the boys and wished me well. In May I enrolled Finn at the Fox School at the back of Kensington Church Street, where Ivor Cutler taught, and pretended that everything would be fine. However, the strain on Victoria was ridiculous, particularly as I carried on my life as a performing poet, which had included the final appearance of the Scaffold at the Albert Hall on All Fools' Day, with the Monty Python team, Barbara Dickson and Alan Price, as well as three nights away in Paris: 'Victoria darling, just popping over to Paris for a few days, conference sort-of-thingy with Charles Causley, Dannie Abse and Jon Silkin. Any problems with the kids just give Brian Patten a ring. *Ciao*.'

In June, my mother, who had been suffering from Parkinson's disease for a number of years, was admitted into Walton Hospital, suffering from bowel cancer, so when the Fox School closed down at the end of the summer term I thanked Victoria for bravely putting up with us all, as well as putting us all up, wished her well and returned to Liverpool.

IT'S ONLY MONEY

I had long been a fan of the Bonzo-Dog Doo-Dah Band when I met Neil Innes in a men's boutique in Carnaby Street in the late sixties. Seeing a thin bloke with long hair wearing round shades and a cowboy hat across the store, I thought I was seeing my own reflection in one of the many mirrors – and so, it turned out, did he. His song 'I'm an Urban Spaceman' had just entered the charts, as had 'Lily the Pink' and we were to meet often over the coming months in television studios where we discovered that each group shared the other's Dadaesque sense of humour. So much so that the Scaffold plus Andy Roberts decided to team up with two of the Bonzos and do some shows together, and over the following months we played to packed houses at the Philharmonic Hall in Liverpool, Manchester's Free Trade Hall and the Dome in Brighton. This fusion of two anarchic groups we called Grimms (Gorman, Roberts, Innes, McGough, McGear, Stanshall) and it appealed to various managements who had no problem in signing us up to a record label. In 1973 we released two albums for Island, *GRIMMS* and *Rockin' Duck*, which you're unlikely to own, which is a pity because the sleeve of the latter is contained in a snazzy cardboard duck, which when removed can be worn on the head to amaze and delight your friends. The original line-up had been given added poetic zest with the inclusion of Brian Patten and Adrian Henri, augmented by various musicians as required, most notably Zoot Money, Ollie Halsall and, on one occasion, Keith Moon, who came on stage towards the end of our show at Kingston Poly and took over from our regular drummer. He was wearing a Viking helmet at the time, which was fairly apt because he raped and pillaged the drums. Coming off to wild applause after kicking over the cymbals and stabbing the snare-drum, he put an arm round a sobbing Mike Giles and said, 'Don't worry, mate, it's only money.'

Money, however, was not a commodity we saw much of. Following a fit of benign Communism at the outset, it had been decided to split all monies equally, and as some shows involved up to a dozen people on stage, plus sound engineers, lighting technicians, roadies, *feng shui* specialists and chiropractors, we were working for the love of it. Also, although on some nights the show was magical, Grimms was no fairy tale, and perhaps a more fitting title might have been ACANI (All Chiefs And No Indians). And some were warring chiefs and when they had taken of the firewater bad things happened. Like at Glasgow University when Brian was centre stage reading his love poems in that distinctive, boy-lost, melancholic voice, and had to contend with empty lager cans lobbed at him from the wings. The lobber was Viv Stanshall, a ginger Gandalf on mescalin and Special Brew, who couldn't understand why Brian was upset: 'Don't worry, dear boy, it's only poetry.'

Like on the coach returning from Manchester Poly late one Saturday night in November 1973, when the Liverpool poet and the Beatle brother finally came to blows. Whereas

Brian had flourished within the Grimms set-up, gaining confidence as a performer and coming up with theatrical ideas that were incorporated within the show, Mike had lost his way. No longer the lead vocalist, his only creative input were songs that the musicians didn't care for, and with his expensive stage suits and penchant for staying in four-star hotels while the rest of us stayed in B&Bs, he became an increasingly isolated figure. When he got off the coach that night and hitched a taxi back to Heswall, Mike had decided, 'I would cease my flirtation with showbiz therewith. Brian poet sent me a lovely apology by post, but my mind was made up. I had stopped being an entertainer.'

Viv had also climbed off, or rather, had been helped off, after the first tour. Although audiences loved him, there could be no denying the morbid fascination they felt as his reputation for being a wild man and a drinker grew with each performance. Will he forget the words? Will the microphone he's swinging hit Neil on the back of the head? Will he fall off stage? Will the next can he throws at Brian be on target?

> He was bright as tartan custard
> Loved the greasepaint and the roar
> He shimmied along a tightrope
> The safety-net nailed to the floor.

We all loved him, too, but he was such an eccentric, an innocent with an artistic ego that made it impossible for him to co-operate with others, and as co-operation was the whole ethos of Grimms, inevitably he sought another tightrope along which to shimmy.

But how we missed him being first in line with his tray at the motorway café. From the depths of whose deranged mind the idea had arisen I'm not sure, but it became the custom after the gig for the coach to call in at a motorway café, usually around two in the morning, where we each had to create and eat the most disgusting combination of food. Haddock and peas covered in custard proved popular, as did quiche and cornflakes. My fairly meek platter of apple pie and bacon was surprisingly tasty, the sweetness of the former offsetting the saltiness to pleasing effect. Other toothsome suppers eaten and enjoyed were raspberry jelly with poached egg and Liquorice Allsorts, and bakewell tart with beans and deep-fried onions. The most surreal part of the event was always the matter-of-factness shown by the girl at the till. Looking up from Viv's tray, which included a plate piled high with lamb chops and Black Forest gâteau covered with prawn curry, and pointing to a cup of tea with two sausages standing up in it, she asked coolly, 'Is that tea or coffee, luv?'

Adrian Henri, following his initial enthusiasm for the project, began to sense that there was one poet too many in the group, and one night after a gig at the South Pole, as we huddled together for warmth, nursing our mugs of cocoa, he stood up and, opening the flap in the side of the tent, announced, 'I am just going outside and may be some time,' then disappeared into that godforsaken plateau of ice where the howling blizzard engulfed him. The tighter, fitter, slimmed-down version of the group now had commercial potential, but we'd already burned our boats as well as the fingers of our first two managers, and, because our albums had sold in their tens rather than in their thousands, Island

Records had thrown in the towel. One management company, however, believed that there was money to be made and signed us up to their record label, Oak. I think it was the name that attracted us, ancient, sturdy and reliable, and they were right, there was money to be made, but if it grew on trees, we didn't get any.

SLEEPERS

A parcel arrived this morning containing ten copies of *Sleepers*, the last album recorded by Grimms, and now reissued thirty years later by Hux Records as a CD. The cover is a shot of the seven who made up the group during its final phase, lying on a railway track as if fast asleep, heads on one rail, feet on the other, and seeing it brought back the memory of what I was thinking when the photograph was taken: I hope a train comes hurtling out of the tunnel. Such a dark, belligerent thought, however, had nothing to do with my fellow sleepers, but with my mental state:

> *I wanted one life,*
> *You wanted another*
> *We couldn't have our cake*
> *So we ate each other*

Immediately after three weeks on the road with Grimms in February and March 1975, I began rehearsals for the series of twelve programmes for BBC's Education department called *Focus*, which involved scriptwriting and presenting mini-dramas dealing with various mathematical concepts. One episode, for instance, had me standing in front of a row of fruit machines at a funfair on Clapham Common on a dark and rainy night, trying to make myself heard above the music and the jeering, as I explained to camera the complex theories of chance. Script meetings and rehearsals were held in London, and the filming was done on location all over the country, so I was rarely in Liverpool. And when I was back home . . .

> *We've had our clichés framed*
> *And hung upon the wall*
> *So now for conversation*
> *We don't have to talk at all.*

Publicity photographs show a very washed-out presenter, angst-ridden and withdrawn, gazing beyond the camera lens as if on the run rather than on location. Instead of being with his sons and sorting out the conflict with Thelma, and helping Brenda, who was facing her own marital problems, to find a nursing home for Mother, whose condition was worsening, where was I? On top of Salisbury Cathedral wearing a safety harness and explaining the theory of gravity.

Brenda had known from an early age what she wanted to do in life and on leaving school went straight into nursing, initially at Walton General and later in a smaller private hospital. She was cut out for the job: fearless and tough, she had a sense of humour, earthy and irreverent, that made her popular with staff and patients alike, and a laugh that was infectious (except, of course, on the isolation wards). When the Parkinson's disease began to squeeze the life out of my mother she moved in with Brenda, her husband Wally and their three sons, and was cared for until cancer eventually killed her. Whenever I was in Liverpool for more than a few days at a time I would take a bus out to Waterloo and spend a couple of hours with her, spinning tales of marital harmony and Scaffold high jinks. Then I would disappear for weeks. 'Our Roger came to see me on Thursday,' Mother would proudly tell anyone who was visiting. 'Always drops in when he can.' And they'd all nod and agree that I was a wonderful son, and Brenda would nod and go to the kitchen to get Mother's medication, before washing her and preparing supper.

'Whenever I feel in need of exercise I put on a tracksuit and write poems about athletics' begins the preface to *Sporting Relations* published by Methuen in 1974 and written during my residency as Poetry Fellow at Loughborough University, a post I'd taken up the previous year, attracted by the prospect of an oasis of calm away from the madness of touring and the debilitating skirmishes at home, where I could wander through the groves of academe writing poems that were gifted from the ether, not wrought from the emotional debris surrounding me. But it didn't work out. (Ever been to Loughborough?) Not only was it an uphill struggle getting science and engineering students interested in poetry, but it became another commitment in an already overcrowded diary. Also, I was lonely. Too old for student parties and, being a non-driver, unable to escape to the pubs in town, my social life became unbearably bleak. Most nights I would head for the Purple Onion, the coffee bar on campus, where I would sit in the corner glowering above a rampart of books. The university was justly proud of its reputation for sport and purple was the colour of the tracksuits worn by the college athletes. Every day I would be out there on the track trying hard to run away from myself. In fact, I spent so much time wearing a tracksuit that I began to feel like a Purple Onion. You know when you're peeling an onion and you don't know when to stop? Is it peeled, or should I take off another layer? You begin with a vegetable the size of your fist and end up in tears with something the size of a garlic clove. That was me.

ONCE I LIVED IN CAPITALS
MY LIFE INTENSELY PHALLIC
but now I'm sadly lowercase
with the occasional *italic*

'*I'm having a baby.*' Isn't that one of the most wondrous lines in the language?

I had known for some time what made women pregnant, and I had always assumed that when the good news was announced I would take the mother-to-be in my arms like I was Jimmy Stewart, and swing her round and round. But somehow I was never prepared: '*You're having a what?*' I'd find myself saying, before recovering my balance to add,'*That's . . . wonderful . . .*'

But that wasn't how I felt. I had always fancied the idea of the lonely poet, a free spirit without the ties that bind ordinary mortals to earth. At each newsflash, and there were four of them, I had to stop myself bursting into tears and heading for the door. I think that for a lot of men children are gifts they are never quite ready for, but which once unwrapped, they can't bear to be separated from. When I went to Cornwall in September 1975 to record what turned out to be Grimms' final album, Finn was three and Tom just over a year, and I was in danger of losing them.

The Sawmills recording studios in Fowey lay at the receiving end of the disused railway line on which we sleepers lay for the album cover, and had been chosen by our new manager for its cheapness and remoteness. Watching him fill the kitchen cupboard with cans of beans and cans of sausages and beans on that first cold, wet morning, I thought back to the summer of 1972 when we recorded *Fresh Liver* for Island Records at the Manor Studios in Shipton-on-Cherwell belonging to Richard Branson, where our producer, Tim Rice, presided over sumptuous dinners served by ravishing young wenches. At the Sawmills, I suspected, rapier-like shafts of wit would not be exchanged over impetuous yet able-bodied wine.

The first four-sixths of the acronym, Gorman, Roberts, Innes and Myself, went into the studio with three other musicians including our key keyboard player John Megginson intent on making an album with a chance of commercial success, which meant no poems and no sketches. 'The Womble Bashers of Walthamstow', a lyric of mine that Neil set to music, although hardly commercial, remains one of my favourite tracks. Remember the chorus? Of course you don't:

> *We're the Womble bashers from Walthamstow*
> *Make Womble trouble wherever we go*
> *From Wimbledon to John o' Groats*
> *We wear Womble-skin fur coats.*

Unfortunately, the BBC refused to play it for fear of upsetting Uncle Bulgaria and his little furry friends who were big on television, and rumoured to have connections with the Balkan mafia. Our other songs didn't make the play list either, because by the time the album was released, our manager had chopped down the oak tree and left the country, taking the acorns with him. Our farewell tour, although we didn't know it was that at the time, had been called *Clowns on the Road*, and now for that group of itinerant poets, musicians and comics, who had been on the road periodically for more than five years, the time had come to hang up their red noses and face reality.

> *Away from the laughter*
> *the lights, the applause,*
> *I'm nobody's fool*
> *Only yours.*

THE LEAVING OF LIVERPOOL

As soon as I walked through the door of Windermere House there were tears of joy. 'Daddy, Daddy,' was the cry, the jumping up and down with excitement, the licking of my face and the wagging of the tail. Confused? Probably not as much as Tom and Finn, whose dad's comings and goings produced a roller coaster of emotions, although not including face-licking or tail-wagging. That would be Bran's department. Finn would have been about two years old when we acquired a pet dog. I say *we* but it was Thelma who decided that what every family needs is a dog and wasn't there a park next door for it to run around, and wouldn't it be company for our little son, and wouldn't she feel safer when I was away from home? Well . . . er, if you say so, love.

There is a track on the Beatles' *White Album* (1968) called 'Martha My Dear', named after Paul's favourite pet. Martha, a big, floppy English sheepdog, produced a litter with the help of another of his dogs, a Dalmatian called Spot (actually, I'm just guessing at the name because we were never introduced), and when Thelma heard from the McCartneys that there were puppies in need of a home, she offered to take one. We chose the name Bran, not because it was full of goodness, or rich in dietary fibre, but because we were pursuing a Celtic trail at the time, christening our first son Finn after the legendary Irish king Finn McCool who had two wolfhounds, Bran and Spot. (Actually, it wasn't Spot either, it was Sgeolan, but nobody could pronounce it.) When our second son was baptised we chose Tom Tara, Tara being the once ancient seat of the High Kings of Ireland. And so, with a bloodline running directly from Celtic royalty through to a Beatle, Bran, whose white coat with black splodges always looked too big for him, would be around for a long time.

Unlike all of my previous pets, I must confess. Yesterday afternoon Matt and I took our new kitten to the vet's for its anti-flu jab and I was telling him how, as far as I remembered, none of my childhood pets ever saw the inside of a vet's surgery. Kittens and puppies arrived, grew up and got run over. That was it, no need for expensive injections or treatments. In a month's time he'll be going back for a snip that will have me weak at the knees, and watching him now, curled up on the sofa like a discarded ginger toupee, I think of a verse written in my teens:

> *Play on young friend, leap and bound*
> *Roll on around the tingling ground*
> *Bite and scratch and act real claw-full*
> *Before the vet does something awful.*

He'll get over it, but the tragedy that befell our first kitten was so heartbreaking, so disquieting, that readers of a nervous disposition may wish to skip the next paragraph. One evening after work, Dad brought home a kitten. It was a complete surprise, and my sister and I were overjoyed when he produced it from his overcoat pocket like a magician. 'Hey Presto!' he cried. That's a funny name for a pussy cat, we thought, we'll soon find a better one. But, sad to say, before we had time to think of a name, our very first kitten had come to a sticky end. Brenda's, in fact.

I watched this tiny ball of electric fluff as it raced across the carpet to skid out of control on the lino and crash into the wall, thinking that cats were even more fun to play with than toy cheese. Again and again he did it until, tiring, he wandered out into the kitchen. Had I followed, it might never have happened. Mum was there getting our tea ready with my sister who would have been a toddler of about eighteen months old. According to my mother, Brenda had been squatting down on her haunches when she beckoned the kitten towards her, and pussy's mistake was to stroll through the dimpled portals of her bonny knees. On turning her head to see where it was going, Brenda toppled backwards and . . .

If you have just rejoined the narrative after skipping the preceding paragraph, what happened was that my little sister sat on a baby kitten and squashed it to death. Splat! Just like that. Sorry.

The one good habit I picked up at Loughborough was the daily jog, and whenever I was home on leave I would put on my purple tracksuit and jog round Princes Park with Bran. The secret of jogging, I have discovered, is not to run too far, or go too fast. On no account must you overtake another jogger, or else the invigorating dawdle will turn into a three-mile sprint, ending in either a cheerless win or a cardiac arrest. Late one morning as I ambled through the park gates at the end of my run I saw two teenage girls waiting outside the house, so I put on a spurt along

Windermere Terrace to impress them. I obviously did because the one holding the autograph book said: 'You're one-of-the-Scaffold, aren't yeh?'

'That's right, yes.'

'We've come for an autograph.'

'A pleasure, girls, just hang on here and I'll nip inside and get a photograph as well.'

'No, we don't want yours, mate, we want Paul's dog's.'

'Pardon?'

The other girl produced an inkpad out of her pocket and, taking Bran's paw, pressed it on to the pad and then on to the page of the book her friend was holding.

'But how can you prove it's Bran's paw print?' I muttered peevishly.

But the camera was already out and the photograph taken.

'And here's one of Philomena with Paul McCartney's dog outside one-of-the-Scaffold's house.'

During the mid-seventies, with Thelma living next door and the boys passing between us, I was at my wit's end. The day-to-day drill left me with little time or energy to write, and I had to turn down any work that meant my being out of town. When I was away I would worry about what was happening at home, and when I was at home I would worry about what was happening at home. I needed advice on how to get organised but there were no local networks for single fathers and no one to whom I could talk, except the dog, of course, and, when I was really desperate, the wardrobe. Had he been able to cook and drive, Bran would have saved me the agonising experience of having to hire and fire nannies.

Two were OK. The hippy singleton with a five-year-old hippy daughter who wanted somewhere nice to live, but there was only so much dope I could passively smoke and so much muesli the boys could eat, so we were relieved when Claudia took over. An art school model, she was a happy-go-lucky American girl who fed them on home-made burgers and barbecue ribs until a photographer snapped her up. The other nannies who passed through were under the impression that there would be weekly showbiz parties and that the job would entail frequent trips to London and New York, as well as a request, eventually, to move into the master bedroom. One girl even volunteered to wear a French maid's outfit around the house. 'With black stockings and things.'

The outfit I chose to wear when I went down to the Philharmonic pub on Saturday 18 September 1977 was a rust-coloured three-piece suit of Irish herringbone and a collarless grandad shirt, very fashionable in a Gilbert O'Sullivan, down-at-heel sort of way. Luckily for me, beauty is in the eye of the beholder and the beholder at the bus stop that evening, waiting for the bus that would never arrive, could see through the rough tweed to the coarse linen beneath. For my part, I could see in her someone strong and centred. The eldest of four children from a close family that welcomed me into its warm and mildly eccentric Yorkshire heart, Hilary Clough was secure enough in herself to allow me to continue my peripatetic life. Twenty-seven years later I don't travel as much, and although she respects what I do for a living and will cast an eye over a poem if asked nicely, she remains healthily unimpressed by the mystique of *la vie poétique*. The existential darkness of the soul, the perpetual angst and ennui cut no ice with her. Whenever I allude to the infinite sadness within, the chaos that gives birth to the dancing star, she tells me to put the kettle on. Suffice it to say that I am grateful to the bus drivers of the Liverpool Corporation Transport Department for going on strike that sunny evening long ago, and now I will leave her be because she doesn't like a fuss. Hilary made me laugh at a time when I really needed to, and we formed a bond that was to be tested by my mother's death two months later, not to mention the spanners thrown into the works by one of our exes. But we determined to find a way out. And the way out was down the M6.

One question I have been asked over the years, usually as an accusation, is: Why did you leave Liverpool? From a Scouser it implies 'traitor', from someone else, 'If the Liverpool you're always banging on about is so great, why did you clear off?' The answer I invariably trot out, 'for domestic reasons', sounds a bit lame, but is nonetheless true. After working for Granada television in Manchester, Thelma got a job with LWT in 1978 and moved down to London with the boys and her partner, and with Hilary considering a post in health education after topping up her Ph.D. with an M.Sc. at the Chelsea College of Science, it was time for me to up sticks and go. Unfortunately, the sticks proved difficult to up, and it was several years before I managed to sell Albatross House and move from our small rented flat in Fulham to a house on the Portobello Road.

'If you can't fight, buy a big house' is inked inside a drawer of the desk at which I'm now sitting, written during the early seventies in a slough of prescient defeatism.

Because buying a big house, like having a baby or wife-swapping, is an activity that couples very often engage in to shore up a failing relationship. When I went back to Windermere House for the last time, to collect Bran, I couldn't get away from it quick enough, in case the new owners arrived with a police escort and a court order for me to resume habitation. Dwarfed by its size and pretensions, I was always cowed by the house and never grew into it, but now, in my mid forties, there was a new beginning. Finally moving away from Liverpool and living in London rather than camping out, would I be dwarfed by the capital's size and pretensions, or would I grow into it?

I knew for a fact that Bran had never been on a train before, but on the journey from Lime Street to Euston he never once looked out of the window, even going over the bridge outside Runcorn, which is always good value. We were in one of those six-seater compartments, you rarely see on trains nowadays, and he spent the whole journey stretched out on the floor, gazing straight up at me. *'You bastard. I can tell by the guilty look on your face that we're not going on holiday. You're taking me to a place that I'm not going to like. You're planning to have me put down, aren't you? Me, your faithful friend for more than a decade. Me, who confronted the burglars the night they broke in through the french windows. Me, who used to babysit Tom and Finn while you sloped off to the pub. Me, who chased the overtakers out of the park while you were jogging. Me, Paul McCartney's dog's dog, for godsake.'*

Although wrong about the dogicide, he got two out of three right, which wasn't bad for a big hairy mongrel with floppy ears; but unlike him, I became very fond of our new home at the Notting Hill Gate end of Portobello Road. The great advantage of living in a street famous the world over for its antiques market is that if you get lost, you can simply ask a passing tourist for directions. Although number 70 was a three-storey terrace-house with four bedrooms, it would have fitted inside the hallway of Windermere, but I liked its compactness, with my study on the top floor overlooking a busy street. My study in Liverpool had been a large, beautiful room with french windows through which you stepped on to a wrought-iron balcony that overlooked a garden the size of a football pitch, stretching down to the railings that separated us from Princes Park with its lake and trees. Beautiful, except for Mother Nature, to whose tender mercies I left the garden, and Mother Superior next door, who feared for the safety of her convent girls as the wild, lascivious jungle encroached.

The Poet's Garden

The garden is looking particularly alright at this time of the year.
There are pinky things everywhere, and sort of red bits in waving clumps.
The lawn is as green as grass and studded with little yellow studs.
Flowers, I think they are called.

I think I may suffer from a kind of floral dyslexia, in that I hardly ever notice flowers. 'Did you remember to water the house plants?' my wife will ask, after a few days away.

'What plants?' I enjoy sitting outside reading, or kicking a ball around the lawn, but the perfumed periphery remains a blur. And although I find pleasure in walking around the garden, with Hilary patiently naming the flowers she has nurtured, I'm ashamed to say that it's in one ear and out the other. 'Mmm, smell this,' she will say. And I do, but it's in one nostril and out the other. Perhaps that coffin-shaped patch of mud in the backyard of 11 Ruthven Road, with its man-eating worms and stinging irises, has a lot to answer for.

During the three days and nights of the Notting Hill Festival the revellers need somewhere to deposit their empty Red Stripe cans and half-chewed corn cobs, so all the houses at the south end of Portobello Road have small patios at the front. And there I would sit with my newspapers on warm Sunday afternoons, watching legions of excitable tourists making their way to the market, only to trudge back hours later like a defeated army, having found it closed. When space was needed I had a key for communal gardens in Ladbroke Square, but dogs had to be kept on a lead and Bran was never to find the freedom he had enjoyed in Liverpool. Nor the respect, for the local dogs were unaware of and unimpressed by his glitzy pedigree, so he began to throw his weight around, pummelling poodles, terrifying terriers, chewing Chihuahuas, to the extent that, pursued by angry neighbours, I was paying vet's fees for half the dogs in Notting Hill.

> *Here lies Bran*
> *Left Liverpool 8 for West 11*
> *Couldn't settle, went to heaven.*

HANSEL AND GRETEL

Susan Sarandon leaned across the table of Elaine's restaurant in New York, and said, 'Louis and I are going on to Woody Allen's party later, and you'd be very welcome to join us, he'd just love to meet you both, wouldn't he, Louis?' Louis Malle nodded. Brian and I agreed it was a very tempting offer, but thanks anyway, we'll just grab a cab back to the hotel, after all, it was nearly eleven o'clock. As I write this I can't believe we were so weary as to turn down an invitation to meet Woody Allen and Jane Fonda, not to mention spending more time getting to know Susan. (Monsieur Malle seemed a nice enough guy, but he was too old and serious for her. What this up-and-coming young actress needed, I reckoned, was to be seen on the arm of a Liverpool poet. This one.) But the arm had to be up early to catch a flight to Toronto, so it left Elaine's restaurant on 42nd Street and went straight to bed.

The Great American Poetry tour of 1979 had been pulled together by Olwyn, a friend of ours who worked for the London Poetry Secretariat, and Clodagh, a fizzy Irish bookseller, based at the time in Yorkshire, who thought there was money to be made in selling our books at the readings. It would be an *On the Road* adventure, with Clodagh driving the hired Buick from college to college across the eastern seaboard, with Olwyn in front map-reading and the two poets in the back being witty and lyrical. We flew from Gatwick on 9 March and checked in at the Chelsea Hotel where the desk clerk amazed me by saying, 'Weren't you here a couple of chapters ago with the Scaffold?' I congratulated him on his surreal memory for faces and asked if this time he could give me a room, if not without cockroaches, at least with different ones and he was happy to oblige.

After only two readings, at Colegate University in Hamilton and Bucknell in Lewisburg, it had become obvious that Clodagh had brought too many books. Whereas at home if we performed to an audience of 300 to 500, a third would buy a book after the show, in the States, even though we had some of the biggest ever turnouts for a poet, the only ones interested in buying books were the professors. Eight gigs stretched over twenty-seven days, including an evening at the Harbourfront Arts Center in Toronto, was never going to make sound economic sense, but now it began to look like economic suicide, and the lack of media coverage meant that our visit would remain a secret beyond the thirty-two walls of the venues we played. I am, by nature, reasonably docile and accommodating, but Brian is less so. I'd had the Irish Christian Brothers beating the virtues of patience and fortitude into me at school, but Brian hadn't. I had been on the road with the Scaffold for twelve years, having to deal with difficult managers, stoned drummers and stroppy landladies, but Brian hadn't. He wanted to go home and said so frequently in the back of the hired Buick.

Thirteen days into the tour we drove the 380 miles from

Lewisburg, crossing the Susquehanna river to stop off in Toledo where we were made welcome by two local poets, Nick Musca and Joel Lipman, who put us all up at their house. At eleven the following morning they dropped Brian and me off at Lucas County jail outside the city, where we would read and run a workshop for those inmates with an interest in poetry. How would we deal with 500 verse-starved convicts, we wondered? After the reading should we divide them into smaller groups for the workshop according to ability or to the seriousness of their offences?

'Hands up those who know what a sonnet is? Good, hands down.'

'Hands up those who are in for first-degree murder? Good, hands down.'

As it happened, only three had volunteered, all drug offenders, and our task was to keep them awake when the medication was wearing off and, once the guard had handed out small plastic beakers of pills, to keep them from climbing up the walls and writing gibberish. On our release at the end of the day we were worn out, and looking forward to a few cold beers and a smoked possum pastie, and were totally unprepared for what lay in store. The birds had flown. On the table in the kitchen was a note from Clodagh saying that Olwyn had flown to Los Angeles, which had always been part of the plan, and she had flown home, which hadn't. It had all become too much for them. Apologies and good luck for the rest of the tour etc. In the corner of the room, like vanities awaiting the bonfire, stood a huge stack of our poetry books.

To this day I'm still not quite sure why they did a runner. I mean, later we would hear rumours of slipped discs, trouble on the domestic front as well as a 'mushrooming of Brian's insecurity', as Clodagh put it in a letter to Jonathan Cape who had supplied the books, but in truth, it came as a bolt from the blue. No hints, no dark mutterings, just a hurried note and the itinerary with details of the remaining venues, as well as the books, most of which Brian and I decided to leave in the safe hands of the Toledo poets to await collection.

Monday 26 March 1979: 7.45 on the road with Nick and Joel, who have gallantly stepped into the breach to drive us to Dayton for tonight's reading at the Catholic University. They are a sort of literary Cheech & Chong, very upfront and easygoing, forever rolling joints and passing round jugs of home-made ale and wine. I realise that Brian and I are not very good at fun, and assume that if Nick and Joel had been Liverpool poets Clodagh and Olwyn might not have fled.

Next morning Hansel and Gretel are left to their own devices as we board the 10.55 a.m. Greyhound bus for Pittsburgh. Previous romantic ideas about Greyhound buses are quickly dashed, for this one is just another smoky coach filled with those who can't afford quicker and more comfortable means of transport. Eight hours later the Mersey chapter of white trash alights heavily at Pittsburgh and heads for the university, where it will be staying for a couple of nights.

We are to take part in an international forum, as well as giving a reading, and so are cosseted in the monogrammed heaven that is the University Club. That evening, over a leisurely dinner of Blue Point oysters followed by fillet of beef with blue cheese, served with whipped acorns and marshmallow, we look at the itinerary and wonder if we should cancel the reading at a New York bookshop, for which there is no fee, and fly directly to Canada.

Friday 30 March: You can't enter the breakfast room without a tie, so the maître d' pulled out a couple of Garrick Club ties from under the counter so that we could sit down to a plate of sausages, buried alive under french toast the size of paving stones, golluped in syrup. Taxi to airport and a one-hour flight in home-made plane to La Guardia airport. It is 70 degrees and humid in New York, ideal conditions for the mushrooming of insecurity.

As it turned out, the reading that night at Books & Co. on Madison Avenue proved to be one of the highlights of the tour, with a large, enthusiastic crowd including our old friend John Brown from Jonathan Cape, his great-uncle Maurice who had been a sweetheart of Ivor Novello, and a young actress none of us had heard of at the time, Susan Sarandon, who invited us to join her for supper the following evening. If only I had listened to my body: *Go to bed reasonably early, Roger, for I need sleep. What I don't need is more fillet of beef with blue cheese, and bottles of red wine and bourbon, and smoky bars, for remember we have a special date tomorrow and who knows, you may get to meet Woody Allen.* But I didn't listen and next day my body was disassembled, my brain inert and my film career in tatters. On Sunday morning a chastened duo flew into Canada and after an easy 2–nil victory at the Harbourfront Arts Centre, which was packed with expats, we shuffled off to Buffalo for the final twitch of the Great American tourette.

Thursday 5 April: Lift to Buffalo with Vic and Gerry, not ice-cream makers, but Canadian poets and friends of Greg Gatenby who programmes the Harbourfront. We pass the Harrisburg nuclear plant with the car windows tightly shut and holding our breath, because there has been a leak recently and people round about are terrified, and rightly so. No one is eating Hershey bars any more because the milk from local cows is said to be infected. For the first time in weeks we read the newspapers in preparation for our return to the real world. In Pakistan, President Bhutto has been executed. At home, Jim Callaghan has been forced to call a general election and in Alabama there is a revival of the Ku Klux Klan.

Saturday 7 April: Arrive Gatwick 08.00. Train to Victoria. Taxi to Euston. Train to Liverpool. Thelma to Crete.

THE LITTLE POOR POETS

Dear Mr McGough,

Our Poetry Festival goes from strength to strength and we are already making plans for the future. Adrian Henri performed this year and was very entertaining, and so of course we can't have another Liverpool poet for at least three years, with that in mind, the committee wondered if you might come and read for us in '88 . . .

Dear Roger,

Please excuse my familiarity but I feel that I know you having listened to you on the radio. Would you come and read for us at the Centre? If you are unavailable on the 24th of next month perhaps Brian Patten would come, or failing that, the other one . . .

Dear Mr McGough,

Our quarterly readings held here in the library have been well received by a small but appreciative audience, due mainly to the calibre of the poets who have read for us, including . . . and . . . However, to close the season we decided to move into the large hall next door for an evening of fun and light verse, pints and poems in the Liverpool manner and wondered if . . .

Tricky things, labels, and the Liverpool tag, though convenient at the time for journalists, became something of an albatross round our necks as our poems, and occasionally our personae, became confused in the public perception. If I had £7 million for every time someone said to me: '*I love that one of yours about the beautiful girl petrol pump attendant on the motorway,* "*I wanted your soft verges / But you gave me the hard shoulder*",' I'd be a rich man. And rather than refute ownership, more likely I would nod and smile modestly, because the enthusiast was so excited about remembering the poem and meeting its author that it seemed a shame to contradict (although I certainly would if it were an Adrian Henri poem with knickers in). Having lived there for most of my life, I remain proud of a city that has always tried to turn anger and confusion into art and humour, but I'm equally aware of the hostility it arouses beyond its parish boundaries. Alan Bennett, in *Writing Home*, talks of his dislike of a people 'who have figured in too many plays, and who have a cockiness that comes from being told too often that they and their city are special. Every Liverpudlian seems a comedian, fitted out with smart answers, ready with the chat and anxious to do his little verbal dance.' I take on the collective Scouse mortification that one of our leading playwrights didn't enjoy his stay there, but, with respect, wonder if, seing a recognisably famous wordsmith, the locals weren't drawn to him like bees to honey, or in his case, lambs to the slaughter. Liverpool has had more than its fair share of media mauling over the years and the fact that it stands up for itself on the verbal dance floor is something to be admired.

If I were a 'Hull poet' or a 'Sheffield poet', what would

that mean? Presumably that I was born or lived in Hull or Sheffield. A 'St Ives poet'? Mmm, writes about coves and seagulls, lots of colour, yellow and blue mainly, and you can almost hear the waves lapping against the bows of his sonnets. A 'Cambridge poet'? Ah, tricky. L=A=N=G=U=A=G=E probably, an egghead without the yolk, writing to slow the reader down and trip him up. But the sobriquet 'Liverpool poet' does not suggest geography, a town on the River Mersey in south-west Lancashire, so much as class, an era and an attitude. Brian, Adrian and I shared many views and influences, but we were never 'the group' that many thought us to be, and since those early days the differences have become more distinctly apparent. Brian in particular felt uneasy with the branding and during the eighties – 'a lost period when I was re-inventing myself. I just wished I knew into what' – he was averse to performing under that banner. So in the 1980s when 'The Liverpool Poets' toured Germany what the audiences usually got was Adrian, myself and Andy Roberts.

And audiences were not sold short, for Andy provided not only a guitar backing to some of the poems, but was a performer who could act when required, as well as sing his own songs, so when we played to audiences for whom English was a second language, the variety on offer enabled the British Council to combine school and university readings with large-scale events in public venues. Like the Richard Strauss Room in the Gasteig Konzertsaal in Munich in May 1989, for instance, when the literature officer from the Council arrived during our tech rehearsal, brandishing a sheaf of programmes and looking very angry. 'Those printers have cocked it up again. I spent ages writing the programme notes, trying to give some idea about the show, and what I wrote was: "Tonight will NOT be an ordinary poetry reading, blah, blah, blah", and what have they put? "Tonight will be an ordinary poetry reading." I'm bloody furious and I'm so sorry about this.' In fact, it didn't matter at all, because the prospect of an unexceptional evening's poetry may explain why the remaining tickets went like hot *Kuchen*.

I never kept a diary or a journal during the time I lived in Liverpool, although I would occasionally put my thoughts down in the hard-backed A4 notebooks used for writing the poems, alongside cartoons, stories, scripts, comedy sketches, shopping lists and running orders. (In fact, my collection of running orders for poetry performances as well as Scaffold and Grimms shows would make a delightful stocking filler should any waggish publisher be interested.) These entries were never a record of places visited, people met or things said, but rather internal jottings, first drafts that might resurface later as poems. But during the years that followed, when I travelled alone, writing became a displacement activity and 'The ALWYCH book' with the *All Weather* cover was always to hand.

Adrian, too, was a compulsively neat scribbler, whose notebooks were filled with drawings as well as tickets for trams and museums, sweet wrappers, *die rechnungs* from favourite restaurants, billets-doux in various languages, all fodder to be used in his collages. I never miss him more than when I'm in a foreign town: his artist's eye for architectural detail, the way he would become transfixed by a shop window display of sweets or cakes. Even butchers' shops would have him window gazing, forever searching for the poet's sausage, '*Blankwurst*'. His surreal, photo-realistic paint-ings of the time reflect mortality by proffering a seemingly contradictory bouquet of raw meat, heavy with blood, and delicate spring flowers, freshly cut: '*Of meat and flowers, I sing / Butchers and gardeners . . .*' I never miss him more than when visiting churches and art galleries, where he would be the enthusiastic guide and fount of all the knowledge you needed.

March 1982, Karlsruhe: Dorte Wiesehofer from the Council ('Hello, I'm dirty' is what we thought she said when introducing herself) took us to the Kunsthalle to see the Grünewald *Crucifixion*. Adrian could hardly contain his excitement, and when we turned into the main gallery and she pointed to the painting on the wall twenty yards ahead, Adrian ran forward, slipped and slid the length of the polished parquet on his back, crashing into the wall to join Our Lady at the foot of the cross.

May 1989, Bonn: In the dressing room before the show at the 'Brotfabrik' (not 'Bread fabric', which conjures up images of sofas made out of bagels, gluten-free cushion covers and self-raising curtains, but 'bread factory', recently converted into a theatre). The stage manager Manfred Klaus comes in to enquire if we need anything else to drink. 'Do you have to drink?' is what he says.

'Oh, yes, we have to,' we chorused, falling off our wholemeal chairs laughing.

It was during that same tour of Germany that yet another slip of the foreign tongue caused mirth and embarrassment, especially during the book signing after the show when everybody had a kind word for us and many offered to take us home for supper, or at least accept a handful of loose change. The British Council office in Cologne had rung the venues of the towns in which we were due to appear, asking them to print posters with details of the event. Unfortunately, the word Liverpool had been misheard, and on arrival in Aachen we were delighted to see posters everywhere advertising 'The Little Poor Poets'.

Holland, too, always kept a welcome in the valleys for the Little Poor Poets.

June 1991, Rotterdam: 'Slept like a clog. Missed breakfast so wandered down to the waterfront and bought a carton of fried fish from a herring stall. An old man sat next to me on the wall and nodded. We watched the seagulls screeching and fighting over fishtails and crusts before he spoke to me in Dutch. I apologised for being English and offered him some of my herring. "No thank you," he said, "I have just passed some potatoes." So we left it at that.'

Back at De Doelen (the concert hall where the festival is taking place) I meet up with Carol Ann Duffy, the naughtiest girl in the class and the most gifted. She is composing a letter to put into Adrian's pigeon-hole. It is from a sixteen-year-old girl 'of the hair blonde and the long leg' who, when not at school, works in a strip club. She loves especially 'BIG poets with horses' tails' and hopes to meet her favourite poet tonight after the concert, where she will be wearing 'the white ankle socks and the black leather miniskirt'. The letter is completely and purposely over the top but Adrian is such a hopeless romantic that on reading it he can hardly contain his excitement, 'I need to calm myself down, I think I'll go back to the hotel room and count my guilders.'

That night, at the opening concert of Poetry International, Adrian, with Andy on guitar, was really out to impress, and before the applause had died down he was off the stage and into the bar before Miroslav Holub, Breyten Breytenbach, Carol Ann or any of us had time to bow, wave or curtsy. Disappointed though he may have been at the non-appearance of the fictitious sixteen-year-old schoolgirl stripper, there was always something for Ade to celebrate, like being within proximity of a bar, for instance, and at midnight-thirty when we all decided to head back to the hotel, he opted to have one more for the road with his new-found Dutch chums.

Surprisingly Adrian, famed for his powers of recuperation, was not down for breakfast and when he failed to appear for lunch we began to worry that perhaps at 4 a.m. in a seedy transvestite club he saw a tall blonde wearing 'the white ankle socks and the black leather miniskirt' sitting at the bar, and mistaking the truck driver for a schoolgirl had introduced himself and, oh dear . . . But later in the afternoon when he emerged gingerly from his room, the tale he told with some relish was horrific, if not quite on the scale of our worst imaginings.

After leaving the concert hall, Adrian had been taken to a string of bars, how many he wasn't quite sure, nor could he remember at what time the students decided to throw in the towel, but he does remember the group farewell hug on the pavement and the offer to drive him back to the hotel on Kruiskade. 'No thanks, the walk will do me good' were his last words which, in retrospect, proved to be widely off the mark. Adrian set off along the main street and turned left. Had he turned right he would have found the hotel a hundred metres up the road, but instead, he kept on walking and walking. It occurred to him at one point that he might have lost his way, but the streets were deserted, so he kept on walking and walking. Then, it seems, he fell asleep, but kept on walking and walking. As Adrian explained later, he didn't black out, but in fact had pleasant dreams, he felt invigorated as he walked, eyes closed, just walking and walking. It was a sudden rush of cold air that jolted him awake, the slipstream of a white van that missed him by a beard's breadth, and as his eyes began to focus he saw a sign ahead saying Amsterdam . . . Amsterdam?

Having fallen asleep in a dream, he awoke to a nightmare, for he looked about him and realised that he was on the inside lane of a motorway. Dawn was blinking and the traffic was slowly building up as our hero had the sense to panic, scamper across the tarmac and scramble up the embankment. He was lost, he was in pain, he was in a foreign country and he could sense one almighty hangover crouching in the shadows behind, waiting to leap out and maul him to near death. But big poets don't cry, they either write a poem or they seek help, and in this case Adrian wisely decided on the assistance option. Through the rising mist, in the far distance he could make out a farmhouse with a light in the window, so he set off across fields not of barley, oats or even tulips, but of hot coals, for each step now was agony, and on reaching the farmhouse he had to bang on the door for ages before it was eventually opened. Having reassured the farmer that he was neither a ghoul nor someone returning home from a fancy dress ball dressed as one of Vincent van Gogh's potato eaters, Adrian was admitted, given bread and coffee, and a taxi was called.

Waking in the hotel bedroom some hours later, he looked at the feet propped up on the headboard and thought he must have fallen asleep wearing a pair of red wooden clogs, but no, they were his feet, bloody, swollen and bare.

On a silent motorway stretching into infinity, lit only by the moon and a sprinkling of stars, a little poor poet shuffles along the hard shoulder in search of the soft verges.

SWIMMING IN THE DREAM

With the exception of a short tour of Sweden, when we were confined to the back of a transit van that took us from Stockholm to Umea in the far north, stopping off at motorway cafés for reindeer steaks with snowberry sauce, travelling in Europe as one third of the Scaffold was a hurried affair. Fly to Milan/Bruges/Amsterdam, car to TV studio to perform hit song on 'Toppi di Poppi' or 'Toppen der Poppen', car back to airport and fly home reading guidebook. We all agreed that next time would be the time when we would stay over for a few days and see the sights, but next times, like snowberries, shrivelled away.

Travelling in Europe as one third of the Liverpool Poets, however, was a more leisurely affair, and because our visits were organised by the British Council rather than record companies, and our audiences were teachers of English and students of literature rather than teenagers who would have preferred the Who or the Kinks, the experience was generally a good one. We earned less for a reading than we would have done at home, the hotels were often only adequate, but audiences were enthusiastic and books flew off the shelves, on occasion hitting the author. There was also the vague ambassadorial feeling that we were spreading the good word, helping to redefine the image of English poetry as a living artform, accessible and entertaining, and not confined to a thatched corner of the BBC World Service. Our three-pronged attack was to prove successful over two decades, but I was very much on my own when the bugle first sounded and the call to arms came.

Stirrings in the breast that could only be defined as patriotism, quickened uncontrollably at a banquet held in Yugoslavia in 1982, on the final evening of an international poetry festival. In May of that year I stood on the corner of a busy street in Sarajevo, my feet fitting comfortably into a pair of footprints carved in a granite plaque, marking the spot where a young Bosnian student, Gavrilo Princip, fired the fatal shots at the Archduke Franz Ferdinand in 1914, and finding it almost impossible to perceive any sense of those violent times. For in that summer of 1982 Yugoslavia was proud of its own brand of benevolent Communism, wherein different ethnic communities lived and worked happily side by side. Or so I was told when I arrived as a guest of the Bosnia-Herzegovina Writers Union to take part in the twentieth jubilee celebrations of 'Sarajevo's Poetry Manifestation'. Poets from Russia, USA, Iraq and Europe were told that: 'Sarajevo opens itself to poets because it has a poetic soul itself, especially in the feeling for freedom, confirmed through centuries of resistance to oppression'. It was to prove a fascinating week for me, with time off in the port of Dubrovnik as well as visits to pretty towns whose names now reverberate within the violent history of the Balkans, Banja Luka, Mostar and Sarajevo itself. It was spring and the green, opalescent rivers flowing through the countryside put me in mind of Perroquet, not the bird, but the drink popular in Provence, consisting of Pernod and crème de menthe. As well as the inevitable four-hour-long poetry readings in the native language, interspersed with folk dancing in national costume, there had been visits to war museums and Tito memorials, and a hatpin factory where the overseas poets read to the bemused workers in the canteen. The young people I met were open and charming, particularly the students who were assigned to us as translators and guides. And take my word for it, there's no better feeling than having two breathtakingly beautiful girls following you around all day hanging on your every word, and falling about with laughter at your silly jokes.

Poets, of course, will be poets and although we all sought 'that interchange of views and information', we quickly broke up into little groups that shared a common language and culture. Petty jealousies arose, as to who had the most poems in the festival magazine, whose biography was the longest, who got the biggest hatpins after the canteen reading, but even then I couldn't help noticing that the greatest rivalries seemed to be among the Yugoslavian poets themselves, hinting at the hairline cracks to be found in the ideal of Slavic unity. On our last evening in Sarajevo our hosts laid on a fine banquet for more than a hundred guests, and once coffee and slivovitz had been served, the Secretary of the Writers Union rose unsteadily to his feet to propose a toast to each of the participating poets and the countries they represented. It soon became obvious that his style was closer to Bernard Manning than to Douglas Hurd as he poked fun at the French and German poets, before comparing the colour of the American poet James Emmanuel's skin to a local wine.

Then he turned towards me: 'Let us now stand and drink

a toast to our distinguished poet from the land of Margaret Thatcher. Thatcherland!' There were giggles as I stood up, fearing the worst. He continued, 'Ladies and gentlemen, let us raise our glasses and drink to . . . Las Malvinas!' A hundred pairs of eyes fixed on me, waiting for my response.

I decided in an instant that this wasn't the time or place to proffer my views on Thatcher or the Falklands fiasco, but whereas up until then John Bull had meant nothing more than a puncture repair outfit, now it pushed out its chest and snarled. Resorting to cheap theatrics, I poured my upheld glass of slivovitz on to the linen tablecloth and sat down. Embarrassment in twenty-seven languages followed, before our host was led over and made to apologise. 'No offence taken,' I lied, squeezing drops of slivovitz from the tablecloth back into my glass.

Ten years later I was at another Slavonic conference of poets, this time in a country that didn't exist, Macedonia, a country with a pistol to its head. The Struga Poetry Festival had been running for thirty years, and with war raging in neighbouring Bosnia and Serbia a decision had to be taken: whether to spend the money on guns or poetry. They chose the latter both for cultural and propagandist reasons, and requested that the British Council send over two poets who were expendable and who would laugh in the face of danger 'to give public readings and become acquainted with Macedonian and other poets for interchange of views and information'. In the days before Brian and I left, at least a dozen people telephoned to wish me luck and a safe return: 'Rather you than me', 'Don't forget your bullet-proof swimming trunks', etc. But I loftily dismissed their anxieties, the British Council wouldn't go to all this trouble and expense to send us anywhere dangerous, would they? Would they? Although, to be honest, we were a little concerned about the prospect of parachuting in after dark, even though they assured us the landing would be well out of mortar range. Some governments, including the American, Dutch and Scandinavian, had decided not to risk their poets and so the eighteen who assembled on the terrace of the House of Poetry overlooking the river to witness the opening ceremony were given a heroes' welcome by the country's president. At nine o'clock on that Thursday evening in August, six rowing boats filled with vestal virgins wearing white robes crossed the Drim (pronounced 'dream'), disembarked on the steps and ran towards us carrying flaming torches, as a Macedonian male-voice choir belted out the national anthem, but when the firework display began and a misdirected rocket screamed across the terrace, everybody thought the Serbs were attacking and ran back into the house.

The workload for Brian and me was not excessive (*On cue, stand and move to microphone at centre stage of concert hall. Read one poem, then move to the right-hand side while famous Macedonian actress reads translation. Return to seat. Sit*) and as the daily symposia were conducted in the local language, we spent much of the time avoiding the hotel food, swimming in the river pronounced 'dream', and wandering around Struga and the surrounding villages, which viewed from afar could have been Tuscan, with their red-tiled houses and rows of cypress trees. But closer inspection revealed the poverty and there were no smells of melting cheese or garlic, only cigarette smoke. And no breathtakingly beautiful interpreters this time, but an earnest and fiercely intellectual university lecturer called Zoran who tried to explain the politics of the region, which were as slippery as the trout in Lake Ohrid. Eight months after the fighting had begun on the borders, paranoia had become muted and given way to a form of ironic apathy. People tried to carry on with their lives as normally as possible. There was food in the shops, but owing to sanctions, industry was winding down and the coming winter, the first as a new republic, would be a testing one. Would there be a spring? some asked. Against such a background, would anybody be interested in poetry?

The answer, of course, was a resounding yes, for Struga was not really a festival about poems or poets, but about the idea of poetry: rhetoric and the oral tradition. Crowds turned up in their thousands to cheer themselves hoarse at the public performances, and for those who couldn't make it the lengthy readings were recorded live and transmitted on prime-time television. Imagine viewers in this country settling down on successive nights to watch four hours of poets reading their poems, often in a foreign language, with no commercial breaks, and no other channels to switch over to. It is easy to become blasé about the role of poetry, living as one does in the West where it is widely available and either enjoyed or ignored, so it is always humbling to experience the fervour with which it is regarded in countries where life is hard and freedom is a river pronounced 'dream'.

CALLING THE TOSS WITH RUSHDIE

One of the benefits of staying in hotels while on the road instead of sharing a flat, as we used to in Edinburgh, is that I no longer have to toss a coin with Brian Patten to see who gets the biggest bedroom and always losing. He swears on his kitten's life that he never used a double-headed coin or sleight-of-hand, but I have my doubts, for as Salman Rushdie once famously remarked, 'Never toss a coin with a Liverpool Poet.'

Allow me to explain: in April 1988, Los Tres Poetas di Liverpool were invited to Granada by the British Council to give public readings and run workshops for teachers, and we were quartered very comfortably in one of the university's halls of residence. For the two other visiting writers, however, the accommodation did not come up to scratch, and on the insistence of Mr Rushdie and his wife, Marianne Wiggins, they were transferred to the Hotel Splendido de Luxe. We enjoyed the sights of this magical city, which included a visit to Lorca's house, and who better to walk with around the Alhambra than the witty and encyclopaedic Salman Rushdie? One evening we went to listen to Salman addressing a packed audience in the ornate Arabic hall at the university, where he read from the manuscript of his new book to be published later in the year. It was called *The Satanic Verses*. There was no hint, not a frisson of the impact this book was to make on the world, and particularly on his own life. To be honest, most of the questions taken from the audience after the reading related to his letters from Nicaragua, and at the restaurant later with the vice-rector of the university and various local writers the conversation ranged from a recent spate of murders at Adelaide Zoo, which fascinated Salman, to Tottenham Hotspur, of whom for some reason he was a great fan.

Having given up smoking and trying to cut down on drink, Brian was not in the best of moods and caught the first flight out of Granada on the Monday. Adrian and I, though, were delighted to stay over as guests of the Council and leave with the Rushdies on Wednesday. We were all duly collected at 8.20 a.m. and driven to the airport in good time to catch the plane to Madrid. In good time, it turned out, to wait an hour and a half for the delayed incoming flight. We knew we were in danger of missing our connection at Madrid to London and Marianne was most concerned about their being late for a reception at the Japanese Embassy later in the evening, but José, our Council Rep, assured them that he would ring ahead and pull all the strings that had little Union Jacks on.

Eventually, we arrived at Madrid with only five minutes before departure and rushed to the Iberian desk in the international terminal, to be told that we were too late to board. 'But this is Salman Rushdie,' I cried, in an 'open sesame' kind of way. But in vain. The man behind the desk was unimpressed and suggested we try British Airways: 'But you must hurry, their plane will depart pronto, pronto.' So we ran the 220 metres to the BA check-in desk to be told that the flight was already full.

'But this is Salman Rushdie,' I cried half-heartedly, not quite believing it myself. 'I'll put you on the waiting list,' said the lady. 'Have you any luggage?' *Luggage?* Of course, luggage. We put our names down, then rushed back to the Iberian desk to learn that our luggage had reached 20,000 feet and was travelling at an average speed of 500 miles per hour. They had delayed departure, apparently, and, unable to contact us while we were faffing around at British Airways, had given away our seats and the plane had taken off.

Daunted, yet unbowed, the four writers made their way back to British Airways to see if there might be a plane leaving Spain within a week or so. The lady behind the desk feigned excitement: 'Good news, there are two seats available on the flight leaving in twenty minutes.'

Adrian and I did what any Scouser would do in those circumstances and chorused, 'Salman, you and Marianne must take the seats, for you have an important engagement this evening at the Japanese Embassy, whereas we are just poor poets with the evening spread out before us like a patient etherised upon a table.'

As Marianne smiled and turned to vault over the desk and run through passport control, Salman held up a hand and, to his eternal credit, said: 'No, that's not cricket, it just wouldn't be fair. We must toss a coin for it.' He produced a peseta and tossed it in the air.

I cried 'Heads' and it came down 'Tails'. 'Off you go, then, you two, and don't eat too much sushi.'

But as the pair moved forward, tickets and passports in

hand, the lady behind the desk suddenly looked up from her computer: 'Oh, I'm terribly sorry, there's only one seat available. Sorry.'

Salman muttered what can only be described as a swear word before helping Marianne to her feet. 'It's between the two of you now, obviously my wife and I can't be separated.' Adrian and I shrugged apologetically as Salman spun the peseta once more. 'Tails,' I cried, as it came down 'Heads'. Adrian shook hands with us all, checked in and giggled through passport control.

We stood watching him disappear and were on the point of moving in search of another airline when the lady behind the desk looked up from her computer: 'Oh no, it's done it again. Computers, honestly! There were two seats after all. And now there's still one available. Which of you will be travelling?' We looked at each other, but there was nothing to be said. No toss of a coin would get Mr and Mrs Rushdie on BA flight 906 from Madrid to London. Laden with unreasonable guilt, but relieved to be on my way, I muttered *adios* and disappeared, leaving my ex-travelling companions etherised upon the concourse.

In the years that followed, whenever I met Salman – and very often it was at a publisher's party or some awards ceremony – he would greet me and then turn to the crowd: 'Be warned, everybody, never toss a coin with a Liverpool poet.'

OPPORTUNITY RINGS

I love it when the telephone rings and someone offers you the chance of changing your life and making a fortune. I don't mean the cold caller breathlessly announcing that you've won a weekend break in Gran Canaria, so hurry to collect the tickets from a hotel in Stevenage where they're selling timeshares, or the recorded message promising wealth untold in northern Nigeria. I mean the genuine enquiry that comes out of the blue and turns your life upside down for weeks or months on end.

Like the one from Brian Brolly at The Really Useful Theatre Company asking if I'd be at all interested in writing some lyrics for a musical that Andrew Lloyd-Webber was currently writing based on the poems of T. S. Eliot. It was called *Cats* and Trevor Nunn believed I might just be the man for the job.

Ermm . . . Yes.

Or the one from Bob Ezrin, managing Pink Floyd at the time, wondering if I had the time to help Dave Gilmour with the lyrics he was writing for the new album.

Ermm . . . I'll be right over.

Like Willy Russell offering me the part of the narrator in *Blood Brothers*, the musical he was writing, due to open at the Liverpool Everyman before transferring to the West End.

Ermm . . . Willy, do I have to sing?

Or the call from New York, where a production company was planning a new musical version of *The Wind in the Willows* and would I provide the lyrics? Of course, this would involve spending time in New York and Washington.

Ermm . . . Now where did I put my passport?

Of the four, the only invitation I turned down, which I have regretted ever since, was the one from Willy. It came at a bad time, for the commitment would have meant my going back to Liverpool for several months when Hilary and I were just settling in to a new life on the Fulham Road. Added to which was the prospect of doing the same show night after night, something that actors are trained to do, but not poets. Could I just do the opening night, I wondered, and understudy for the remainder of the run? That way I would get the glory and the champagne, and a cosy dressing room in which to spend my evenings writing poems and learning Italian. Then again, if the show proved to be a success (and at the time we had no idea just what a huge hit it would be) and the critics heaped praise on my performance, reminiscent of my early days in *Luther* at the Playhouse – 'The musical really came alive when the Narrator, played by McGough, brought on the stool and set it "sans pareil" stage left' – would it lead to other parts in other West End musicals? Of course not. So I said no. I have not mentioned, of course, the fear of failure. Of being up there on stage with the likes of Barbara Dickson and proper actors and singers, and being crap. So I said no, and did nothing else of note during the period I could have been rehearsing and appearing in the first ever production of *Blood Brothers*, one of the greatest musicals of the twentieth century.

Pink Floyd had been beavering away for the best part of a year, in a houseboat on the Thames that had been converted into a recording studio, and although they were pleased with the music tracks laid down, some of the band were not happy with Dave Gilmour's lyrics. Roger Waters had quit and at the time seemed irreplaceable. All this, Bob Ezrin imparted to me over the phone, as well as saying that the group had discussed the problem and agreed on bringing in another writer, that writer being me. Great! I thought. 'Although, I must point out', he went on, 'that Dave thinks the lyrics are fine.' Shit! I thought. And so it was not only with sharpened pencils and a rhyming dictionary that I turned up next day at Dave's house in Maida Vale, but with a great deal of trepidation. What gives me the right to monkey around with someone else's thoughts and feelings put into words, I asked myself. Well, first and foremost he's a musician, and so the writing may be a trifle clumsy, with the words obscuring the meaning, and so perhaps I can hack away at the undergrowth and let the light shine through. Could I help make the lyrics as memorable as the music? That was to be the challenge as we sat down together and looked at the lyrics in the cold light of silence.

'What are we trying to say here?'

'Mmm . . .'

'This one's about war isn't it?'

'Yep.'

'For or against?'

'Against, definitely.'

'Good, then let's see if we can try and bring that out . . .'

The drummer, Nick Mason, had a daughter in the same class as Finn, and when he was around we'd chat about the pros and cons of Ackland Burghley Comprehensive in Tufnell Park; but alone with Gilmour I felt as welcome as a tax inspector and was not surprised when Ezrin rang a few weeks later to say that the band had agreed to go along with Dave's original lyrics. Apologies all round, but two tickets for the Floyd concert at Wembley were as good as on their way.

Unfortunately, I never did get to sit down at the piano next to Andrew Lloyd-Webber, because the decision had been taken to stay with the original lyrics, but had I been able to give voice to the characters fashioned in the Eliot image, I'm sure we might have squeezed in one or two when Mrs Eliot's back was turned:

> *There's many a cat in the cats'* Who's Who
> *Who rue the cat they once did woo*
>
> *From Felixstowe to Edinbraw*
> *Titled toms have held her paw*
>
> *Miaowed her praises, sworn true love*
> *By the light of the milky moon above*
>
> *Alone now, Miranda mopes in her flat*
> *An ex-sex-kitten, now a tired old cat.*

Occasionally, on cold, grey mornings when I'm writing out a cheque for the council tax, or packing an overnight bag to travel somewhere for a reading when I'd rather stay home by the fire, I think about the 'What ifs' and the

'Nearlys'. What a difference a few points or a nano-percentage of *Cats* or the Floyd's LP *A Momentary Lapse of Reason* would have made to my life. Would the kids have gone to private schools? Would I have had a facelift? Would Hilary still be driving an old Peugeot? Would I pay a ghost to write this while I'm relaxing on my private island in the Caribbean? Of all the arts, poetry is the one you don't pursue if it's money you're after. Paint, sculpt, compose or play a musical instrument and if you're any good there's a ready market for your talent, but write a poem? It's not currency, it won't increase in value, it can't be hung on the wall and if it's memorable it can be carried round in the head, so why pay for it? Poetry has been good to me and I've been fortunate, but had I wanted to make money I'd have chosen a different path. All the same, it's nice to dream.

In December 1982 the telephone rang with an American accent and William Perry, over from New York for a few days, was keen to meet up for a chat about a new musical he was involved in. Over supper at Thierry's on the King's Road, he and his partner Jane Iredale, born in England but now settled in the US and running a casting agency, told me about their plans to adapt *The Wind in the Willows* into a musical that would open at the Folger Theater in Washington the following year. Their production company, Great Amwell, had introduced me to the American television public in a half-hour show devoted to my work, starring Jim Dale, and they were keen to have me on board, especially when I didn't throw my napkin on the table and storm out of the restaurant when they told me that Mole would be female. Initially it was a lovely project to work on. I liked Bill's music, which was tuneful, and he had clear ideas about what the lyrics should do; and Jane, who was writing the book, welcomed my input and happily added my dialogue to the script. But now let me cut to the chase.

The Chase: It was just after midnight on Wednesday 3 August 1983, two days before we opened at the Folger Theater, when I left the bar I'd gone to with a few of the cast after a late rehearsal and, refusing an offer to walk me home from a pair of weasels, set off. Within minutes I was away from the brightly lit cafés and bars and crowded streets, and walking along an empty sidewalk overhung with trees. The air was hot and humid, and the only noise was the drip-drip of moisture from the branches and my own hurried footsteps. They appeared out of the shadows: a tall young black with a basketball-player's stoop and a short guy who looked like an Argentinian football legend. 'Hey, man, shlanna bea gimmer,' growled Maradona. 'Pugga ma hon.' He's talking to me in Gaelic, I thought, but when he pulled the knife I leaped off the sidewalk and sprinted up the road. I heard them swearing and giving chase, but they were so stoned they soon gave up and I reached my apartment safe, sound and soaking wet.

The Folger Theater, a copy of Shakespeare's Globe built within a modern complex, is a compact 270-seater and proved an ideal venue to stage the musical. Directed by an Englishman, John Neville-Andrews, the production ran for nine weeks and reviews ranged from encouraging to 'Bound to be a smash! See it now before it becomes next year's *CATS*!' (Bob Mondello, 'Close-up' Channel 7), 'One of the most delightful and entertaining nights I've ever been privileged to share in the theater' (Arch Campbell, Channel 4 News). And although there were hints that cuts needed to be made, with perhaps a little honing here and there before it transferred to New York, no one could have foreseen the wreckage that was to become of *The Wind* on Broadway.

THE WIND IN WASHINGTON

1 April 1983: Pan Am Flight 101 out of Heathrow at 11 a.m. It is Good Friday and two hours away from New York the sky darkens and the plane shakes with biblical intensity. Apparently we are unable to alter altitude because of the busy flightpath, so pre-landing snacks are to be postponed for fear of pouring hot coffee into clenched laps. I fall to earth a hundred times. Eventually, after flying upside down for a hundred miles, the plane lands safely at JFK where I fail to cut the mustard with Immigration and am led away to a small office where an inspector is unimpressed by the fact that I went to Paul McCartney's twenty-first birthday party. Following twenty minutes of careful questioning, it transpires that I am, in fact, me and, let loose into the community, I take the Carey bus to the Sheraton Russell Hotel on Park Avenue and on to meet up with Bill and Jane at their office on Madison Avenue. Next morning we travel by train and car to Austerlitz, a pretty little town on the borders of New York State and Massachusetts where Bill and Jane have a house. Outside New Amsterdam we pass a scrapyard the size of a football pitch, a graveyard for yellow school buses, some lying on their sides like elephants. Rusting carcasses. No school today.

The idea of coming here to the boondocks is to escape

the temptations of the Big Apple and hunker down to writing new lyrics. Robert Frost used to live only an hour's drive away and I mention how I'd love to walk in his woods 'lovely dark and deep', or visit our nearest village, Stockbridge, where Norman Rockwell lived and painted, but there is no response. In fact, I am left very much to myself, with Bill downstairs at the piano and Jane outside setting squirrel traps.

Knowing her passion for all creatures great and small, I asked her one morning what she did with the rotting corpses and, not detecting the irony, she explained that these were 'Have a Heart' traps, that merely caged the little critters. Once she had nabbed a few she would drive them to another part of the state and let them loose, presumably on some other animal lover's property.

I use my jet lag to advantage by rising before dawn and getting down to work while my fellow writers sleep. Being made of wood, the house stretches itself and comes to life as the sun rises. You can hear the bones creaking as it tones up its muscles for the day. 'Lumbering up', you might say. With no distractions I get a lot done, including new verses for 'Large Families' and the 'Wayfarer's Song' but the claustrophobia kicks in and I'm glad when they decide to return to New York on Wednesday. Back at the office on Madison Avenue, the idea is to work together, but their other productions take up most of the time and I leave on Saturday having achieved nothing I couldn't have done at home.

Sunday 7 August 1983: In my room in the Capitol Hill suite killing time before the nine o'clock flight tonight from Dulles airport. Still in recovery from the opening night hangover (preceded by the press night hangover, preceded by the pre-press night hangover etc.). The show, I think, is a success with excellent reviews so far, although still awaiting the *Washington Post*. The music and the choreography were impressive, as were the performances, particularly Vicky Lewis who plays Mole. She's no bigger than a mole but certainly prettier, and what a voice! Yes, I do regret not having been around during rehearsals and when I brought the matter up with Renny (one of the producers) he agreed but said the expense hadn't been included in the budget. Paranoia sets in with an uncharitable, sinking feeling that perhaps Bill and Jane wanted me out of the way, because now all but four of my lyrics have been added to, so the credits for future productions will read: 'Book by Jane Iredale, Music by William Perry, Lyrics by Roger McGough and William Perry'. But I mustn't get above myself, it's only fame and money after all. Looking out of the living-room window just now, I thought I saw Maradona and Michael Jordan stroll by. Do they know I'm staying here? Are they biding their time until I leave the building, to jump out and apologise for trying to mug me in their stoned pseudo-gaelic patois?

Sunday 4 December 1983: Good flight except for a little turbulence before dinner and a little flatulence after.

This time I don't have to scuttle to the shuttle, because an eight-seater black limo is waiting, courtesy of the producers, with genial Dan at the wheel to drive me into the city. This is the lyric writer's life, I think, waving majestically to the locals as we speed along, safe in the knowledge that no one can see me behind the smoke-blackened windows. The Milford Plaza, just down the road from Times Square, lacks the faux bookish charm of the Sheraton Russell but is bustling and lively, and in next to no time I have stuffed my travellers cheques under a loose corner of the carpet in my room, showered and hit the town. The plan now is to take the show to New Haven for a week, then on to Boston prior to New York, all of which sounds good to me. Over the following few days I spend time in a recording studio with the cast, who are making a tape that will be used to attract backers for the show, as well as meeting Peter Hunt, the new director. I feel it is very important to fight my corner, or else my input, not to mention my lyrics, will be sidelined in the rush to get to Broadway. But he's hard to pin down and, having been appointed by Jane, who is also a producer, he is careful not to tamper overmuch with her script, which I feel needs tampering with, very overmuch. Only through harassing Renny and Michael from the management team do I manage to pin down the director for a meeting on the day before I leave town. We confer in the back of his limo and over a swift Martini in his hotel before he leaves for an important dinner date. He seems to have little time for wilting poets, but does agree that cuts and additions to all lyrics should not be made without reference to me. No more should my co-writers slip in references to baseball, Daytona Beach and other all-Americanisms that are out of place in the English Wild Wood that Kenneth Grahame had created. Ho, ho. We shall see.

I think the Liverpool Poets might have made a decent fist of *Wind in the Willows*, had we staged it in England, with Adrian as Mr Badger, Brian as Ratty and myself as Mole.

However, we chose to devise our own shows instead, and during May 1984 we toured *Gifted Wreckage* and in March the following year *It's for You*. Both shows comprised us reading our own poems, as well as sharing each other's. There were sketches, usually with a literary theme, musical accompaniment supplied by Andy Roberts, lighting cues, and in the case of *It's for You* a stage set in the form of a one-dimensional, bright red telephone box. But where were Bill Kenwright and Cameron Macintosh when we needed them? We had written a show that only we three poets could perform and although it had legs, two of them (Badger's) were getting tired. It would not run and run, unlike the *Willows* with a fair wind behind it, and deep down I always cherished the hope that success on Broadway would bring home the gravy.

THE WIND ON BROADWAY

Monday 23 September 1985: The TWA flight scheduled to depart Heathrow will be delayed by an hour, so I sit slow-motioning by the departure gate. I seem to go into a trance once I enter an airport building. My breathing slows down as if to reduce my pulse rate, a way of combating anxiety, for this summer has had more than its fair share of planes dropping out of the sky. I try to muster some enthusiasm for the trip, but fear the invitation is a generous but token gesture on behalf of the management, for *The Wind* opens on Broadway in early December, and I assume the script and lyrics are already cast in stone, which I fear may cause the show to sink like one. Nearly two years have passed and I feel distanced from the whole project. 'Distance' being the operative word, I suppose. And talking of operative, my stomach feels like it's been kicked. Nobly, I decide to forgo cocktails and spirits on the flight, and eight hours later in the back of the luxury limo wonder whether, nobly, I should have forgone the beer and wine as well.

The script waiting for me at the Excelsior Hotel on West 81st Street makes for a disappointing read. Some of the songs that worked well in Washington have been cut and replaced by new songs and lyrics that do not spring from the Wild Wood, as well as a long soliloquy for Ratty about his leaving home when young. For reasons that may have been financial or because the actors weren't available, the show didn't get a run out in those small provincial theatres where a good deal of pruning and shipshaping could have taken place, but has been reconstituted to suit the sophisticates on Broadway. I read the script again and decide on my plan of action for the meeting next morning: I will get on my high horse, and fight for Kenneth Grahame and the purity of the book. I will defend the Wild Wood and the creatures that live in it to my dying breath. I will insist on my lyrics being reinstated.

Then I'll capitulate.

Wednesday 25 September 1985: The 'Recall Auditions' are held in a large studio on the corner of Broadway and 19th where I sit at a long table with the new director, Ed Berkeley, two guys from the Johnson-Liff casting agency, the choreographer Randolyn Zinn (now there's a name to plié with), as well as Bill and Jane, various assistants and their assistants. Of the original cast only Vicky Lewis is retained as Ms Mole; the other principals – Toad, Badger and Ratty – are advised to seek alternative employment. As usual, everyone has their own plans for the evening, so I drift back to the hotel and listen to the tape of Bill's new songs. The show is too far down the line now for me to save the Wild Wood, so I push my high horse out of the window on the twenty-seventh floor, order room service and settle down to work on a lyric about Toad doing the cancan. It's just another day for a jobbing lyricist.

On Monday morning I turn up to watch the singers and dancers audition for parts in the chorus and it's mind–

boggling, because each one comes over like a star, and it's fascinating to see how Vinny Liff of the casting agency assembles a group that, hopefully, will spend the next six to twelve months together. The secret lies in his little black book of backstage gossip:

> We can't use Larry, he's HIV positive. And Pierre may be as well.
> Karen's recovered, but she's still carrying a torch for Toni.
> If you choose Mark, you can't have Meryl because of what happened in Philadelphia.
> Chico and Robert have had a major fallout, so it's one or the other.
> Joleen may be pregnant.
> Errol is still doing coke, and Esther's weight loss could be pathogenic.

I had fondly imagined that the best singers and dancers would be chosen, but as they are all multi-talented and equally gifted, the deciding factor proves to be their social and, hitherto, private lives. It's a revelation, but one that should come as no surprise if you think about it. At one point the ethnic mix required by law was mentioned and I piped up with the theory that as most of the cast would be wearing masks or heavy make-up, nobody would be able to spot the difference between whites, blacks and hispanics, but an assistant's assistant explained, as a mother might to a wayward toddler, that I was missing the point. Before leaving I enjoyed the excitement as the successful auditionees were given their contracts. Pink ones for small parts and members of the chorus worth $600 a week, and white ones for principals, upwards from $1,200.

At 10.30 the following morning we go to view the Nederlander Theater on 41st and Broadway, formerly known as the Billy Rose Theater and before that the National, home to many a Rodgers and Hart musical, a huge 6,000-seater. Unfillable, surely, why can't we find a neat little theatre off-off-off-off Broadway, about the size of the old Traverse in Edinburgh and let the show run for twenty-seven years? Although I suspect that Bill and Jane might agree, there seem to be dark mutterings of the producer's licence running out, so it's make-or-break time for them. I am cheered, though, on leaving, to see that people are already queuing up for tickets. (Well, one old man with Rastafarian dreadlocks curled up with a bottle of wine on the step by the front entrance, but that's a start, surely?)

Wednesday 2 October 1985: The budget can no longer afford shiny black limos for limey poets to swan about in, so I take a yellow cab to JFK airport like common-or-garden people do. The driver does nothing but moan about the long drive back, about the rain and the traffic jams, about the hurricane and about the fact that there will be no incoming flights for hours and therefore no passengers to pick up. Encouraged, I throw in a moan about the size of the Nederlander and the problems we might have filling it, but he's so 'me, me, me' that I get no sympathy.

I wish I could have stayed on longer for the start of rehearsals, but that means a lot of hanging about, and I've got to be back for *Book Tower*, the kids' programme I'm presenting for Yorkshire TV. In retrospect, I wrote some good lyrics under pressure, but had the usual problems getting them past Jane, who on one occasion raised objections to the word 'spleen' I'd used in a verse, to rhyme with 'tureen'. 'No one here will know what a tureen is,' she argued, 'and anyway, there's no such word as "spleen".' She was surprised when Ed explained the meaning, having assumed that it was Liverpool slang, but even so I fear it will be shuffled off to the Great Couplet cemetery on the borders of New York State and Massachusetts.

Sunday 10 November 1985:

> *Here I am,*
> *48 years of age*
> *and never having gone to work in ladies underwear*
>
> *Never run naked at night in the rain*
> *Made love to a girl I'd just met on a plane . . .*

Arriving in New York still hungover from yesterday's birthday celebrations and hopeful that I can be of use, because this time the producers were very keen to have me here. In fact, one of them rang me over the weekend to see if I could fly out right away: 'We need your input, Raaajer.' Unfortunately, I had to be in Leeds filming *Book Tower* until yesterday. In the production office there is good news and bad news. The good news is that NBC will be filming a couple of songs from the show for the Macy's Christmas party and parade. Four minutes' worth of free advertising on a show watched by 70 million! Who cares about the bad news? I hear you ask. The bad news is that Ed is a worried man. The first half is overrunning and the cuts being suggested are cosmetic rather than drastic, and at the stage in rehearsals when he should be in sole charge, it appears to be a case of direction by committee. 'I can't work with the rewrites,' he yells at Renny. 'They're unsayable by actors.' So the reason I'm here is to rewrite the rewrites, and at this late stage to join Ed in his battle to recapture the spirit of the original Washington production.

The following morning Bill takes me aside for a little tête-à-tête in which he explains that the show will be re-anglicised when it moves to Europe, but this is America and over here audiences become irritated by too many foreign references. Foreign? England? Surely not. Spend the afternoon gazing blankly at Jane's lyrics for one of Toad's songs, in which he sips camomile tea, performs yoga and beats himself with strips of cactus.

Wednesday 13 November 1985: All hands trooped down to Macy's for their Christmas party, where the cast sang one of Bill's new songs, 'Christmas Carol', probably for the last time in public because Ed wants it cut from the show. The champagne flowed and it was fun to watch Jerome Robbins flitting about like a small silver rabbit as people tried to cage him in conversation. Almost every single person I spoke to said, 'Hey, I love your eye-glasses!' which made me think it must be time for a new pair, but it was party time so I recalled the question-and-answer session after a children's poetry reading in Hong Kong some months before, when a boy had stood up and asked, 'Mister Roger, why do you wear green spectacles?' to which I had replied, 'Because I'm short-sighted.'

This probably wasn't the most suitable occasion to talk

business but time was short, so I cornered Renny and offered to work on the script and do all the rewrites that Ed wanted, and to do it for free, gratis. 'It won't cost you a cent and I don't want a credit, or points, I just want the show to work.' Renny listened, admired my glasses and said he'd get back to me.

Saturday 16 November 1985: I'm leaving this afternoon and probably won't be back before the show opens, and as I haven't heard back from Renny I write a letter to Bill wishing him and Jane all the luck in the world, suggesting a few alterations to the lyrics and urging them to have faith in the director.

At 5.45 it's out into the swishing rain and a cab to the Carey bus terminal opposite Grand Central. On the way we pass the Nederlander, which is a buzz of activity with lights and billboards going up and posters already proclaiming the advent of a brand-new musical for Broadway: *The Wind in the Willows*.

The plane is delayed by fifty minutes because the baggage handlers don't like being out in the rain. Good flight except for a group of Zambians in the row behind who fart silently and venomously throughout. Whether singly or communally I was never to discover. Arrive Heathrow 9 a.m.

Postscript: Hilary was working at the time as an assistant producer on BBC TV's *Tomorrow's World* and had arranged to have a week off so that we could attend the opening on 14 December, and consequently I booked a room at the Excelsior and flights with People's Express airline. But only provisionally, for after returning home there had been an ominous silence from across the Atlantic, no phone calls, faxes, nada, so I rang Renny to learn that Ed Berkeley had been sacked and replaced, and that the opening had been postponed until the following week.

My waters told me that the wind that was about to blow through the willows was a hurricane, so I decided to give my first ever, and no doubt one and only, Broadway opening night a miss. I cancelled the flights and hotel room, and took Bran for a run in Princes Park, where I kicked leaves joyously, as if my X-rays had proved to be clear and I had nothing to worry about.

Wednesday 1 January 1986: Instead of going to New York, Hilary and I went to Liverpool and checked in at the Adelphi where a telegram arrived on Saturday night with news that the show was closing the following day after only four performances. In retrospect there had been a great deal of time and energy wasted, working in some cases with people whose enthusiasm was greater than their talent. But there were good people, too, and clever ones, and I'd hugely enjoyed my trips to the US, where I had gained some insights into the workings of theatre and into the human heart. I may have missed out on earning $6,000 a week, but on the credit side I gained four box files of unusable scripts and three exercise books filled with song lyrics. *Variety* magazine signed off its review with: 'Mean old Broadway is the wrong arena for this anthropomorphic fantasy, but smaller musical theaters and children's theaters might please their audiences with it.' And here comes the lining (though copper rather than silver), the Rodgers and Hammerstein Organisation bought the rights and a version of the show is occasionally performed in the States as well as over here. Poop Poop!

At that awkward age now between birth and death
I think of all the outrages unperpetrated
opportunities missed

The dragons unchased
The maidens unkissed
The wines still untasted
The oceans uncrossed
The fantasies wasted
The mad urges lost.

LETTER FROM THE COMIC

> *Royal Sussex County Hospital*
> *Friday 13 February 2004*

Dear Roger,

As you can see from the address, things aren't going according to plan. I'm afraid I've had a bit of a heart scare – chest pains that had me admitted here last weekend. I'm still having tests, and it looks like I'm going to be in here for a while yet. A bypass seems to be on the cards, so one way and another I'm going to be out of action for a while. A hospital book is looming, but I don't know how it ends yet.

Pete McCarthy's letter came as a nasty shock because we'd met only the week before at Ottakar's Bookshop in Putney when he turned up at a reading I was doing, followed by a book signing to promote my new *Collected Poems*. Recognising Pete, the store manager had come over all excited and persuaded him (not a difficult task) to sign all available copies of *McCarthy's Bar* and *The Road to McCarthy* which, unlike my collected poems, were both in the top-seller list, and I was delighted to note that Pete sold more copies of his books that evening than I did of mine. (Did I say *delighted*? What I meant was *nauseous, splenetic, embittered, peeved, incensed,* in a fraternal sort of way.)

Later, in a tapas bar down the road, Pete, as ebullient as ever, was looking forward to returning to the States and promoting the paperback edition of his new book.

After a busy and successful career in television, which included writing gags and scripts for Mel Smith and Griff Rhys Jones and presenting *Travelog*, the Channel 4 guide for independent travellers, he settled down in 1998 to write the first of his two big sellers. I used the word 'fraternal' earlier and there was something of that in our relationship, as there is between Brian Patten and me, although a different kind of one. Not only were Pete and I from similar backgrounds, but we shared the same birthday, 9 November, and because I was fifteen years older and he'd been a fan of mine since the days of the Scaffold, when as a schoolboy he'd come up on stage at the Liverpool Everyman Theatre to have the piss taken out of him and receive a badge from PC Plod (aka John Gorman), Pete never saw me as a rival but as someone who would take pride in his success. And I did.

Although his habit of ringing me twice a week to bring me up to date on the meteoric sales figures of *McCarthy's Bar* and divulge details of the huge advances for his next book did put fraternity to the test, I was chuffed that a mate of mine was well on the road to becoming an author of international repute. His wife and his three young daughters loved horses and the countryside, and in 2003 Pete felt secure enough to move into a beautiful manor house in the Sussex Downs. The future could not have looked brighter.

Tuesday 2 March 2004

Dearest Roger,
  Well, they finally let me home from hospital on Sunday,

after fixing me up with an angioplasty last week. So far, the heart seems fine. It was good to talk to you on the phone, and thanks again for the delightful letter you sent.

Unfortunately, though, it doesn't end there. Routine bloodtests during my time in hospital showed up some irregularities, and I'm afraid they have now confirmed the presence of cancer in my system. Diagnoses are continuing, but it seems likely I will begin a course of chemo in two or three weeks' time. They haven't written me off just yet, and rest assured I will be fighting with every fibre of body and spirit.

In August 1986 *McGough & McCarthy* opened at the Assembly Rooms during the Edinburgh Festival and was well received despite our blurb in the programme: 'Imagine a stage on which there are two people (well, one some of the time) saying things. This gives you just some idea of the sort of whacky, way-out antics these two popular performers get up to. Entrances, exits, slow fades and blackouts, this show has got the lot. The jester and the muse in flagrante.' The conceit of the show was the interplay between the stereotypical sensitive poet and the pushy stand-up comic, which gradually revealed, through a series of sketches, a scheming poet and a gullible, innocent comic. Probably the best material was co-written and based on our experiences as teachers, and as pupils at the hands of the Irish Christian Brothers.

(*Enter Brother McCarthy interrupting McGough's routine about life in a monastery*) 'So, McGough, is this the best you can do, sneering at the religion that made you what you are?'

'Just a bit of fun, sir.'

'Too clever for religion now, are we? It's all those non-Catholic authors you're mixing with.'

(*Shamefaced, McGough regresses to boyhood*) 'I can still remember everything I was taught, sir.'

'Ah, we'll see about that. And what country did the Virgin Mary come from?'

'Ireland, sir.'

'Correct. And Jesus?'

'The same, sir.'

'And what religion was he?'

'Jew, sir.'

'What sort of a Jew?'

'A Catholic Jew, sir.'

'And what religion was the Good Samaritan?'

'Catholic, sir.'

'The Angel Gabriel?'

'Catholic.'

'Cain and Abel? . . . It's a trick question.'

'Cain was a Protestant and Abel was a Catholic.'

'Very good. King Herod?'

'Protestant, sir.'

'Pontius Pilate, Judas Iscariot, Attila the Hun, and all the inhabitants of Sodom and Gomorrah?'

'All Protestant, sir.'

'Very good. And Adolf Hitler, President Marcos and the Yorkshire Ripper?'

'. . . Er, I think they were all Catholics, sir.'

(*Producing black leather strap*) 'All Protestants, McGough. And do you know what you are? A snivelling little guttersnipe. What are you?'

'A snivelling little guttersnipe, sir.'

★

We played each night to packed houses and reviews were good, so we were faced with the pleasing problem of where to take it next. A transfer to the West End would have been nice, but we had a better offer, three weeks at the Melbourne Comedy Festival.

The Troubadour on Brunswick Street, a folk club that always seemed to be recovering from a hangover, was in retrospect not the ideal venue for the show. Appearing on the same bill were two other artists, Joe Dolce, who had lobbed an oddball number one hit into the UK charts in 1980 called 'Shaddap You Face', and a rotund gentleman who recited uncomical 'Jolly Swagman' verse. 'Dingo' Rawlinson was one of those performance poets who suffered from a syndrome known as 'the-next-poem-will-be-the-one-that-grabs-them', an affliction that affects many people faced with an increasingly restive audience. They start off badly, and instead of retreating to the safety of the dressing room they wag their tails and scamper into a billabong. In his case, each heckle, yawn, or jeer was a challenge, a bone tossed into the water for him to retrieve. Consequently, Pete and I invariably started late and had to soothe an audience too often tired and emotional, including, on the second night, twenty undertakers. (And what would be the collective noun? A dirge of undertakers? A dispatch? A moribund? An unction?)

Most nights there would be a percentage of poms who knew us from the UK, or at least had heard of us, and it was like playing at home, but often the locals were nonplussed, wondering when these two guys on stage were going to sing a folk song for godsake. One night I was in the middle of a poem when a voice barged in from the darkness: 'Ay, mate, who wrote them poems yer readin'?'

At this point I realised that I wasn't Billy Connolly or Ken Dodd, armed with a quip that would fell the heckler and bring the room to its knees in a gale of laughter. But I needed time to think . . . 'Pardon?'

'I said who wrote them fockin poems?'

'Erm, I did.'

'Then why are you reading them out of a book?'

'Er, well, because I haven't learned them off by heart.'

'Oh, I see, OK, mate, yer can carry on now.'

At 12.30 on Friday the official launch of the Comedy Festival was held at the town hall and I had to reply to the Mayor's welcoming speech on behalf of the overseas visitors, or 'Ovies' as we were known. Barry Humphries on his home turf dropped aphorisms like Oscar Wilde after a good lunch, and there was a dinkum sprinkling of local and national comedians. The 'Ovies' included Pam Ayres, Mel Smith and the Comedy Festival's guest of honour, Peter Cook, and we were encouraged to enjoy the unlimited grog until 5.30 when tequila sunsets would appear at a cocktail party fifty yards down the road. Unfortunately, this was an invitation Pete and I couldn't take up as we had a show that evening, so we stuck to water and drank like fish.

A good friend of ours, William Burdett-Coutts, who had produced our show at the Assembly Rooms in Edinburgh was also in town and he came to the Troubadour that night with Peter Cook and his wife Lin, and Mel Smith and his lady Pam. Now Mel was an old pal who had worked with both Pete and me, so we rather hoped for a few kind comments from him after the show. Peter Cook, however, was an altogether different proposition for, although I had been a huge fan of his since *Beyond the Fringe* and continued to be in awe, I was pretty sure we wouldn't get along. For a start he couldn't remember that we had met three years earlier at the First International Nether Wallop Arts Festival, a wacky concert party devised by Stephen Pile and filmed for LWT, which featured local turns performing with the likes of Michael Hordern, John Wells, Rick Mayall and Jenny Agutter. Recalling that weekend, I think mainly of Jenny Agutter, but I also remember my comic hero in someone's sitting room, breaking the leg off a Queen Anne chair for a laugh (and not a cheap one). Of one thing we could be certain, if Peter Cook hated the show he wouldn't shy from telling us. Now it is certainly possible that their critical faculties had been marred by an early Riesling in the mayoral parlour, followed by Chardonnay, Shiraz and a rainbow of cocktails to ease them into the warm glow of evening, not to mention the one and a half bottles of vodka and three bottles of champagne they'd consumed during the show notwithstanding (and they did have problems in that area), they were fulsome in their praise. 'Brilliant,' said Peter. Suddenly we were all luvvies.

William, knowing when he was beaten, called a cab, but Pete and I were starving and, having missed out on a day's drinking, had a lot of catching up to do, so Peter Cook invited us back to the Regency Hotel. When it comes to room service I am not very good at ordering. I ring the number and, grateful when someone answers, beg and grovel for whatever scraps might be available. Mel Smith, however, is very good at ordering and in no time at all we were tucking into Regency Burgers, crayfish omelettes, oysters (three dozen), four bottles of champagne and two bottles of brandy, as Peter Cook wisely pointed out 'just to be on the safe side'.

At about 2 a.m. came the rock'n'roll moment when Peter suddenly picked up the large cut-glass goblet containing sweets from a side table and ran towards the window. He's going to throw it at the moon, I thought, but I hope to God he opens the window first. He did, and then poured out hundreds of sweets that fell like foil-wrapped snowflakes on to the pavement seventeen floors below. The goblet was filled with the remainder of the brandy and champagne, then passed round. But Captain Cautious could not be tempted and, leaving Pete, Peter and Mel to carry on doing what Ovies do best, decided to forgo a cab and walk back to our more modest hotel, the Travel Inn. The street outside the Regency was surprisingly devoid of sweets. Had the hotel cleaners been alerted? Had the 'garbos', the city's proud garbage collectors, already swept the streets? Had a kangaroo with a sweet tooth, unable to believe her luck, stuffed her pouch and hopped back into the bush? The answer, more prosaically, was to do with convection and wind currents, and for half a mile I followed the milky way, silver-wrapped sweets, like stars on the black tarmac guiding me home.

Saturday was a day of glorious technicolor and at the invitation of our friendly Oz promoter, John Pinder, the two Petes, Mel and I went to the races at Moonee Valley, where I couldn't wait to mix with the crowds, take in the atmosphere and enjoy the sunshine and fresh air. On arrival Peter Cook led the way. To the VIP enclosure, I assumed, no doubt, as being the Festival's Lead Ovie probably he had a ministerial marquee at his disposal, or at least a box overlooking the track. Instead, he located a noisy, smoke-filled bar, where he and Mel found a table within sight of a black-and-white TV screen showing the afternoon's races, ordered the first round and placed their bets. Having never been to a race meeting before, I left them to it and went out to watch the real thing and turn a flutter into a small fortune. After all, I was of Irish stock and for sure, wouldn't I be able to spot a winner by the wild look in the eye and the twitch of a neatly turned fetlock? And that's only the jockey. Approaching the Tote while reading the race card, I was gripped by an uncontrollable desire to put all the money I was carrying, $250, on an accumulator: Roger's Cert in the 2.20, Summer with Monika in the three o'clock, Lily the Pink in the 3.30 and Said and Done in the four o'clock; but on reaching the window, it seemed like a bit of a gamble, so instead I placed $2 on the favourite and $2 on the outsider with the highest odds. The favourite romped home and, beginner's luck, I was already only a dollar down. My good fortune continued throughout the afternoon and, by employing extreme caution and careful management, I ended up $15 in the clear. When it was time for the last race I couldn't wait to join my fellow high rollers in the bar to buy a round of drinks and explain my sure-fire method of punting for geeks, called 'Wagers without Fear'. Peter Cook had already won $500 and had lost interest, but Mel was losing, so he dug deep into his wallet and placed $700 to win on an outsider.

'Don't, Mel, don't.'

It came second, and whereas I might have screamed and hurled myself through the window like a large cut-glass goblet, Mel said 'Bugger' and asked if he could borrow $20 to buy a round. I lent him fifteen with pleasure, and over a vodka and orange explained my method of carefree gambling, pointing out gently that to risk so much money on an outsider . . .

Mel turned towards me, that face like a wonderfully expressive pudding, and took my arm: 'Roger, you don't understand, do you? You just don't understand.'

After three weeks at the Troubadour, *McGough & McCarthy* transferred to the much larger Universal Theatre as part of a programme called enticingly *Wogs, Dykes and Poms*. The Wogs were a comic trio composed of an Italian, a Spaniard and a Greek, known as Wogs out of Work, the Dykes were five ladies, light-hearted and gay, and the Poms were two very tired Brits who wished they'd resisted the invitation to exceed their welcome in Melbourne. One in particular, whose wife Hilary was eight months pregnant. Although I have dwelt on drink-related escapades, obviously with an eye on tabloid serialisation, I valued most the quiet times that I spent with Peter Cook and Lin, a coffee on Lygon Street, lunch in a Chinese restaurant, when madness was on hold and wit became the man, and there was loose talk of keeping in touch once we were back in dear old Blighty, but almost inevitably we never did. It had been very much an Ovies sort of thing.

On 15 May 2004 I saw Pete McCarthy for the last time when I went to visit him at the recently acquired manor house. He showed me round the former abbey, the paddock and beautiful grounds, but with little enthusiasm: 'I spent twenty happy years in a three-bedroomed house in Warrington, so what on earth possessed me to buy this? Ego, bloody ego.'

'No, Pete, you bought it for the family, and you'd worked hard, and . . . well, at the time . . .'

But there would be no time. The cancer had spread to the liver and even though Pete said there was no pain, only the fatigue brought on by the chemo, he was depressed and bewildered. Sitting on a bench watching Irene playing with the girls across the lawn, we talked about transiency, the belief in God that he was trying to rekindle, and the inevitable: why me? If he could work out a reason for the cruel visitation, perhaps he could find a way of getting rid of it. Should he continue to fight with every fibre of body and spirit, or resign himself to the fate at which doctors hinted? It was an afternoon of spring sunshine and the scene held a terrible beauty by knowledge of its swift and inevitable passing. The leaves would not fall from the trees, there would be no roaring fires in the drawing room, he would not see his daughters growing older. When it was time to leave, Pete walked me across the forecourt to the five-bar wooden gate where we said goodbye and, wearing a grey fleece, even though it was still warm in the late afternoon, the lad from Warrington walked slowly back into the shadow of the beautiful house that haunted him.

November the Fifth

As I write this, a bonfire is being lit in the garden next door.
While above, planes filled with strangers I will never meet,
are flying to places I will never visit. Tonight is Guy Fawkes
night,
and rockets fail in glorious technicolour on their journey to the
moon.
I am wearied of writing eulogies for friends who have gone too
soon.

News of a sudden death pulls the earth from under our feet.
Unprepared, we are crushed and bewildered.
But when dying is a slow and painful inevitability
we look on helplessly, and hope for miracles.
We either choke on prayer, or else we rage
and refuse to imagine a future without them there.

I am wearied of writing eulogies,
and this is one I thought I'd never have to write. It's so unfair.
Midnight now, and still a smell of burning in the air.
The bonfire has been put out, and for a few hours at least,
the sky, free of planes can settle down for the night.
Cheers mate, and God Bless.

WHAT'S IN A NAME?

Having been to Majorca several times in the sixties, laddish package holidays with John Gorman and Hewo in Magaluf and Arenal, and quieter family holidays with Thelma, Nathan, Finn and Tom, I had assumed that the island was one huge package resort, a ring doughnut with high-rise hotels sugaring the coast all around and nothing in the middle. But if Robert Graves, a man not noted for his love of hotdogs and Tetley's bitter, had settled on the island, then perhaps my geography was no better than that of the two tanned girls from Nottingham I talked to at Gatwick on my return.

'Where have you two been?'

'San Antonio.'

'Where's that?'

'I don't know, we flew.'

And later this year I'll be returning to Majorca, where Hilary and I will spend our time trying to prevent our teenagers getting up to what we got up to when we were their age. But this time we'll be heading to the north-west of the island, to a village that does not display its charms or its residents too readily. For one of the many delights of Deyá is that most people who drive through the village are not tempted to stop. There is no beach, for instance, the

Cala is a tiny, secluded, difficult-to-get-to cove at the foot of a cliff, favoured by masochists who relish the challenge of stumbling over rocks and sharp pebbles to swim with jellyfish. The heart of Deyá itself lies away from the main road, up the hill to the church of Saint John the Baptist, where, in the graveyard that overlooks the village and the sea, is a rectangle of sun-bleached cement inscribed simply: 'Robert Graves, Poeta'.

But the grave wasn't there on my first visits and in 1984 I was invited up to the Graves house for afternoon tea by Pauline Scudamore, a good friend of the family and Spike Milligan's biographer. Robert, the revered and distinguished man of letters, had struck up an unlikely but deep and lasting friendship with Spike Milligan, and over the years kept up a warm correspondence that Pauline had now edited, and a casual reader who didn't know either man might assume from the letters that Robert was the comic genius and Spike the poet.

We sat out on the terrace overlooking the olive grove where, beneath the overhang of a thirty-foot cliff, a small theatre space had been constructed by the poet's family, which made a magical venue for the poetry events that became a regular feature of my visits. Up to fifty people would make their way down the rocky path to the amphitheatre, some with babies and cushions, others with candles and wine, to sit and listen to poems, and the chime of goat bells echoing round the hillside, as the sun, like a giant ensaimada, set into the sea beyond.

I doubt if ensaimadas, the round sweet pastry indigenous to the island, were on the menu for afternoon tea, but there were sandwiches, home-made cakes and, as the shadows lengthened, red wine. Robert's wife, Beryl, was there with their children, William, Lucia, Juan, and Tomás, as well as friends of the family including David Templeton, an artist who was to produce a series of moving sketches of the poet during his final months. At this late stage the great man was lost within himself and sat upright in a cane chair wearing his famous black sombrero, a tartan blanket covering his knees, grey haunted eyes gazing wordlessly out into the far distance. But he was handsome still and, having spent a lifetime being admired for those imperious good looks, he posed for David with exalted indifference. He said not a word while those around him chatted about the comings and goings in the village, about plans to widen the road to Soller, not ignoring the man in their midst but rather including him in the warmth of their banter, and occasionally Lucia would say 'Wine, Robert?' and her father would sip from the glass held up to his lips. Eventually it was time to make a move and we stood to say our thanks and goodbyes. 'Roger and Hilary are going now, Robert,' announced Beryl and, turning to me, said, 'Give him your hand, Roger.' So I went over and took his right hand in mine. If I was expecting a brief and feeble handshake, I was in for a surprise, because for a man of eighty-nine he had a fearsome grip and seemed determined not to loosen it. I stood before him, my hand in his, as the minutes ticked by, aware that I was holding the hand of the man who had held the hand of Thomas Hardy, who in turn had held the hand of Tennyson who had held the hand . . . more minutes were ticking by and, unsure of the etiquette, I wondered if it would be considered rude to use my left hand to extricate myself. 'He can always tell a poet's hand,' said Beryl, and everybody smiled and nodded. It was indeed a lovely thought, but I reckoned on something more basic. My hands have not been hardened and calloused over the years with good honest toil; they are not hairy or muscular and could be mistaken in the dark for a young maiden's. As he clasped my hand, I believe he was transported back through the darkness to a time when he was holding the hand of a new lover:

> *Child, take my hand, kiss it finger by finger!*
> *Can true love fade? I do not fear death*
> *But only pity, with forgetfulness*
> *Of love's timeless vocabulary*
>
> *And an end to poetry*
> *With death's mad aircraft rocketing from the sky.*
> *Child, take my hand!*

Robert Graves (from 'The Moon's Last Quarter' 1973)

I spent yesterday morning wondering how to spell my name, which is a bit worrying at my age. One of the best jobs I had last year was to write a poem that would be inscribed on a fountain to be built in Williamson Square, opposite the Playhouse Theatre in Liverpool. My gift to the city as it tarts itself up in readiness for its role as European Capital of Culture in 2008.

Not for us the Trevi fountain, but a large rectangle bordered by squares of black granite with the letters inlaid in steel, above which water and light will be projected. A tricky one, this, because the poem has to work from wherever the reader happens upon it, so narrative ballads are out for a start, and a haiku simply will not do.

Inevitably, whenever I'm invited to write a poem, I look to the heavens for inspiration, I seek the sublime. As when the BBC World Service commissioned a poem in the year 2000 to celebrate the millennium total eclipse of the sun. It was August, and I wasn't sure I could pull it off because I was leaving the next day for Majorca and the family holiday. Without access to information about astrophysics and the history of eclipses, what could I find to write about? Where would I start? I started the very next morning, in fact, when I strolled into the village of Deyá armed with a pencil and notepad. I sat down at a table in Las Palmeras and ordered a café con leche and an ensaimada. The girl put the coffee on the table in front of me, then went back to the kitchen, leaving me still looking to the heavens for divine inspiration. She returned and placed an empty plate before me, and I watched as the shadow of the ensaimada passed over it like a . . .? like a . . .? before she transferred it to the plate. Inspiration, not from heaven but from the kitchen. But inspiration nonetheless. I felt as Wordsworth did when he beheld the daffodils, like William Blake before he shot the tyger. Inspiration. An eclipse, but an everyday, common-or-garden eclipse. By the end of the holiday I had written a poem which pleased the BBC, and *Everyday Eclipses* became the title of my next book. (I felt sorry for the ensaimada, though. Having provided the initial inspiration for the poem, it ended up on the cutting-room floor because pastries, like bottles of syrupy green liquor with twigs in, don't travel well.)

And so with the fountain poem. Where shall I look to for inspiration? To Liverpool's great maritime past? To its history as a great seaport? To the Beatles and the cultural explosion of the sixties? Can the essence of all this be distilled into ninety-six words? No. So, what is the first thing that comes to mind when you picture a fountain? Water. That seemed like a good idea, after all there's loads of the stuff swishing around Liverpool. And so the word 'water' became my ensaimada, the key to unlocking the poem, which came out as a children's chant in the tradition of 'We all sail on the alley alley-o'. I also tried to bring in the hissing sounds of a fountain jet with the shushing and the sissing sounds of the words. The poem begins:

Water is fountainous is gymnast is flash Water is mountainous is scallywag is splash Water is mysterious is playhouse is dream Water is serious is stargazy is steam

and continues in similar vein around a rectangle measuring 170×75 metres. Obviously I'm hoping that the poem will be read from the beginning, but I can foresee puzzlement slow-burning into resentment as someone approaching the fountain from the wrong end and walking anti-clockwise tries to make sense of 'steam is stargazy is serious is Water dream is playhouse is mysterious is Water splash is scallywag is mountainous is Water'. '*Call that poetry? My five-year-old could do better. Load of rubbish.*'

I enjoyed writing the poem once the initial fear had worn off, and I hope that the tourists and the good folk of Liverpool, as they cross Williamson Square when the water is switched off, will, in the words of W. B. Yeats, 'Tread softly because you tread on my dreams.'

Whenever I tell people what I've been up to they invariably say, 'How wonderful to have your words and your name set in granite for posterity.' But I think to myself, 'Ho ho! This is Liverpool we're talking about, my home town. Posterity? I'll give it six months before some scallywags have dug up the letters and carted them away to play Scrabble with.'

Which brings me back to wondering how to spell my name. The architect rang up to see how I wanted McGough to be spelled at the end of the poem. Should the c be large or small? Is it MC or Mc, or with the c like a parrot on M's shoulder, M^c? I'd never thought too much about it really, as I vary it when signing my name, so I looked it up in the *Oxford Book of Twentieth Century Verse*. It's there on page 348: 'McGough'.

CELEBRITY

Is the poet an observer or a commentator? Auden described himself as 'a pen for hire', and Betjeman was very happy to present TV programmes that had little to do with poetry; but if poetry is about the minutiae, the intimate detail seen from a unique perspective, exploring the rhythms and structures of language, where what you say is less important than how you say it, then surely he or she should avoid the media marketplace? Is there a conflict between the private role and the public role of the poet? Please don't feel obliged to answer these questions, but they were occupying my attention in the back of a cab last Friday afternoon on my way to Broadcasting House to take part in a discussion on Radio 4's *The Message* with Michael Schmidt of Carcanet Press and the Irish poet and professor Brendan Kennelly, with Jenni Murray in the chair. I assumed that Brendan, a familiar face on Irish TV adverts, like myself would be on the side of Auden and Sir John, while Michael, a critic and editor, would be in the puritan corner. However, that proved not to be the case and the discussion, though short, was lively and Michael Schmidt was very generous about my attempts at writing to order, particularly on screen. At least, I think he was because, to be honest, my mind wasn't one hundred per cent on the job.

I was scheduled to arrive at the studio at 4.15 in good time for the programme, which goes out live at 4.30, and in the cab wondered if the conversation might touch on 'the poet as celebrity, and the dangers therein', a topic that always had me reaching for a short verse called 'Fame':

> *The best thing about being famous*
> *Is when you walk down the street*
> *And people turn round to look at you*
> *And bump into things*

And when the studio laughter had eventually subsided, I would refer back to my Scaffold days and the shallowness of instant celebrity, the claustrophobia of public recognition. I might even recall the incident in the bedding department of John Lewis in Liverpool some years after the group had broken up, when I was approached by a middle-aged lady who said: 'Excuse me, excuse me, I've had this little bet with my husband, can you settle it for us?'

'Well, I'll try.'

'Didn't you used to be Roger McGough?'

'Er, yes.'

'I thought so, that's a duvet cover he owes me.'

Much more consoling, I would aver, to be known as a voice or a name on a dust jacket than as a face. Pausing to let Brendan or Michael throw in a few words of support, I would impress the listeners with my experiences of the previous evening when I had attended the opening night of Victoria Wood's new musical *Acorn Antiques* at the Theatre Royal in the Haymarket. Celebrities were there in abundance, and real ones, stars of stage and screen who by dint of talent and hard work had achieved wealth and fame, and as they fizzed on the red carpet leading up the steps into the foyer, flash bulbs flashed, and the cordoned-off crowd gasped and applauded. The poet and his wife slipped in unnoticed.

It was close to midnight when we said goodbye to Victoria after the opening-night party at the Café Royal and, amazingly, the autograph hunters were still out in force, as head down, I dragged Hilary out into Piccadilly. I'm not completely autographobic, in that I am happy to sign a book or an album sleeve, but I don't like writing my name in autograph books or on bits of paper for people who don't know me from Adam, but who might be able to sell it to someone who does. I thought I'd got away with it, until some ageing hippies cornered me at the traffic lights, where I obliged with a few thumbnail squiggles. Then the cry went up, 'There's someone!' Before the pack could descend, the someone was across the road and hailing a taxi. Then two young men came out from nowhere: 'Please, you must sign.'

'I'm sorry, we're in a terrible hurry.'

'But you must, ve are coming all the way from Hamburg.'

I accepted the Edding 380 permanent marker on offer and began the pathetic ritual. 'Do you know who I am?'

'It doesn't matter, you party mit Julie Valters und Sir Ian McKellen. You must be very famous.'

Back in the cab on the way to Broadcasting House, I was refining the above dialogue for the delight of my studio companions, not to mention the listening millions when my mobile rang. It was Sue Boardman, John Gorman's partner: 'Roger, where are you?'

'On my way to the BBC.'

'Radio Merseyside?'

'No, Radio 4 in London.'

'You're not coming to Liverpool, then?'

'What for?'

'The show at the Philharmonic with the Scaffold?'

'But that's not until next month.'

'It's tonight.'

'Shite!'

In January I had received an e-mail from John saying that the Scaffold had been asked if they would take part in a tsunami fund-raising concert at the Philharmonic Hall in Liverpool on 11 February. He could make himself available, and Mike was keen, so would I be up for it? I hesitated because relations between Mike and myself had been strained since I'd ducked out of a reunion gig at the Everyman Theatre two years before, but here was a chance to build bridges, ford rivers, grapple hooks, sew on patches and so on, so I said yes and made a note of it in my diary. The trouble was that I put it down as Friday 11 March. Whether this sleight-of-mind was a senior moment, or my subconscious secretary wilfully getting it wrong, I don't know, but once 'Scaffs' appeared in the little box designated 11 March it was writ in stone, for the e-mail dropped below the plimsoll line and there was never a contract, a phone call or a piece of paper to make me question the date.

'I'll hand you over to John,' said Sue and, curled up on the floor of the cab I whined, grovelled and mumbled my apologies. It was obvious that I'd made a stupid mistake, but nonetheless I'd put them in an embarrassing position.

SCAFFOLD REBUILT ran the headline in the local paper,

'The 60s band will re-form for one night only at the *Liverpool Echo* tsunami concert . . .' next to a photograph of Mike 'looking forward to turning the clock back with the Scaffold'. Obviously, neither he nor John would ever speak to me again and no doubt the keys to the city would have to be handed back in to the town hall. Once in Broadcasting House I rang the arts editor of the *Echo*, blubbed my pathetic tale and asked him to convey my sincere apologies to all concerned, before racing into the studio to record *The Message*. My brain certainly wasn't the finely tuned instrument that I like to pretend it is, and as a counterpoint to Michael Schmidt's erudition and Brendan Kennelly's mellifluous musings, I provided the high-pitched keening and strangled sobs.

The cab was still outside waiting to run me back to Barnes, where I planned to get drunk and lie low for a year or two, then Hilary rang: 'Just get on a train and go.' Why hadn't I thought of that? What is it about wives that enables them to see the bleeding obvious? In a trice, out of a trance. 'Change of plan,' I said to the driver, 'Euston Station.'

I arrived at the venue just prior to the interval, and when I walked into the Green Room, instead of having stale sandwiches and beer cans hurled at me for being the dozy git that I undoubtedly was, everybody cheered and applauded. I was the hero home from the war and suitably bedraggled, for I was dressed for radio, not for stage. So Mike lent me his elegant black overcoat to cover my grey woolly jumper and after a quick run-through in the dressing-room with our backing band, The Chip Shop Boys, it was time to follow Mel C. on to the platform of the huge auditorium where I had recited poetry as a schoolboy on Speech Days. But this time it wasn't John Masefield's 'Cargoes', or 'The Pied Piper of Hamelin' that had the audience shuffling in their seats, but 'Thank U Very Much', 'Liverpool Lou' and 'Lily the Pink' that had them if not dancing in the aisles, at least waving their arms and singing along. For just under ten minutes I was a celebrity and after the show, as I slipped through the stage door, had anybody thrust an autograph book in front of me I would gladly have signed. But nobody did.

SAYING AND DOING

In the fourteen months I have been working on this book I have written 103,352 words, which is a lot for me. If you think about it, an average poem of mine consists of eighty-two words, which means I could have written well over a thousand poems during the time it has taken me to complete this. A slim volume retailing at £9.99 might contain on average fifty poems; therefore, instead of slaving away at *Said and Done* which sells in hardback at £17.99, I could have had twenty-five books of poetry lined up on the runway awaiting take-off at regular intervals over the next few decades, or had the series published and put into the shops right away, and twenty-five new collections at £9.99 would cost you nearly £250, so I hope you realise what a bargain you're holding in those (*delete where inapplicable*) carefully manicured/pudgy/hairy/liverspotted/loving/hands.

To those who believe that poetry is merely chopped-up prose, may I counter with my experience as someone who has always found it easier to write in verse. The poem usually either happens or it doesn't, and if it doesn't then no amount of mouth-to-mouth or chopping up will breathe life into it. *Schlimmbesserung* is a fine word meaning to make something worse by trying to improve it, as in overextensive revision, but prose seems to benefit when reworked and repolished so that it can be read at a pace at which the reader feels comfortable, usually quickly, whereas a poem won't offer itself up to a speed read. A poem creates a sort of relaxed tension, the reader hovering between boredom and anticipation, whereas prose makes a narrative promise: '*Stay with me, it will be worth the journey.*' The process has been a learning curve for me, trying to avoid the elliptical, replacing the full stop with a comma and extending the idea. You wouldn't believe the exhilaration I feel when a sentence runs over on to a second, even a third line. Words, out of control falling over a cliff. And the thrill of the paragraph! I'm also using a laptop, which is pretty courageous for somebody who is anti-magnetic. Inklings of poems can arrive at any time and there is always pen and paper to hand, so when writing I can see it taking shape, the crossings out and the rearrangement of lines, the alternative rhymes, all there on the page in front of me. But the job in hand required so many revisions that I would never have got beyond the second chapter if I hadn't learned to type.

The learning curve also half-mooned into an alcohol-free zone. Very often when writing a poem I reach the point where it cries out for a drink. My brain has come to a crossroads and just wants to stretch out on that bench over there – no, not that one, the one by the tree – but when the alcohol kicks in, suddenly imagination takes flight, perhaps to nosedive shortly afterwards, but it's always a trip worth taking. I have pictured the creative process as something like two parts of the brain at work on a poem: Magenta, who is often skimpily dressed, comes up with all the wild ideas; and Max, who wears a three-piece suit, is in charge of quality control. His role is not to be underestimated, for although a stickler for tradition, he counts the syllables, makes sure the rhymes chime and generally keeps an eye and an ear on things. Sometimes, though, Max can be a bit of a bore, and his one failing is that he can't hold his drink, so after a glass or two of the magic potion he falls asleep and Magenta dances in with a bouquet of fanciful flights clasped to her shimmering bosom. But there's something Presbyterian about the memoir that demands stricter control, for there is a past to be taken into account with dates, names and faces that you have elected to represent. Poems should be honest without necessarily being truthful, and the 'I' doesn't have to be the author's voice, but in an autobiography the 'I' must take its responsibilities seriously, even if the reader doesn't.

> *Here I am*
> *as old as Methuselah*
> *was when he was my age*
> *and never having stepped outside for a fight*

> *Crossed on red, pissed on rose (or white)*
> *Pretty dull for a poet, I suppose, eh? Quite.*

It isn't so much growing old that's a bore, but the common sense that comes with it, the increasingly futile need for self-preservation that stops you having another drink, that says no to the chocolate fudge surprise, that nods towards the umbrella and whispers 'just in case'. Since the onset of my fifties, having nursed the scenario of a law-abiding, bookish middle age, segueing into a ruttish, dissolute, fun-filled routine before the final curtain call, the realisation, slow to dawn, that the show's director has something less energetic in mind comes as a bit of a blow.

I am not the author of my life, but its ghost-writer, kept at a distance, trying to create a more believable me, and I wish I'd been able to come up with someone more outrageous. Someone who had gone to the edge and beyond. A wild extrovert, able to pick up a large cut-glass goblet filled with purple onions and throw it through a window at the Savoy. Able to go up to those sports journalists in the Brown Bull and say, 'Stop getting that young footballer pissed so that you can write about his problem.' Able to tell John Lennon/Keith Moon/Allen Ginsberg to go back and apologise. Able to accept generously the gifts on offer ('*The door clicks shut behind him, he turns: "Tania, I really don't think . . . Mmm . . . Mind you, on second thoughts . . ."*') Has writing been a form of displacement activity to keep the encroaching darkness at bay, or merely an excuse not to get too involved in real life?

'*What did you do in the Great War, Daddy?*'

'*Well, wrote a few decent poems, actually.*'

Like many writers, excluding Hemingway and Genghis Khan, I'm a *sayer* who would rather have been a *doer*. But there's still time to change, because it's never too late to rise up and become a flame, as lightning out of a thundercloud, and that's what I intend to do. But unobtrusively, so that no one will notice. And certainly not my family. It's bad enough your father writing his autobiography and people coming up to them and saying '*Was your father really alive during the Great War?*' And '*Did he really have an affair with Michelle Pfeiffer?*' Without '*Was that your father I saw this morning, surrounded by flames appearing on a cloud above*

Hammersmith Bridge?' No, they can rest assured I'll keep my attention-seeking to the written page.

I might have wished otherwise, but my guardian angel (whose name is Max, by the way) always managed to keep me in check, and although I was able to give him the slip occasionally, thanks to Magenta, I was never quite able to let go completely and join in the fun. Picture the scene: *The early sixties. It is late summer, after midnight and a group of us sit around a fire on a beach in Devon drinking wine and cider, somebody strumming a guitar, when suddenly a girl strips and runs naked into the sea. Everybody follows suit and, not wanting to be last in, I unbutton my jeans. Then pause, somebody had better stay behind and keep an eye on the clothes, common sense. Listening to the screams and laughter, I throw another piece of driftwood on to the fire and take a long, untroubled swig of scrumpy.* Thanks Max (or, to give him his full title, Maximus Cautious, a captain in the Brigade of Guardians).

But that was a long time ago, and now it's April and the sun is shining and I've nearly finished writing about myself. This may sound naïve, or worse still, faux-naïf, but I have only recently come to the realisation that once I've submitted the manuscript, it is only a matter of time before it appears in book form and that some people will read it. I will no longer be able to pretend that I was merely thinking aloud, the words will be there, the ink holding them in place, page after page. Close friends, lovers, relatives may feel misrepresented, or slighted that I didn't spend more time with them, and speaking as someone who isn't as clever as he thinks he is, I'll have to prepare myself for the brickbats, the slurs and the shattered roof slates that will come winging my way from the professionals. I can't do anything about the former except feel guilty, but I've already taken steps to help me deal with the latter, by ordering another glass paperweight from New Mexico, containing a scorpion with lobsteresque claws and a tail like a curled rattlesnake.

In a couple of hours' time I'll be able to put away the diaries and the journals and the newspaper cuttings, and begin to live again in the present. Might convert the garage into a studio and start painting again, for in my youth I wanted to paint Beauty, but the paint always got in the way; maybe now I'll be content just to paint. And who knows, I might just be tempted to accept the invitation that has arrived to attend a literary festival in a town I can't pronounce, in a country far, far way. Might even pick up a hammer and hit the nail on the head. In other words, start doing.

Enough said.